T0127551

Footprint Handbook
Zanzibar
& Pemba
LIZZIE WILLIAMS

This is
Zanzibar
& Pemba

The idyllic, balmy, tropical (there is no end to the superlatives) Indian Ocean islands of the Zanzibar Archipelago lie 25 to 50 km off mainland Tanzania. Consisting of many small islands – some inhabited, some no more than tiny sandy atolls or islets – the two largest and most significant are Unguja (the main island, referred to informally as Zanzibar) and the quieter and more traditional Pemba. The archipelago is rightly famous for its palm-fringed, pearly white-sand beaches, interspersed with picturesque fishing villages, and coral reefs teeming with life and colour: perfect ingredients for a sun, sea and sand holiday.

And then there is the intriguing history of the Swahili coast. For centuries, the archipelago was part of the extensive trade network that spanned the Indian Ocean and, carried by the annual monsoon winds, ocean-going dhows (white-sailed boats) visited the islands from Arabia, Persia, India and as far away as China. The distinctive

coastal language and culture of the Swahili was created by this multi-fusion of peoples, while Islam was introduced to the shores of East Africa. On Zanzibar Island is Stone Town, considered one of the oldest still-functioning settlements on the East African coast. Here the atmospheric narrow winding streets with their minarets, carved doors, 19th-century palaces and grand Swahili mansions are a highlight of any visit to the islands. Elsewhere, roads are lined by banana palms, mangroves and coconut trees and the countryside is blanketed with the scent of fragrant spices – cloves, nutmeg, cinnamon, pepper and many more. It was the ruling Arabs of the 18th century who recognized the islands' spice potential and, using slaves to cultivate and harvest them, developed it into a prosperous trade that led to Zanzibar's informal name as 'The Spice Islands'.

Lizzie Williams

Best of
Zanzibar
& Pemba

❶ Stone Town

Absorb the atmosphere in the maze of winding alleyways in the charming historic capital of Zanzibar Island. Join giggling schoolchildren scurrying across courtyards, chattering Swahili women hurrying home from market, and men idly gossiping on *barazas* (stone benches). Page 48.

❷ Darajani Market

This crammed bazaar is a riot of noise and colour, and sells everything from saucepans and traditional kangas (sarongs) to raw meat and the island's tropical fruit – try and catch the lively fish and seafood auctions here every morning. Page 49.

❸ Forodhani Gardens

Every evening this lovely Stone Town park, in front of the Old Fort, becomes a buzzing food market when vendors fill their tables with an assortment of tasty snacks – eat freshly grilled fish, giant crab claws or a local version of pizza in the glow of oil lamps. Page 57.

❹ Sunset from Stone Town

As Stone Town faces west, it offers
glorious sunset views over the Indian
Ocean – best enjoyed with a drink in hand
(a 'sundowner') on a rooftop terrace of a
hotel or restaurant, or take to the water
under a billowing white sail on a dhow
sunset cruise. Pages 71 and 75.

❺ Spice tours

This popular half-day excursion to the
plantations in the interior of Zanzibar
tickles the senses, and foodies and anyone
who loves to cook will find out how their
favourite spices are grown and harvested.
Page 80.

❻ Zanzibar north coast

Zanzibar's most lively resorts of Nungwi
and Kendwa on the north coast offer
everything you would want for a typical
beach holiday – all-day swimming
and water sports (the tide doesn't
retreat far), and an excellent choice of
accommodation, restaurants and beach
bars. Page 92.

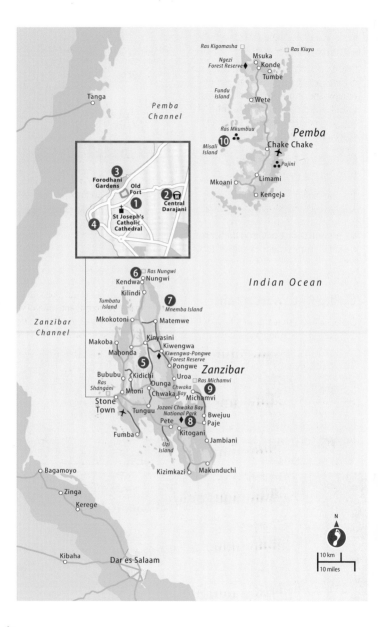

Ras Kigomasha □   □ Ras Kiuyu
          Msuka
Ngezi   ○ Konde
Forest Reserve ◆
          Tumbe

Fundu
Island   ○ Wete

Pemba
Channel

Ras Mkumbuu
Misali   ⑩ ∴
Island   Chake Chake ○

          ∴ Pujini

Mkoani ○ ○ Limami

          ○ Kengeja

Tanga ○

Old Fort inset map:

③
Forodhani
Gardens   **Old**
               Fort
                         ② Ⓜ
                    Central
               ①   **Darajani**
          St Joseph's
④   **Catholic**
          Cathedral

Indian Ocean

⑥ □ Ras Nungwi
Kendwa ○ Nungwi
     ○ Kilindi

     ⑦
Tumbatu   Mnemba Island
Island

Zanzibar   Mkokotoni ○ ○ Matemwe
Channel

Makoba ○   Kinyasini ○
     Mahonda ○   Kiwengwa
          ⑤   Kiwengwa-Pongwe
               Forest Reserve ◆
Bububu ○   ○ Pongwe
     ○ Kidichi ○ Uroa   **Zanzibar**
Ras   Dunga ○ □ Ras Michamvi
Shangani □ ○ Mtoni Chwaka ○ ⑨
          Chwaka Bay Michamvi ○
Stone   ○ Tunguu Jozani Chwaka Bay
Town ✈   National Park ○ Bwejuu
               Pete ◆ ⑧ ○ Paje
Fumba ○   ○ Kitogani
          Uzi   ○ Jambiani
          Island

○ Bagamoyo

○ Zinga   Kizimkazi ○ ○ Makunduchi
     Kerege ○

○ Kibaha

     Dar es Salaam ○

N
▲

10 km
10 miles

❼ Snorkelling and diving at Mnemba Island

Boat excursions go to this tiny island – part of a marine conservation area – from Nungwi and resorts along the northeast coast to see the array of tropical fish and large marine creatures on its surrounding spectacular coral reef. Page 105.

❽ Jozani Chwaka Bay National Park

The only national park on the islands, Jozani is home to the rare and endemic Zanzibar red colobus monkey and there's an excellent chance of seeing these playful creatures on a visit here. Explore on nature trails and boardwalks over mangroves. Page 112.

❾ The Rock Restaurant

Ocean views, fresh sea air, a menu of delectable seafood and fine wines in an

extraordinary setting – this tiny restaurant is literally perched on top of a coral islet about 50 m offshore near Pingwe on Zanzibar's southeast coast. Page 122.

❿ Pemba

Little-developed and rarely visited, Pemba has amazing diving in the Pemba Channel and around Misali Island, traditional fishing villages, mangrove forests and miles of wild coastline. It also offers a large dose of privacy and exclusivity in its few lodges. Page 124.

Stone Town

Route planner

The combination of the finest beaches in East Africa as well as a number of its best dive sites makes Zanzibar and Pemba the perfect destination for the classic sun, sea and sand type of holiday. Zanzibar (Unguja) in particular offers a multitude of resorts, ranging from the last word in luxury to simple thatched cottages in the sand. And if you can peel yourself off the beach, the lazy days can be broken up with an exploration of charming Stone Town – a UNESCO World Heritage Site for its historical importance – and visits to the forests and spice plantations of the island's interior.

Pemba is Zanzibar's sister island, where the mainstay of the economy is farming and fishing and the people live fairly simple and traditional lives. Despite many years of isolation from the outside world, it is receiving a small but growing number of foreign visitors, led mostly by scuba-diving tourists seeking the uncrowded and unspoiled coral reefs off the island. Its infrastructure is far more basic than that on Zanzibar Island, and it's much harder to get to and around, but the beautiful beaches, natural forests, outstanding diving and its simple isolation are just some of the attractions on offer.

The port city of Dar es Salaam on the mainland is a fast-growing developing East African city, which, despite an interesting colonial history and balmy Swahili atmosphere, doesn't have a great deal of sights per say – especially not when Zanzibar is so tantalizingly close – but it does serve as the springboard to the islands by ferry or plane and is the location of Tanzania's largest airport. By routing through Dar, visitors have the option of adding a wildlife safari to Tanzania's national parks and game reserves in the north or the south of the country. Zanzibar is usually the final destination on such a safari/beach combination holiday in order to enjoy doing nothing after the rigours of the road. But then again it's an equally standalone destination too, where it's impossible not to relax next to the turquoise ocean and soak up the sun.

Four to seven days

If you only have a few days – say at the end of a safari or and overland tour of East Africa – it's quite possible to see Zanzibar's major sites and relax on the beach for a couple of days. All visitors arrive in **Stone Town** – either by the fast ferry from Dar es Salaam or by plane from the mainland to Abeid Amani Karume International Airport, 7 km southeast of Stone Town. If your time is short (and you really want to get to the beach), you may choose to be whisked away straight to the coast – **Paje**, **Jambiani**, **Bwejuu**, **Nungwi**, **Kendwa** etc. But this would be a shame, as staying for at least one night in Stone Town is really worthwhile; not only to explore on foot, but to sleep in a wonderfully restored hotel, perhaps with a rooftop, and enjoy a good meal, sunset drink and a spot of shopping at the charming curio shops dotted around the warren of streets. To get to the coast, you can combine a minibus transfer with a morning **spice tour**. These fun and informative excursions take about four hours and the tour operators will arrange for you to get to the beach after lunch. Finally at least one dhow trip is recommended – you can take an excursion on these romantic white-sailed boats around the island and it's the perfect way to enjoy the Indian Ocean.

One to two weeks

The optimum time to really relax is at least one week on the beach. You can lazily while away the days sunbathing, walking along the sand, enjoying the beach bars, seafood lunches and reading a book on the patio of your beach cottage. The more active can try their hand at water sports. **Snorkelling** is easy around the island in the warm and clear ocean, even for children, and there's plenty of colourful underwater marine life to see – either from in front of your hotel or on a boat trip to the coral reefs. Experienced divers have a choice of **dive sites**, and Zanzibar is an ideal place to learn (PADI Open Water courses typically take five days). **Kiteboarding**, too, is a growing sport, especially on the beach at Paje where there are a number of kite schools, so if you've never tried this before, conditions are ideal for beginners and there's plenty of tuition. Other day trips from **Stone Town** or the resorts go to **Jozani Chwaka Bay National Park**, where you can hunt for the entertaining and cheeky Zanzibar red colobus monkeys, learn about the mangroves that line much of the coast and enjoy a respite from the heat on cool forests paths.

There's no reason not to mix it up a little and stay at a number of destinations around Zanzibar – transfers are straightforward and *dala-dalas* across the island are fun and a good way to meet local people. While many visitors are on all-inclusive packages, you don't have to stay in your chosen resort every night if another part of the island appeals and you don't mind the additional expense. Then there's **Pemba**; although the ferries between Zanzibar and Pemba only go twice a week, there is the option to fly which only takes 30 minutes. Once there, the towns on the island hold little interest, and the easiest option is to get taxis/transfers straight to the resorts. Divers here will be well rewarded with excursions to virtually unexplored reefs where some of the larger marine species such as whale sharks, turtles and sharks can be seen.

Tip...

If you want to add a wildlife safari (coverage of the nearby safari destinations is outside the scope of this guide), allow a minimum of four days for a trip to the Serengeti National Park and the Ngorongoro Crater in the 'Northern Circuit', up to a week if you want to add another couple of the parks, see Footprint *Kilimanjaro & Northern Tanzania Handbook*.

ON THE ROAD
Improve your travel photography

Taking pictures is a highlight for many travellers, yet too often the results turn out to be disappointing. Steve Davey, author of Footprint's *Travel Photography*, sets out his top rules for coming home with pictures you can be proud of.

Before you go
Don't waste precious travelling time and do your research before you leave. Find out what festivals or events might be happening or which day the weekly market takes place, and search online image sites such as Flickr to see whether places are best shot at the beginning or end of the day, and what vantage points you should consider.

Get up early
The quality of the light will be better in the few hours after sunrise and again before sunset – especially in the tropics when the sun will be harsh and unforgiving in the middle of the day. Sometimes seeing the sunrise is a part of the whole travel experience: sleep in and you will miss more than just photographs.

Stop and think
Don't just click away without any thought. Pause for a few seconds before raising the camera and ask yourself what you are trying to show with your photograph. Think about what things you need to include in the frame to convey this meaning. Be prepared to move around your subject to get the best angle. Knowing the point of your picture is the first step to making sure that the person looking at the picture will know it too.

Compose your picture
Avoid simply dumping your subject in the centre of the frame every time you take a picture. If you compose with it to one side, then your picture can look more balanced. This will also allow you to show a significant background and make the picture more meaningful. A good rule of thumb is to place your subject or any significant detail a third of the way into the frame; facing into the frame not out of it.

This rule also works for landscapes. Compose with the horizon two-thirds of the way up the frame if the foreground is the most interesting part of the picture; one-third of the way up if the sky is more striking.

Don't get hung up with this so-called Rule of Thirds, though. Exaggerate it by pushing your subject out to the edge of the frame if it makes a more interesting picture; or if the sky is dull in a landscape, try cropping with the horizon near the very top of the frame.

Fill the frame
If you are going to focus on a detail or even a person's face in a close-up portrait, then be bold and make sure that you fill the frame. This is often a case of physically getting in close. You can use a telephoto setting on a zoom lens but this can lead to pictures looking quite flat; moving in close is a lot more fun!

Interact with people

If you want to shoot evocative portraits then it is vital to approach people and seek permission in some way, even if it is just by smiling at someone. Spend a little time with them and they are likely to relax and look less stiff and formal. Action portraits where people are doing something, or environmental portraits, where they are set against a significant background, are a good way to achieve relaxed portraits. Interacting is a good way to find out more about people and their lives, creating memories as well as photographs.

Focus carefully

Your camera can focus quicker than you, but it doesn't know which part of the picture you want to be in focus. If your camera is using the centre focus sensor then move the camera so it is over the subject and half press the button, then, holding it down, recompose the picture. This will lock the focus. Take the now correctly focused picture when you are ready.

Another technique for accurate focusing is to move the active sensor over your subject. Some cameras with touch-sensitive screens allow you to do this by simply clicking on the subject.

Leave light in the sky

Most good night photography is actually taken at dusk when there is some light and colour left in the sky; any lit portions of the picture will balance with the sky and any ambient lighting. There is only a very small window when this will happen, so get into position early, be prepared and keep shooting and reviewing the results. You can take pictures after this time, but avoid shots of tall towers in an inky black sky; crop in close on lit areas to fill the frame.

Bring it home safely

Digital images are inherently ephemeral: they can be deleted or corrupted in a heartbeat. The good news though is they can be copied just as easily. Wherever you travel, you should have a backup strategy. Cloud backups are popular, but make sure that you will have access to fast enough Wi-Fi. If you use RAW format, then you will need some sort of physical back-up. If you don't travel with a laptop or tablet, then you can buy a backup drive that will copy directly from memory cards.

Recently updated and available in both digital and print formats, Footprint's Travel Photography by Steve Davey covers everything you need to know about travelling with a camera, including simple post-processing. More information is available at www.footprinttravelguides.com

When to go

Thanks to its location just south of the equator, Tanzania's coasts and islands have a moderate climate and long sunny days for most of the year. Daytime temperatures average between 25 and 32°C, with an average of seven to eight hours of sunshine. This is ideal holiday weather for most of the year, although, officially the summer and winter peaks are in December and June respectively. On Zanzibar high temperatures are cooled by ocean breezes, particularly on the north and east coasts, so it is rarely overpoweringly hot, although humidity levels peak just before the rains arrive which some visitors find uncomfortable. There are short rains, *mvuli*, usually from November to December, which come intermittently as light showers in the mornings and late afternoons and are punctuated by stretches of clear skies and bright sunshine. The long rains, *masika*, are usually from the end of March to the end of May. Even in these months, however, it doesn't rain every day and there is an average of four to six hours of daily sunshine, but day-long tropical storms may occur, especially in April and May. The driest months are from June to October when the sky is beautifully clear and blue and this is the best time to visit Zanzibar. In terms of accommodation and flights, high season on Zanzibar is from September to January as this is the time Europeans visit looking for some winter sun; it gets especially busy around the Christmas and New Year period when you will need to make reservations well in advance.

Tip...
The best time to dive here is between October and April before the long rains; the best time to fish is usually from August to the end of March.

Weather Zanzibar and Pemba

January	February	March	April	May	June
32°C	32°C	32°C	30°C	28°C	28°C
24°C	24°C	25°C	25°C	23°C	23°C
5mm	6mm	14mm	32mm	28mm	5mm

July	August	September	October	November	December
27°C	28°C	28°C	30°C	31°C	31°C
22°C	22°C	22°C	22°C	23°C	24°C
2mm	3mm	4mm	6mm	17mm	13mm

What to do

from scuba-diving to dhow excursions

Diving and snorkelling

Undoubtedly one of East Africa's greatest tourism assets is the vast area of coral reefs that stretch south from the equator. There is an abundance of tropical reef fish as well as large pelagic fish, and, if lucky, you will encounter barracuda, manta rays, whale and reef sharks, hawksbill and green turtles, and schools of dolphins are often seen. The best diving areas are found off the islands of Pemba, where there are dramatic drop-offs, and Zanzibar where there are fringing reefs and coral gardens. On the mainland, you can dive at the offshore islands around Dar es Salaam. The best time to dive is between October and April before the long rains, when the average water temperature is 27°C and visibility ranges from 20-30 m, increasing to 50 m around Pemba. Conditions are ideal for first-timers, and there are many PADI dive schools. Non-divers can enjoy the reefs by snorkelling from the beach or a boat, which can be arranged at all the coastal resorts. See the listings for details of local operators.

Fishing

Deep-sea fishing is popular with tourists on the coast and islands, especially in the deep Pemba Channel. This reaches depths of 823 m and is home to three varieties of marlin – black, blue and striped – as well as sailfish, spearfish, swordfish, yellowfin tuna, tiger shark, mako shark and virtually every game fish popular with anglers. A gentle north current runs through the channel, acting much like a scaled-down version of the Gulf Stream, which is forced up by the lip in the north of the channel, also referred to locally as the Sea Mountain, which creates rips and eddies that bring nutrients to the surface and concentrates the fish in a very tight area. The fishing season is usually from August to March. A number of operators offer excursions in customized boats with tackle and equipment, and some offer tuition for beginners. The listings sections have details of operators.

SIX OF THE BEST
Zanzibar dive sites

Pange Reef

Pange is the first sandbank west of Stone Town, and is a popular spot for dhow trips with lunch and snorkelling. The reef itself lies in shallow calm waters with a maximum depth of 14 m and is ideal for learning to dive. There is an enormous variety of coral and lots of tropical reef fish such as clown fish, parrotfish, moorish idol and many others. Just off the sandbank at 12 m, lies the the wreck of *The Great Northern*, a British steel cable-laying ship, which was built in 1870 and sank on New Year's Eve 1902. It has become a magnificent artificial reef and is also a good spot for night dives, where you may see cuttle fish, squid, crab and other nocturnal life.

Bawe Island

A 25-minute boat ride from Stone Town, Bawe suits all levels of diver and has a lovely reef stretching right around it with a maximum depth of 18 m. Here you will find beautiful corals, such as acropora, staghorn, brain corals, and a large variety of reef fish plus octopus and turtles. For advanced divers only, the wreck of the *Royal Navy Lighter* at 30 m lies in the sand just off Bawe's reef and the gaps around the hull are home to large groupers and eels, while crocodile fish and stone fish hide in the surrounding sand.

Leven Banks

On the north coast, this site is popular with advanced divers as it lies near the deep water of the Pemba Channel. Leven is a 'coral mountain' about 6 km long. Depths are 14 to 40 m with great visibility and this is a very enjoyable drift dive but there are often strong currents. You can see the real big stuff from the open ocean here including manta rays, whale sharks and several big predatory fish. On the mountain you can find very large moral eels and octopus surrounded by schools of tuna and trevally.

Kiteboarding

Kiteboarding (or kitesurfing) is the latest craze on Zanzibar. The best beaches, with cross-shore winds, wide flat sandy beaches, shallow waves and virtually no obstructions, are at Paje on the east coast and Ras Nungwi on the north coast. The wind is best from April to November when it picks up to 12-20 knots in the afternoon. The kite centres (of which there are many at Paje) can organize lessons for beginners and also rent out equipment to experienced boarders. Some also offer other activities such as stand-up paddle-boarding (SUP), windsurfing and wake-boarding. Details of local operators are given in the listings.

Spice tours

The exotic spices and fruits that are grown in the plantations around Stone

Kendwa Reef

Running parallel to the beach at Kendwa on the north coast, this shallow dive site with a depth of 8 to 10 m is a great place for snorkelling, and is ideal for beginners or qualified divers interested in a long shallow dive. It's a nursery area for young fish and other marine life including turtles and you will see many small reef fish, seahorses and beautiful anemones hiding in the coral garden. Frequent visitors include squid, cuttlefish, Spanish dancers, pipefish and a variety of rays. This spot is a favourite for night dives.

Mnemba Island

On the east coast of Zanzibar and reached from Nungwi or Matemwe, this small, privately owned island is surrounded by a large circular reef and is part of a marine conservation area. It has stunning aquarium-like conditions on the west side, and good wall diving on the east side with a wide range of sites varying in depth from 10 to 30 m with visibility of up to 20 m. It is suitable for both beginners and advanced divers and great for snorkelling too. Bottlenose dolphins often visit the waters and green turtles lay their eggs on its white beaches, and from July to September humpback whales and whale sharks can be spotted.

Hunga Reef

Whereas many of Zanzibar's reefs are fringing reefs around the islands, Hunga is in the open sea four nautical miles due west from Nungwi and is made up of a series of interconnected pinnacles consisting of hard and soft corals at an average depth of 18 m. Schooling fish and big pelagic fish can often be found here such as barracuda, tuna, parrotfish, snapper and trevally. Lucky divers may also spot sharks, eagle and manta rays but these sightings are very rare. The sandy bottom also has a variety of species including crocodile fish, stonefish and scorpion fish. It is an ideal spot for underwater photography but is for experienced divers only.

Town have attracted traders from across the Indian Ocean for centuries, and there's ample opportunity to dazzle the senses on a spice tour. It's also a good opportunity to see the rural areas in the interior of the island and connect with local people. Without a guide, you will never find nutmeg sitting on the forest floor, think to peel the bark off a cinnamon tree, or know how to open a jackfruit or custard apple, but these are some of the fun things to do on a spice tour. The guide will carve off a root, branch or bark and then ask you to smell or taste it to guess what it is. Along the way, local children will scamper up a palm to cut a fresh green coconut for you. Almost all the ingredients of the average kitchen spice rack can be found on this tour, and you can buy packaged spices including turmeric, tandoori, vanilla beans, masala, hot chillies, black pepper, cloves, nutmeg, cinnamon sticks or powder, ginger and others. Most Stone Town hotels and practically every tour operator will offer some version of the spice tour by a/c minibus. A half-day tour costs around US$35 per person for two people including lunch; the cost goes down the more people in the group. Longer tours include additional visits to the slave caves and beach at Mangapwani. They generally leave Stone Town around 0900 and return 1300-1400. Tour operators can also arrange to drop you at one of the resorts after the spice tour.

Water sports

As well as diving and snorkelling, many hotels and resorts on the coast organize jet skiing, parasailing and sea-kayaking, and many types of boat are available from an inflatable banana boat or a glass-bottom boat, to catamaran sailing and a sunset cruise on a traditional white-sailed dhow. Details of local operators are given in the relevant listings.

Where to stay

There is a wide range of accommodation on offer, from secluded 'barefoot luxury' retreats from US$300-1000 per couple per day, to mid-range family-orientated beach resorts for around US$150-250 for a double room, standard Dar es Salaam city hotels used by local business people for around US$50-150 per room, and basic thatched beach cottages favoured by backpackers for around US$20 per person per day. Note camping (and sleeping on the beach) is illegal on the Zanzibar Archipelago, but there are campsites in Dar es Salaam, where you can also conveniently leave a vehicle and your camping gear while you visit the islands.

Hotels in Dar es Salaam usually keep the same rates year-round, but beach resorts (and safari lodges if you are going on safari) have seasonal rates depending on weather and periods of popularity with overseas (especially European) visitors. Generally, accommodation booked through a European agent will be more expensive than if you contact the establishment directly. Most of Tanzania's hoteliers have websites and there are many Tanzanian-run hotel and lodge groups, and all the local airlines can be booked directly too. However, some all-inclusive package holidays to Zanzibar that include flights and transfers, booked in your own country, can be very good value. How you choose accommodation rather depends on what sort of holiday appeals to you and how much independence and flexibility you prefer.

Price codes

Where to stay	Restaurants
$$$$ over US$300	$$$ over US$30
$$$ US$100-300	$$ US$15-30
$$ US$50-99	$ under US$15
$ under US$50	Prices for a two-course meal for one person, excluding drinks or service charge.
Price of a double room in high season, including taxes.	

Beach resorts

The popularity of Zanzibar as a sun-sea-and-sand holiday destination means that beach resorts ring almost the entire island. By contrast there is only a clutch on Pemba, but then again Pemba is not as easy to visit. Room rates vary considerably depending on their level of luxury and the type of clientele they target. A secluded honeymoon suite can cost US$300-1000 per couple, while a double or family room in a large resort can be US$150-250 per day with breakfast. Rates are more if you opt for full board (or all-inclusive), which usually includes three meals a day, some soft drinks and perhaps free activities such as snorkelling or children's clubs. Most places on Zanzibar have been built in a style that reflects the traditional architecture of the islands – low thatched cottages – although there are still a few old-fashioned 'blocky' places. Rooms themselves will have everything you expect of a regular hotel room (with the addition of mosquito nets), and whatever the design, you can expect to have a patio or balcony. However, having a TV is not that usual – why would you want to stay in your room – and Wi-Fi is sometimes only available in public areas. Obviously good access to the beach itself is the paramount here – generally you pay more for a room on the beach or with an ocean view than for a unit that is located in the garden of the property. At the lower end of the budget, in most of the popular coastal areas around Zanzibar you'll find establishments offering very basic cottages. While they are fairly bare and lack facilities, they often also have a patio to relax on and are close to the beach, restaurants, bars and water sports facilities. Given that camping is not permitted on the islands, this is the cheapest accommodation and if you are prepared to share a room with three or four other people rates can be as little as US$20 per person per night with a basic bread/eggs/fruit breakfast.

> **Tip...**
> Credit cards are widely accepted at the larger and more expensive hotels and resorts, but may attract a surcharge of around 5%. Hotels at the cheaper end will only accept Tanzania shillings, but in the tourist areas, they may also accept US dollars. On all hotel bills, VAT at 20% is added and is included in the bill.

Hotels

The quality of hotels in Tanzania varies widely. Hotels at the top end charge US$200-300 for a double room and for this you should expect good en suite facilities, a/c, DSTV (satellite TV), Wi-Fi, or internet access elsewhere in the hotel, and breakfast. Mid-range hotels cost around US$100-200 and offer the same but won't be as luxurious or reliable or have as many extras such as a swimming pool. Rooms in the US$50-100 range are often the best value

Bargaining over accommodation

If you just walk into places on Zanzibar, you can often negotiate room rates down if it's out of season or things are quiet. However, forget about it over December and January – peak season for European visitors – when by contrast you should have made a reservation in advance in any case. Always be friendly when negotiating and, if you are successful, anything within 20-40% discount can be possible at the mid-range hotels and resorts, but at budget places (where prices are already tight) don't expect more than 10-20% discount. Other tactics to employ to get room rates down include opting not to have breakfast; negotiating a better price if there is more than two of you (putting extra beds in rooms is common practice); or saying you don't mind having the smallest room or the one farthest away from the beach.

with comfortable accommodation in self-contained rooms, hot water, fans, possibly DSTV, breakfast and perhaps a decent restaurant. At the budget end there's a fairly wide choice of cheap hotels for US$20-50. A room often comprises a simple bed, basic bathroom that is sometimes shared, mosquito net and fan, but may have an irregular water or electricity supply; it is always a good idea to look at a room first, to ensure it's clean and everything works. It is also imperative to ensure that your luggage will be locked away securely for protection against petty theft. There may be a restaurant serving local food or basics such as chicken or fish and chips, and breakfast could be included but may not be substantial with perhaps a cup of tea/coffee, bread and fruit.

Hotels in Dar es Salaam cover all of the above, and in Stone Town on Zanzibar too. However, Stone Town's hotels have the added advantage of almost all being housed in wonderfully restored historic houses. The benefits of staying at these is the charming ambience, and the sometimes beautiful furnishings such as traditional Zanzibari four-poster beds, usually swathed in billowing mosquito nets, Persian rugs, chandeliers and antique bric-a-brac. The disadvantage is that some rooms may be a bit pokey, and noise in Stone Town can be a problem for some visitors – the tightly packed alleyways are constantly busy and are dotted with mosques from which muezzin calls ring out early in the morning.

Tip...
The word *hoteli* in Kiswahili means a cheap stall/café for food and drink, rather than lodging. It is better to use the word guesthouse in Kiswahili, *guesti*, when enquiring about accommodation.

Food
& drink

from *ugali* to Swahili prawn curry

Food

Tanzanians are largely big meat eaters, and a standard meal is *nyama choma*, roasted beef or goat meat, usually served with a spicy relish, although some like it with a mixture of raw peppers, onions and tomato known as *kachumbari*. The main staple or starch in Tanzania is *ugali*, a dish of maize flour, millet flour or sorghum flour cooked with water to a porridge or dough-like consistency, which, under various names, is eaten all over Africa. It is fairly bland on its own, but makes a filling meal accompanied with a tasty sauce or stew. Other starch includes *wali* (rice), *matoke* (boiled and mashed plantains) and *chapati* (an unleavened flatbread originally imported from India).

Eating out

Local hotels and restaurants tend to serve a limited and somewhat unadventurous menu of food like these meat and starch dishes, or maybe stews and boiled vegetables or grilled chicken and chips. There is little choice of dishes specifically made for vegetarians on menus and you may have to make special requests. However, there is a much greater variety of restaurants in the cities and tourist spots; in particular Dar es Salaam has a good choice of individual restaurants (not connected to the hotels) that are enjoyed for their creative menus. Restaurant prices vary depending on where you are eating; it is quite possible to get a plate of simple hot food in a basic restaurant for US$5, while the expensive places with gourmet cuisine will cost more like US$30-40 per person with drinks. The service in Tanzanian restaurants can be somewhat slower than you are used to and it can take hours for something to materialize from a kitchen. Rather than complain just enjoy the laid-back pace and order another beer.

Swahili cuisine

While cuisine on mainland Tanzania is not one of the country's main attractions, the coastal and island regions, however, are a different matter. They have the best choice of food thanks to the abundant availability of seafood and the unique Swahili style of cooking. Like the language and culture, Swahili cuisine has been influenced over the centuries by Arabic, Indian and European elements, and is further enhanced by the spices and tropical fruits grown on Zanzibar and Pemba. You can expect the likes of aromatic curries using coconut milk, fragrant cardamom-infused steamed rice, fish and calamari grilled in chilli and ginger, delicious bisques made from lobster and crab, and pancakes and chapatis topped with freshly prepared fruit and locally sourced honey.

Beach resorts

Most of the larger beach resorts offer breakfast, lunch and dinner buffets for their all-inclusive guests, some of which can be excellent while others can be of a poor standard and there's no real way of knowing what you'll get. The most important thing is to avoid food sitting around for a long time on a buffet table, so ensure it's freshly prepared and served. With any luck there'll be a good choice of hot and cold breakfasts, fresh fruit and vegetables, meat and fish main courses, and perhaps home-made bread, pastries and desserts. Vegetarians are catered for, and children too, are looked after – there will always be something on a buffet that will satisfy even the fussiest of little eaters.

Streetfood and markets

Throughout Tanzania, various dishes can be bought at roadside stalls and from street vendors who prepare and cook over charcoal – in fact eating at the nightly food market at Forodhani Gardens is one of the highlights of Stone Town (see page 57). It's pretty safe, despite hygiene being fairly basic, because most of the items are cooked or peeled. **Savouries** include: barbecued beef on skewers (*mishkaki*), roast maize (corn), samosas, kebabs, hard-boiled eggs and roast cassava (looks like white, peeled turnips) with red chilli-pepper garnish. **Fruits** include: oranges (peeled and halved), grapes, pineapples, bananas, mangoes (slices scored and turned inside-out), paw-paw (*papaya*) and watermelon.

Most food is bought in open air markets, which as well as a fantastic choice of fresh fruit and vegetables (Tanzania is very fertile), also sell eggs, bread, fish and meat. Other locally produced and imported food items are sold in supermarkets; some are small shops with crammed shelves, while Dar es Salaam features large modern chains like Nakumatt.

Drink

Sodas (soft drinks like Coca-Cola, Fanta and the like) are available everywhere and are very cheap, and are bought in cans or cheaper refundable 300 ml bottles. Bottled water is fairly expensive, but is available in all but the smallest villages. Tap water is reputedly safe in many parts of the country, but is only really recommended if you have a fairly hardy traveller's stomach. In cafés, freshly squeezed fruit juices are often available, and they are quite delicious, but remember they may be mixed with tap water. Coffee, when freshly ground, is the local Arabica variety that grows on the lower slopes of Mount Meru and Kilimanjaro, which has a distinctive, acidic flavour. Most of the upmarket cafés and hotels have coffee machines for cappuccinos, espressos and the like, but also look out for traditional Swahili coffee vendors with large portable conical brass coffee pots with charcoal braziers underneath (often seen at bus stations and markets, and on Zanzibar, around the streets of Stone Town). The coffee, sold black in small porcelain cups, is excellent, and instead of adding sugar is often accompanied by a slice of peanut brittle or sugary cakes made from molasses. *Chai* (tea) is drunk in small glasses and is served milky and sweet with the ingredients boiled together, but is surprisingly refreshing.

Local beers (lager) are decent and cheap and are sold in 700 ml refundable bottles. Brands include Kilimanjaro and Safari lager, tasty Tusker imported from Kenya or Castle from South Africa. Imported wines are on the expensive side, but there's a good choice of European or South African labels. Imported spirits are widely available, and local alternatives that are sold in both bottles and sachets of one tot include some rough vodkas and whiskies and the much more pleasant Konyagi, a type of scented gin distilled from sugarcane. Cocktails (or mocktails) on Zanzibar are inventive, delicious and usually loaded with fruit; best enjoyed at a beach bar or from a terrace at sunset.

Dar es Salaam

Dar es Salaam, meaning 'haven of peace' in Arabic, is far from peaceful these days and is a fast-growing city of more than four million. It is Tanzania's main entry point by air, East Africa's principal port, a thriving business centre and administrative base for the country (even though its status as capital city was removed in 1973). German and Swahili buildings sit alongside gleaming tower blocks, with the Indian Ocean as a sparkling backdrop to the city. Everything from *ngalawas* (tiny white-sailed fishing boats) to massive container ships makes their way in and out of the harbour.

But, by African standards at least, it retains a relatively relaxed, unassuming atmosphere, helped somewhat by its sultry and balmy Indian Ocean location. There are only a handful of sights to visit, the most interesting architecture is of the 'faded colonial grandeur' category, and the coast of mainland Tanzania, while pleasant, is not by comparison as fabulous as across the water on Zanzibar. Nonetheless, Dar (as it's simply called) is a good place to simply watch urban Tanzanian life go by and people are relaxed and friendly. It is also home to some excellent international standard hotels and restaurants, and, should the urban bustle prove too much, nearby beaches to the north and south of the city provide an easy escape. Dar is of course the springboard for ferries or flights to the islands of Zanzibar and Pemba, and you could do worse than spend a day or two here on the way.

Essential Dar es Salaam

Getting there

Air

To get to the city, organize your taxi from the stand in the main hall and not with the touts. A large board here has a list of hotels/destinations with fares: to the city centre, ferry terminal, and Ubungo bus station, these are set at a fixed rate of US$30. Taxi drivers prefer TSh rather than US$. Most hotels can also prearrange transfers. The drive usually takes around 40-60 minutes, but during 'rush hour' in Dar, 0800-1000 in the morning and 1600-1900 in the evening, traffic is very congested. From the public bus stop on Julius K Nyerere Road (a five-minute walk from the terminal building), there are also regular *dala-dalas* which cost no more than US$2 but are very crowded and there is the possibility of petty theft. (From the city centre to the airport, these depart from the New Post Office stand on Azikiwe Street.) If you arrive after dark, the only sensible option is to take a taxi.

Bus

The long-distance bus terminal is on Morogoro Road in the Ubungo area, 6 km to the west of the centre. It is served by the new **Bus Rapid Transit (BRT)** and *dala-dalas*; both of which follow Morogoro Road into the city centre. A taxi (a better idea if you have lots of luggage) will cost in the region of US$8.

Getting around

Bus

The government's **Dar es Salaam Rapid Transit (DART) Agency**, Dar es Salaam's **Bus Rapid Transit (BRT)** is currently under construction. At the time of writing much of the first phase, a 21 km network on three trunk routes with a total of 29 stations, was largely complete. A single fare is expected to cost around US$0.50. The most useful section is the Kimara–Kivukoni route. This starts at Kimara on the city outskirts on Morogoro Road, and goes all the way into the city centre via the Ubongo bus terminal, past the Zanzibar/Pemba ferry terminal and along Kivukoni Road to Kivukoni. It ends at the Kigamboni car-and-passenger ferry. The BRT, in the most part, follows dedicated bus lanes and has self-contained stations. For updates check DART's website: www.dart.go.tz.

Dala-dala

These are cheap at around US$0.50 for a short journey. The front of the vehicle usually has two destinations painted on the bonnet. The main terminals (stands) in the city centre are at the **Central Line Railway Station** (Stesheni) and the **New Post Office** (Posta) on Azikiwe Street.

Taxi

Taxis are readily available in the city centre and are parked on just about every street corner. They cost around US$2-3 per kilometre. Any car can serve as a taxi; they are not painted in a specific colour but many have a thin green strip along the side. If you are visiting a non-central location and there is no taxi stand at the destination, you can always ask the driver to wait or come back and pick you up at an allotted time. Also get the driver's cell phone number. Taxis do not have meters so always negotiate fares before setting off on your journey. A short journey within the city centre should cost no more than US$3-4, and a longer journey to the Msasani Peninsula around US$8-10.

City centre

Despite Dar es Salaam having a burgeoning population, the older part of the city centre itself is a fairly compact grid of streets. It is broadly hemmed in by Bibi Titi Mohammed Street to the west and south, and Sokoine Drive (which branches into Kivukoni Road) along the harbour to the east. While there are plenty of newer buildings, this is the historical core of Dar where there is a mishmash of architectural styles from varying eras.

The main sights are within walking distance from one another, and a couple of hours' wandering might start on Sokoine Drive opposite the ferry terminal at the beautifully restored **St Joseph's Cathedral** ① *open for Mass several times a day, check the website for times, www.daressalaamarchdiocese.or.tz/st-joseph-cathedral.* One of the most striking buildings in Dar es Salaam, dominating the harbour front, it was built by the Germans between 1897 and 1902. It has a classically Gothic exterior with red-tiled roofs and gleaming white spire, and the impressive vaulted interior has a fine arrangement of arches and gables.

Some 300 m southwest down Sokoine Drive from the cathedral, at the junction of Morogoro Road, is the **Old Boma**. Built in 1867 to accommodate the visitors of Sultan Majid (the site of his long-gone palace was between here and the shore), it features a fine Zanzibar door and coral-rag walls. It's presently undergoing a restoration by the **Dar es Salaam Centre for Architectural Heritage** (DARCH). On the opposite corner is the very handsome German-built **City Hall**, which has an impressive façade and elaborate decoration.

Another 400 m further down Sokoine Drive on the corner of Railway Street is the **Railway Station**, a double-storey building with arches and a pitched-tile roof, the construction of which began in 1905 for the Central Railway line. On the roundabout at the top end of Railway Street is the **Clock Tower**, a rather boxy concrete construction erected to celebrate the elevation of Dar es Salaam to city status in 1961. A right turn here leads 800 m along busy Samora Avenue with its many shops and restaurants to the **Askari Monument** on another roundabout at the junction of Maktaba Street. The bronze statue, in memory of all those who died in the First World War, but principally dedicated to the African troops and porters, was unveiled in 1927 and was cast by Morris Bronze Founders of Westminster, London. From here, follow Maktaba Street back to the harbour front and Sokoine Drive and on the left is the **Azania Front Lutheran Church** ① *open daily for services in English, Kiswahili and German, check the websites for times, www.azaniafront.org.* With its distinctive red-tiled spire and tiled canopies over the windows to provide shade, it was built in a vaguely Bavarian style by German missionaries in 1898. Opposite is the **Cenotaph**, again commemorating the 1914-1918 war and dating to 1927. Another 200 m from here takes you back along Sokoine Drive to the cathedral and ferry terminal.

Kigamboni Market and Banda Beach The eastern part of the city centre resembles an eagle's head (it is said the Msasani Peninsula is one of the eagle's wings). At the tip of the eagle's beak is the pier for the car-and-passenger ferry that goes over to Kigamboni (see below). Next to the ferry is the **Kivukoni Fish Market** ⓘ *Barack Obama Dr (formerly Ocean Rd), dawn-1500, if you want to see the auctions be there by 0700.* It was constructed in the British period for the use of the governor (it's just south of State House), although a fish market has been on this site since time immemorial. Once part of an old fishing village called Mzizima, the village met its demise when Seyyid Majid began to build Dar es Salaam in 1865, although the fish market survived. Although an extremely smelly place, it's a lively place to visit, and is well organized (in a chaotic sort of way), with

Dar es Salaam centre

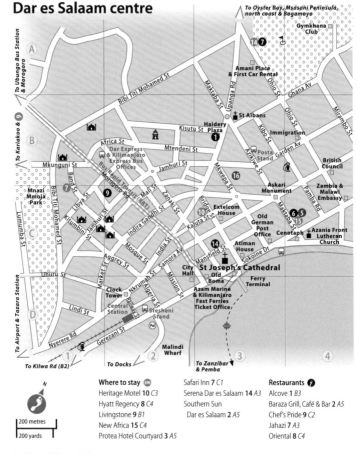

zones for fish cleaning, fish frying, one for shellfish and vegetables, another for firewood and charcoal, an auction hall for wholesale vendors and buyers, and a maintenance area for the repair of boats, fishing nets and other tools of the trade. There is an astonishingly wide variety of seafood to buy, from blue fish, lobster and red snapper to calamari and prawns. Be warned though, the vendors are quite aggressive and you'll need to haggle hard. The complex is one of a kind and provides employment for hundreds of fishermen and caters to thousands of daily shoppers. Just north of the market is a stretch of sand known as **Banda Beach**, a well-known place for sittin' on the dock of the bay. Fishing boats, mostly lateen-sailed *ngalawas*, are beached on the shore.

To ③ , Aga Khan Hospital, Oyster Bay, Msasani Peninsula, north coast & Bagamoyo

Chimera Rd
Barack Obama Rd
UK Embassy
Botanical Gardens
Samora Av
Karimjee Hall
Shaaban Robert St
National Museum & House of Culture
Luthuli Rd
Banda Beach
Madaraka St
State House
Bus Rapid Transit (BRT)
Kivukoni Rd
High Court & Magistrates Court
Magogoni St
Kivukoni Fish Market
To Kigamboni & southern beaches▼

Botanical Gardens

Botanical Gardens ① *Samora Av, sunrise-sunset.* Although now hemmed in by modern buildings around the junction of Samora Avenue and Luthuli Road, the Botanical Gardens were one of the glories of Dar es Salaam in the German era – the flamboyant trees and *Oreodoxa* (Royal Palms) still border it. The gardens was created in 1893 by a well-known German doctor, Professor Franz Stuhlmann, who also became the first Director of Agriculture, and made various experiments on plantation crops and tree species of different types here. It was the place where colonial administrators came to sit and rest in the evening, and today it's a welcome escape from the city, and the peacocks give it an exotic air. It is one of the few places in the world to see the coco-de-mer palm tree, apart from the Seychelles.

Sawasdee **6** *C4*
Serengeti **7** *A3*
Sno-cream **14** *C3*

Level 8 **11** *C4*
Onyx Lounge **5** *C4*

Bars & clubs 🎵
Club Bilicanas **16** *B3*

Tip...

Tip...
The terrace at the Baraza Grill, Cafe and Bar (see Restaurants, below) at the Southern Sun Hotel directly overlooks the gardens and is a good place for a drink or meal, especially at night when some of the trees are floodlit.

BACKGROUND
Dar es Salaam

Zanzibar period 1862-1886

Dar es Salaam ('haven of peace') was founded and named by Seyyid Majid, Sultan of Zanzibar. He chose it as his mainland port thanks to its sheltered natural harbour, which would act as a focus for trade and caravans operating to the south. The slave-trading centre of Bagamoyo to the north was already well established, but local interests there were inclined to oppose direction from Zanzibar, and the new city was a way of ensuring control from the outset. Construction began in 1865 when streets were laid along the shoreline around what is now Sokoine Drive, along which were mosques and grand buildings including the elaborate Sultan's Palace.

Dar es Salaam suffered its first stroke of ill-luck when Majid died suddenly in 1870, after a fall in his new palace, and was succeeded as Sultan by his half-brother, Seyyid Barghash. Barghash did not share Majid's enthusiasm for the new settlement and, indeed Majid's death was taken to indicate that carrying on with the project would bring ill-fortune. The palace and other buildings were abandoned, and the fabric of Dar rapidly fell into decay. Nevertheless, despite the neglect, Barghash maintained control over Dar es Salaam. Some commercial momentum had been established too; the Sultan's coconut plantations were maintained and the local Zaramo people traded gum copal (a residue used in making varnishes), rubber, rice and fish for cloth, ironware and beads. By 1887, the population had expanded to around 500.

German period 1887-1916

In 1887 the German East African Company under Hauptmann Leue took up residence in Dar es Salaam, and occupied the residence of the Sultan's governor, whom they succeeded in getting recalled to Zanzibar. The Zaramo, Swahili and Arabs opposed this European takeover, culminating in the Arab revolt of 1888-1889. But this revolt was crushed, and the German government took over responsibility from the German East Africa Company in 1891, and Dar es Salaam was selected as their main centre for administration. From 1900 to 1916, several fine civic buildings were built on Wilhelms Ufer (now Kivukoni Road), the area behind the north harbour shore was laid out with fine acacia-lined streets and residential two-storey buildings with pitched corrugated-iron roofs and first-floor verandas, while behind the east waterfront were shops and office buildings. A dockyard was built just to the south of Kurasini Creek, where the present deep-water docks are now situated.

British period 1916-1961

In the 45 years that the British administered Tanganyika, public construction was kept to a minimum on economic grounds, and business was largely carried on in the old German buildings. Although the governor's residence, damaged by naval gunfire in 1915, was remodelled to form the present State House, and in the 1920s, the British built the Selander Bridge causeway, which opened up the Oyster Bay area to the north of the city centre for residential construction. As was to be expected, streets names were changed too; some after early explorers like Speke and Burton, although Bismarck Strasse was changed to Versailles Street – it was the Treaty of Versailles in 1918 that allocated the former German East Africa to the British.

The settling by the various groups living in the city into distinctive areas was consolidated during the British period. Europeans lived in Oyster Bay. The Asians lived either in tenement-style blocks in the city centre or in the Upanga area between the city and Oyster Bay. African families built Swahili-style houses, initially in the Kariakoo area to the west of the city.

Independence 1961-present

Despite the construction of government buildings, during the early years of Independence, Dar es Salaam managed to sustain its enviable reputation of being a gloriously located city with a fine harbour, generous parklands, tree-lined avenues (particularly in the Botanical Gardens and Gymkhana area), and a tidy central area of shops and services. But after the Arusha Declaration of 1967 (the government's policy on socialism and self-reliance), the city went into steady decline. Many shops and commercial buildings were nationalized, roads fell into disrepair and the harbour became littered with rusting hulks, and after 1973 when the government decided to move the capital to Dodoma, much of the public infrastructure was neglected. By the early 1980s, Dar es Salaam reached a low point, not dissimilar from the one reached almost exactly a century earlier with the death of Sultan Majid.

But by the early 2000s things began to improve and a comprehensive civic management plan led to restoration of the road system, historical buildings were refurbished, public squares and spaces re-landscaped and even the Botanical Gardens were restored. Additionally while government decided to move to Dodoma, big business did not, and in recent years Dar has witnessed a major construction boom. Bank and corporate headquarters are rising in tower blocks on the city centre's skyline, while the outskirts are expanding with estates of apartments and manufacturing suburbs. Additionally, Dar es Salaam's harbour, the most important in Tanzania, is now prominent for entrepôt trade with landlocked countries such as the Democratic Republic of Congo, Rwanda, Burundi and Zambia.

Despite this, and like other East African cities, today's Dar has an ever-growing urbanization rate (currently the population is increasing by about 8% per year). As such there are major infrastructural problems; a huge proportion of people live in slums, the limited transport systems are overloaded, the chaotic traffic has to squeeze along not enough roads, and there is occasional power rationing. But things are changing to relieve the challenges: a third terminal is being built at Julius Nyerere International Airport, a new bus rapid transit system is under construction, and another cargo port has been proposed for Bagamoyo to ease the congestion in Dar.

National Museum and House of Culture ⓘ *Shaaban Robert St next to the Botanical Gardens, between Sokoine Dr and Samora Av, T022-211 7508, www.house ofculture.or.tz, 0930-1800, US$3, children (5-16) US$2.* Next to the Botanical Gardens, the original National Museum, a single-storey stone building with a red-tiled roof and arched windows, was constructed as the King George V Memorial Museum in 1940. A larger, building was constructed in 1963, and the old building was (and still is) used as offices. The museum has ethnographic, historical and archaeological collections, the old photographs of Dar are particularly interesting, and there are traditional craft items, headdresses, ornaments, musical instruments and witchcraft accoutrements on display. Fossils from Olduvai Gorge include those of Zinjanthropus – sometimes referred to as Zinj or 'nutcracker man' – the first of a new group of hominid remains collectively known as *Australopithecus boisei*, discovered by Mary Leakey. The coastal history is represented by glazed Chinese porcelain pottery and a range of copper coins from Kilwa. In the garden is a sculpture in memory of victims of the 1998 American Embassy bombing.

Kigamboni and the southern beaches
The shores close to the city centre are not particularly safe or pleasant for swimming, thanks to water pollution caused by the ships making their way in and out of port and rubbish on the beaches. The much nicer and cleaner beaches, backed by particularly tall coconut palms, are at Kigamboni on the opposite side of Kurasini Creek to the city centre. Although currently reached by the Kigamboni car-and-passenger ferry near the fish market (departs at regular intervals 0400-0100, US$1 per vehicle and US$0.40 per person, five minutes), by the time you read this, the **Kigamboni Bridge** that is presently under construction is likely to have been completed. For now foot passengers can walk directly on to the ferry from the city side and catch taxis and *dala-dalas* on the other side that follow the beach road. The simpler resorts within a few kilometres of the ferry accept day visitors for a fee of around US$3-7 and they are fine places for a seafood lunch on the beach (a couple of which are recommended in Where to stay, page 38).

Msasani Peninsula
Most visitors to Dar es Salaam end up gravitating to the Msasani Peninsula located just a few kilometres north of the city centre. Despite its access across the (usually horribly congested) Selander Bridge, a causeway over the Msimbazi Creek, and it being completely on the opposite side of the congested centre to the airport, this is where the best hotels, restaurants, nightlife and shops are located.

The Msasani Peninsula is bounded by the ocean on the east and Ali Hassan Mwinyi Road to the southwest. It is divided into three neighbourhoods: Oyster Bay to the south, Msasani to the west and Masaki at the northern tip of the peninsula. Oyster Bay was the first suburb, established in the interwar period by the British to become the main European residential area in the colonial era (Rita Hayworth had a house here). Today, although the construction boom of recent years has taken hold, it retains a relaxed genteel atmosphere among the leafy streets of spacious houses that remain; many of which are now diplomatic missions. Over time the suburb

Msasani Peninsula

spread north along the Msasani Peninsula (once only the site of a Swahili fishing village) and now this area is one of the wealthiest in Dar es Salaam; it features luxurious villas and apartments popular with diplomats and embassy staff, ex-pats and government officials and politicians. The peninsula is also the location of the Dar es Salaam Yacht Club, along with the Gymkhana Club, one of the principal sports' clubs in the city, private schools and hospitals, as well as good hotels and restaurants.

The Slipway ① *Yacht Club Rd, T022-260 0893, www.slipway.net, shops Mon-Sat 1000-1800, Sun 1000-1500, restaurants and bars later.* The principal attraction on the Msasani Peninsula is The Slipway, a shopping and entertainment development in a converted boatyard on the northeast side facing Msasani Bay. The pleasant waterfront here has four restaurants – facing west, so an ideal spot for sunset – while there are a number of boutiques and specialist shops, a souk-like craft market selling textiles, beadwork and the like, and hotel rooms (see Where to stay, below).

From here there are boat trips to uninhabited **Bongoyo Island**, which lies 2 km north of the Msasani Peninsula and is the most frequently visited of the four islands of the Dar es Salaam Marine Reserve (the others are Mbudya, Pangavini and Fungu Yasini). It's a great and relaxing

Where to stay 🛏
Coral Beach **5** *A1*
Mediterraneo Hotel
& Restaurant **7** *D1*
The Oyster Bay **3** *C2*
Q Bar & Guest
House **1** *C1*
Sea Cliff **4** *A2*

Slipway **9** *B1*

Restaurants 🍴
Addis in Dar **1** *D1*
Azuma **2** *B1*
Café Classico **2** *B1*
Epi d'Or **4** *A2*
Karambezi Café **11** *A2*

The Mashua
Waterfront **2** *B1*

Bars & clubs 🍸
News Café **3** *A2*
Q Bar **4** *C1*

ON THE ROAD

Tingatinga art

It is easy enough to recognize Tingatinga paintings for their powerful images and vivid colours. Canvasses are crowded with exaggerated figures of birds, fish and all manner of African creatures, with giant heads and eyes, that roam rainbow landscapes and brilliant seas. This style of pop art was created in the dusty backstreets of Dar es Salaam by Edward Tingatinga in the late 1960s. Born in 1937 in the Tanga region of southern Tanzania, he went to Dar in 1959 in search of work. After attempting several jobs, he worked on building sites and began painting murals on the walls. He then progressed to boards and canvasses and used an enamel bicycle paint that is especially glossy. He sold his paintings underneath a baobab tree at the Morogoro Stores in Oyster Bay which attracted the rich Europeans. He took on several young apprentices and taught them his unique style. Tragically, in 1972, only four years into his discovery of art, he was shot dead by police who accidentally mistook his car for the getaway car in a local robbery. But his students continued to practice the Tingatinga style and took on more apprentices. Today you can buy Tingatinga-style paintings all over Tanzania and Kenya from both craft markets and upmarket souvenir shops. In 2010, *Tinga Tinga Tales* was commissioned by BBC's CBeebies and the Disney Channel aimed at four to six year olds. This TV show's delightful cartoon characters are based on the Tingatinga style and tell African stories, such as 'Why Elephant Has a Trunk', 'Why Aardvark Has a Sticky Tongue', 'Why Wildebeest Stampede' and 'Why Vulture is Bald' and are now watched by children worldwide. Edward Tingatinga would no doubt have been impressed by the success of his legacy.

day trip for swimming, snorkelling and sunbathing, and boats from the Slipway take 30 minutes (US$20 return, which includes entry to the marine reserve, at 0930, 1130, 1330 and 1530, returning at 1030, 1230, 1430 and 1700). The island has a rocky shore but there are two lovely small sandy beaches and simple seafood meals (grilled fresh fish and chips) and cold drinks (including beers) are available from kiosks, from where umbrellas and sun loungers can also be hired.

Mwenge Carvers' Market ① *On the opposite side of Bagamoyo Rd and accessed from Sam Njoma Rd, 8 km north of the city centre. 0800-1800. Taxis cost about US$10 from the city centre, or take a dala-dala from the New Post Office (Posta) to the Mwenge dala-dala stand at the Sam Njoma Rd junction.* This large community market, a major tourist attraction of Dar es Salaam, is where to come to buy Makonde carvings, animal knick-knacks and Tingatinga paintings. The perk of shopping at Mwenge is the sheer volume of crafts to choose from, and you can watch the carvers at work at more than 200 stalls. Prices are highly negotiable – be sure not to give in too quickly and even let the vendors pit over prices among themselves. Makonde carving is probably the best known artwork produced in

Tanzania and originates from the Makonde people in the southern coastal region. Carvings are traditional, human and demon-faced ceremonial masks and 'tree of life' statues are common, and contemporary and more in tune with the tourist market; such as animals commonly seen on safari, spoons, bowls and the like

Listings Dar es Salaam *maps pages 30 and 36*

Tourist information

Tanzania Tourist Board
IPS Building, 3rd floor, Samora Av/Azikiwe St, T022-211 1244, www.tanzaniatouristboard.com.
This is not a drop-in tourist information office but the website has some reasonable information.

Where to stay

Dar es Salaam has an excellent choice of accommodation from international chain hotels to cheap local board and lodgings.

For access to the Zanzibar ferry, it makes sense to overnight in the city centre, but accommodation on the Msasani Peninsula or the beaches to the south of the city make for a more relaxed and quieter stay. If driving, check on the security of any parked vehicle. If you're pre-booking, ask about transfers from the airport, even at the budget end.

City centre

$$$$ Hyatt Regency
Kivukoni Rd, T0764-701 234, www. daressalaam.kilimanjaro.hyatt.com.
Occupying a commanding position in the centre of the city overlooking the harbour, this 8-storey hotel enclosed in blue glass offers 5-star luxury with contemporary decor, 180 rooms and excellent restaurants (see below). There's

also a spa, a beautiful swimming pool on the 1st floor, a gym, shopping arcade and casino. Rates start from US$405.

$$$ New Africa Hotel
Corner Azikiwe St and Sokoine Dr, T022-211 7050, www.newafricahotel.com.
Central and within walking distance of the ferry terminal, great harbour views from the higher floors. 126 rooms with DSTV, Wi-Fi and comfortable made-for-hotel furnishings. Not badly priced given its location (a double starts from US$170). Facilities include 2 restaurants (the **Sawasdee**, see below, is well-known for its Thai food), bar, casino and a lovely indoor heated swimming pool.

$$$ Protea Hotel Courtyard
Barack Obama Dr, next to the Aga Khan Hospital, T022-213 0130, www.proteahotels.com.
A quality hotel with good facilities, a bit more character than some of the larger hotels and with excellent food and service. The 52 rooms, with a/c, DSTV and Wi-Fi, overlook a central lush garden and swimming pool, there's a bar, restaurant and 24-hr coffee shop.

$$$ Serena Dar es Salaam Hotel
Ohio St, T022-211 2416, www.serena hotels.com. Doubles from US$210.
A landmark on Dar's skyline, the Serena has 230 spacious rooms have all mod cons, the best are at the rear overlooking the lovely gardens and very large swimming pool surrounded by palms.

There's a full range of facilities, including a shopping arcade, gym, restaurants (see page 40), a popular bar, coffee shop and a bakery.

$$$ Southern Sun Dar es Salaam
Garden Av, T022-213 7575,
www.tsogosunhotels.com.
An excellent upmarket offering from the quality South African chain Tsogo Sun Hotels, nice location next to the Botanical Gardens (the peacocks regularly fly into the hotel's gardens) and close to the National Museum. 152 well-equipped rooms, gym, swimming pool and a popular restaurant (see Restaurants, below).

$$ Heritage Motel
Corner Kaluta and Bridge sts, T022-211 7471, www.heritagemotel.co.tz.
Easy to locate in the city centre in a tall, yellow building and conveniently located for the ferry terminal, this has 50 simply furnished but comfortable and spotless single/double/triple rooms with a/c, DSTV and Wi-Fi, though some are a little cramped. There's a restaurant and bar and secure parking.

$ Livingstone Hotel
Corner Amani and Livingstone sts, T022-218 1462, www.livingstone-tz.com.
A 7-storey pink block with 60 well-maintained budget rooms that have a little bit more decor (mirrors and pictures) and are larger than most, all with a/c and fan, TV, and some have fridges and balconies. The restaurant is reasonable, and there's Wi-Fi and good service. Doubles from US$60.

$ Safari Inn
Band St, off Libya St, T022-213 8101, www.safariinn.co.tz.
Popular with backpackers with 40 rooms with reliable hot water in a square

concrete block down an alleyway (security guards are at the entrance), continental breakfast is included but there's no restaurant. Wi-Fi in reception, luggage storage and helpful staff. Doubles are US$18 and a single is US$13.

Kigamboni and the southern beaches

$$$-$ Kipepeo
7 km south of the Kigamboni ferry, T0732-920 211, www.kipepeovillage.com.
One of the more relaxed and friendly beach resorts in this area, with 20 rustic en suite huts built on stilts in a grove of coconut palms, plus cheaper beach bandas for US$28 for 2, sharing good ablutions and hot showers with campers. Overlanders can leave vehicles for a small daily fee while they go to Zanzibar. Very good food and drinks are served on the beach or at the rustic thatched beach bar.

$ Mikadi Beach
2 km south of the Kigamboni ferry, T0754-370 269, www.mikadibeach.com.
Popular campsite in a grove of coconut palms right on the beach. You can hire a tent or there are 14 simple reed and thatch double bandas with mattresses and mosquito nets, 2 with en suite bathrooms. Also clean ablutions, a swimming pool and a very good bar that gets busy at the weekends and offers simple home-cooked meals. For a small fee you can park vehicles here whilst you visit Zanzibar.

Msasani Peninsula

$$$$ The Oyster Bay Hotel
Toure Dr, T022-260 0530,
www.theoysterbayhotel.com.
Considered Dar's finest boutique hotel with 8 stylish and massive (70 sq m) suites in a whitewashed villa facing the

Indian Ocean, the emphasis here is on luxury and relaxation. There's a quiet lawned garden, with swimming pool and outdoor eating terrace, and the interior is furnished with a mix of contemporary and antique African crafts. Rates are from US$730 for a double full board.

$$$$-$$$ Hotel Sea Cliff
Toure Dr, T022-260 0380,
www.hotelseacliff.com.
Stylish whitewashed hotel with thatched *makuti* roof set on a low cliff in manicured grounds on the northern tip of the peninsula. 94 spacious and modern a/c rooms with ocean view, and 20 cheaper units in garden cottages. Try the **Alcove Restaurant** and the beautifully positioned **Karambezi** café bar overlooking the bay (see Restaurants, below). There's also a swimming pool, gym, casino and shopping mall.

$$$ Coral Beach
Coral La, T022-260 1928,
www.coralbeach-tz.com.
Mid-range option in good location overlooking Msasani Bay. 62 smart rooms with DSTV and Wi-Fi, some with balconies and ocean views, bright and breezy lobby area, restaurant and bar overlooking the swimming pool and a tiny man-made beach, gym, sauna and jacuzzi.

$$$ Mediterraneo Hotel & Restaurant
Kawe Beach off Old Bagomoyo Rd, 8 km north of Oyster Bay, T022-261 8359,
www.mediterraneotanzania.com.
Relaxing set up in pretty gardens, with 21 simple and brightly painted bungalow-style rooms with cool tiled floors and shady verandas from US$150 for a double and extra beds available. The fantastic restaurant is right on the beach and offers a varied and inventive menu of Italian home-made pasta,

pizza, seafood and Swahili-style buffets, and there's a swimming pool, chilled lounge/bar with cushions and upturned wooden dugout canoes in the sand. Boat trips to the islands are available.

$$-$ Hotel Slipway
At The Slipway, see page 35, T022-260 0893, www.hotelslipway.com.
Part of the Slipway, with 39 smallish but modern a/c rooms with DSTV, some with kitchenettes, arranged around an inner courtyard in the shopping/leisure development. There's no pool but great location next to shops and restaurants (some rooms can be noisy); also used as 'day rooms' which they let out during the day for people who have returned to Dar from safari or from Zanzibar and are not flying out until the evening.

$ Q Bar and Guest House
Haile Selassie Rd, T0754-282 474,
www.qbardar.com.
Smart 4-storey block next to the popular bar (see Bars and clubs, below), with 20 comfortable and spacious, good-value but, quite often, noisy rooms with a/c, fridge, cool tiled floors and Tingatinga paintings on the walls. There's also an 8-bed dorm room (US$15 per person) with a/c, mosquito nets and private lockers. Separate breakfast room for guests on the 2nd floor.

Restaurants

Most of the hotels have restaurants and bars. While the city centre has a fair number of good places to eat, many of these are only open during the day, cater for office workers and do not serve alcohol. The best places for dinner and evening drinks are on the Msasani Peninsula.

City centre

$$$ Jahazi
Serena Dar es Salaam Hotel, Ohio St, see Where to stay, above37. Open 1200-1500, 1900-2300.
Upmarket Mediterranean and seafood restaurant with bright contemporary decor and good service, well-known for its seafood chowder and a grilled calamari. The hotel's other restaurant, the Serengeti (24-hr) has themed nights every day of the week such as Oriental, Tex-Mex or Indian, plus good-value buffet breakfasts and lunches. **The Island Trader Bar and Restaurant** (0900-2000) offers casual dining next to the pool.

$$$ Oriental
Hyatt Regency, Kivukoni St, city centre, see Where to stay, above. Open 1230-1430, 1900-2230.
Very smart 1st-floor restaurant serving a pricey but superb and varied Southeast Asian menu – try the dim sum or beautifully presented sushi – with an excellent wine list and impeccable service. Bookings advised.

$$$ Sawasdee
New Africa Hotel, corner Azikiwe St and Sokine Dr, see Where to stay, above. Open 1900-2300.
Exceptionally good and very authentic Thai food cooked by chefs from Bangkok, elegant decor, attentive service and fantastic setting on the hotel's 9th floor, with wonderful harbour views.

$$ Alcove
2nd Floor, Haidery Plaza, Kisutu St, T022-213 7444, www.alcovetz.com. Mon-Sat 1200-1500, daily 1900-2230.
Long-established and smart Indian and Chinese restaurant, more upmarket than most in the city centre, offering tasty Indian kebabs, tandoori and masala dishes; the long Chinese menu is equally good. They have another branch in the **Hotel Sea Cliff** (see Where to stay, above).

$$ Baraza Grill, Cafe and Bar
Southern Sun Dar es Salaam, Garden Av, see Where to stay, above. Open 1000-2200.
A deservedly popular restaurant with upmarket African decor serving a mix of Swahili and continental food, including pastas, curries, grills, seafood and vegetarian dishes, the weekend brunch goes on until 1300. There's an outdoor terrace onto the pool area and a relaxed bar, and at night the Botanical Gardens next door are partially floodlit around the hotel.

$ Chef's Pride
Chagga St, just off Jamhuri St. Open 0800-2300.
A perennial favourite with budget travellers and locals alike, this split-level restaurant offers tasty food, fast service and is always packed so you may have to wait for a seat and share a table, offering Chinese, Indian and Tanzanian dishes; try *matoke* (savoury bananas) with beef stew or fresh fish in coconut.

$ Sno-cream
Mansfield St, T022-210 2129. Open 0900-midnight.
Established in Dar in, this old-fashioned ice cream parlour is within a short walk of the ferry terminal serving excellent ice cream, including incredibly elaborate sundaes with all the trimmings, plus iced coffees and chocolate malts. Ideal on a hot day in Dar and you can come here while waiting for the ferry.

Msasani Peninsula

$$$ Addis in Dar
35 Ursino St, off Old Bagamoyo Rd, Oyster Bay, T0713-266 299. Mon-Sat 1730-2230.
Charming Ethiopian restaurant with an outside terrace, great place to try spicy beef, lamb and chicken stews, and plenty of choice for vegetarians. Everything is served on woven platters and scooped up with *injera*, a sponge-like bread. Ethiopian honey wine and coffee afterwards completes the experience.

$$$ Azuma
The Slipway, T022-260 0893. Tue-Sun 1800-2300.
Japanese and Indonesian restaurant, authentic cuisine with elegant decor and good views over the bay. Very good sushi. If you book ahead, the chef will come out from the kitchen and prepare food at your table.

$$$-$$ Karambezi Café
Hotel Sea Cliff, see Where to stay, above. Mon-Fri 0630-1030, 1200-2200, Sat and Sun 0630-2200.
Beautiful setting on wooden decking on a low cliff overlooking the ocean. The menu is varied, with pizzas, pastas, seafood and grills and a good selection of wines. It's a fine place for weekend brunch, to share a seafood platter, or a cocktail at sunset.

$$ The Waterfront
At The Slipway, see page 35, T022-260 0893. Open 1200-2400.
Great location on the waterfront offering sunset views over the ocean and a broad terrace with sea breezes. Grills, burgers, salads, pizza, a varied selection of seafood and a popular bar.

$ Epi d'Or
Haile Selassie Rd, at the junction of Chole Rd, T022-260 1663, www.epidor.co.tz. Tue-Sun 0700-2230.
Bistro-style café and French bakery with outside terrace tables, serving very good sandwiches, with imaginative fillings, pastries, croissants, cappuccino and fresh juice, and there's Wi-Fi. There are some beautiful cream cakes in the chilled cabinet here, and it's a popular spot for Sun brunch. The dinner menu includes wood-fired pizzas and Lebanese mezzes.

Bars and clubs

Many of the hotels and restaurants mentioned above crank it up late in the evening with live music or a DJ, especially at weekends when tables are cleared away for dancing.

Level 8
Hyatt Regency, Kivukoni St, city centre, see Where to stay, above. Open 1700-0100.
A luxurious bar on the 8th floor of the Hyatt, with rooftop terrace and mesmerizing views of the port and downtown Dar at night (go here for sunset). Subtle lounge music and occasional live jazz, 90 cocktails plus champagne and cigars.

News Café
Baines Singh Av, Msasani Peninsula, T0767-451 778. Mon-Thu 0800-2300, Fri-Sun 0800-0100.
Equally good for a family brunch as it is for late night drinking, this contemporary café/bar has an upbeat soundtrack, hip, colourful decor, a breezy outdoor patio, and offers cocktails, coffees, light meals and all-day breakfasts. Live bands and DJs play on weekend evenings and Sun lunchtime.

Q Bar

Haile Selassie Rd, Oyster Bay, also see Where to stay, above, T0754-304 733. Open 1700-0200.

A friendly and popular expat venue, with good bar meals, cocktails and shooters, pool tables, lots of TVs – gets packed when European football is showing – live music on Wed and Fri, and Sat is 1970s soul night.

Shopping

There are plenty of shops in the city centre, particularly along Samora Av and its surrounding streets, a short walk from the ferry terminal. The closest large supermarket to the ferry, Nakumatt (0800-2000), is on Julius K Nyerere Rd, about 1.5 km beyond the Central Line Railway Station towards the airport.

Bookshops

A Novel Idea, *at The Slipway (page 35), Yacht Club Rd, Msasani Peninsula, T022-260 1088, www.anovelideatz.com. Mon-Sat 0900-1900, Sun 1000-1800.* The best bookshop in Dar by far, with a full range of new novels, coffee table books, maps and guide books.

Curios and crafts

In the city centre, traditional crafts, particularly wooden carvings, are sold in various shops along Samora Av to the south of the Askari Monument, and from stalls along Ali Hassan Mwinyi Rd near the intersection with Haile Selassie Rd. For materials such as *kangas*, colourful, sarong-like pieces of cloth with Swahili proverbs along the hem, try the southern end of Jamhuri St, where there are many textile shops. On the Msasani Peninsula, the craft market at **The Slipway** *(page 35)* has a good choice of carvings, beaded items, textiles and Tingatinga paintings.

Jewellery

For tanzanite, the beautiful blue-violet gemstone only mined in Tanzania, try **Lithos Africa**, in the **Hyatt Regency Hotel** (see Where to stay, above, T0753-603 666, www.lithosafrica.com).

What to do

Diving

Diving takes place in the **Dar es Salaam Marine Reserve** off the north coast, which includes the 4 uninhabited islands of Mbudya, Pangavini, Fungu Yasin and Bongoyo. All dive sites are accessible from the shore within 25 mins by boat. The best time to dive is Oct-Feb when visibility is excellent and dives average 20-25 m. Although the variety of fish is good, it's not exceptional as it is in Zanzibar and Pemba, and the marine life has suffered from the consequences of illegal dynamite fishing off the coast here. Nevertheless, moray eels, blue-spotted stingrays, lion scorpion and crocodile fish may be spotted on the reefs. Of particular note is Ferns Wall, on the seaward side of Fungu Yasin Reef, where you'll find large barrel sponges, gorgonian fans and 2-m-long whip corals. Reef sharks are often spotted here. Another favourite is Mwamba, a unique reef comprising large fields of pristine brain, rose and plate corals. **Sea Breeze Marine**, *T0754-783 241, www.seabreezemarine.org.* PADI-affiliated, offering single dives and Open Water courses. Excursions by boat go from both **The Slipway** (page 35) or **Hotel White Sands** (page 38).

Golf

Gymkhana Club, *Ghana Av, T022-212 0519*. Established in 1916 as a horse-riding club, this has a full range of sporting facilities, including an 18-hole golf course, tennis and squash courts, and cricket, football and rugby pitches. Visitors can obtain temporary membership to play golf and the pro-shop rents out clubs. Here, because of a shortage of water, you will be playing on browns not greens.

Sailing

Yacht Club, *Yacht Club Rd, Msasani Peninsula, T022-260 0132, www.daryachtclub.com*. The club organizes East Africa's premier sailing event, the Dar to Tanga (and back) Yacht Race every Dec. Although it's a members-only club, visitors can contact them to rent kayaks and SUPS (stand-up paddle-boards) from a kiosk on the beach for about US$7 for 4 hrs, and there's a restaurant and bar. It's just north of The Slipway.

Transport

Air

Julius Nyerere International Airport (**JNIA**) is 13 km southwest of the city centre along Julius K Nyerere Rd, T022-284 2402, www.taa.go.tz. The airlines have desks at the airport and there are a range of facilities including a cafeteria and bar, 24-hr bureaux de change and ATMs and, airside, duty free and souvenir shops. For those international visitors requiring a visa for Tanzania (see page 165), the visa desk is just before immigration at international arrivals. The airport is served by a number of international airlines (see page 145) and domestic and regional carriers (see page 148). These include **Air Excel**, **Air Tanzania**, **Auric Air**, **Coastal Aviation**, **Fast Jet**, **Precision Air**, **Regional Air** and **ZanAir**. Between them they link Dar es Salaam to other cities in **Tanzania**, **Zanzibar**, **Pemba** and **Mafia Island**, **Arusha** and **Kilimanjaro** from where they connect with a circuit of the airstrips in the **Serengeti National Park** and other safari destinations in **northern Tanzania**, the safari destinations in southern Tanzania such as the **Selous Game Reserve** and **Ruaha National Park**, and some fly between Dar and **Nairobi** and **Mombasa** in Kenya, to destinations in **northern Mozambique**, and to **Johannesburg** in South Africa.

Bus

The main long-distance bus terminal is on Morogoro Rd in the Ubungo area, 6 km to the west of the centre. It is well organized and modern, with cafés and

shops, and is reasonably secure as only ticket holders and registered taxi drivers are allowed inside; nevertheless watch out for pickpocketing. For a few shillings you can hire a porter with a trolley for luggage. However, the ticket offices are on Morogoro Rd outside, which means that if a taxi drops you here, then you are very likely to be pounced upon by a crowd of touts who want to take you to their preferred bus company. Hang on to your luggage tightly and ignore them. A taxi from Ubungo into the city centre should cost around US$8. Outside on Morogoro ad, you can also catch the **Bus Rapid Transit (BRT)** or *dala-dala* to the centre, though again these are crowded and there is a problem if you are carrying a large amount of luggage.

Buses go to destinations across the country and will only leave when completely full. **Note** Buses are not permitted to travel at night in Tanzania, so except for those to nearby destinations, departures are early in the morning. As such, Ubungo gets very busy from as early as 0500 (when it's still dark), when buses are preparing themselves to leave their overnight parking spots, and the roads around Ubungo are teeming with people being spewed from taxis and *dala-dalas*.

Car hire
Car hire can be arranged through most of the many tour operators in Dar es Salaam or try the companies below. All can arrange pick-ups and drop-offs at the airport. For more information about renting a car and driving, see Practicalities, page 151.
Avis, (who use local agents) T022-276 1277, www.avis.com.
Europcar, at the Serena Dar es Salaam

Hotel, Ohio St, T022-266 4722, www.europcar.co.tz.
First Car Rental, airport T022-284 2738, Amani Place, Ohio St, opposite the Serena Dar es Salaam Hotel, T022-211 5381, www.firstcarrental.co.tz.
Green Car Rentals, Nukrumah St, along Nyerere Rd, T022-218 3718, www.greencarstz.com.
Sam's Car Rentals, New Bagamoyo Road, Mbezi Beach, T022-277 3610, www.samscarental.com.
XCar, Mwai Kibaki Rd, opposite Shopper's Plaza, Msasani Peninsula, T0753-254 660, www.xcarrentals.com.

Ferry
Ferries to and from Zanzibar and Pemba go from the ferry terminal on Sokoine Dr, opposite St Joseph's Cathedral. After disembarking from the ferry, taxis are readily available on the main road outside, as are stops for the new **Bus Rapid Transit (BRT)**.

There used to be several ferry companies with services to Zanzibar and Pemba but these days the monopoly is run by **Azam Marine & Kilimanjaro Fast Ferries**, T022-212 3324, www.azammarine.com. They operate a fleet of 8 fast purpose-built catamarans, and the trip to Zanzibar is generally reliable and pleasant and takes on average of 90 mins, though the newer boats being put into service will reduce this to just 40 mins. The ticket office is open 0600-2000; ignore the touts hanging around outside the ferry terminal who may follow you to the office to claim credit and take commission – it is easy enough to book a ticket on your own. Fares for non-residents greatly exceed those for residents, though they are not overly expensive and are inclusive of port tax. Payment for tickets for non-residents is in US$ cash, though £ and € cash may be accepted at a push, and in theory also in Visa/MasterCard (but do not rely on this). The 1st class tickets entitle you to a comfortable seat on the very top deck, which has a/c and a snack bar, while economy class tickets are on the lower decks and the outside areas with bench-type seating – the latter is advised for anyone who suffers from sea-sickness.

Daily departures from **Dar to Zanzibar** are at 0700, 0930, 1230 and 1545; from **Zanzibar to Dar**, 0700, 0930, 1230 and 1530. On Wed and Sat they also operate a service from **Zanzibar to Pemba** at 0700, which arrives in Pemba at around 1000. The return boat departs Pemba at 1230, and arrives back in Zanzibar at 1430. However, schedules to/from Pemba change regularly (on occasions, there may also be the option of getting a ferry from Dar to Pemba on the same day), so check with Azam for the current situation. Fares between both Dar and Zanzibar, and Zanzibar and Pemba, are: economy class US$35, children (under 12) US$25, 1st class US$40 per person.

Zanzibar

The very name Zanzibar conjures up exotic and romantic images. The main town, Stone Town, with its intriguing winding alleyways and old Arabian townhouses, is steeped in history and full of atmosphere, while Zanzibar's coastline offers some of the best beaches in the world, where it is impossible not to relax on the palm-fringed beaches next the Indian Ocean.

Zanzibar attracts hundreds of thousands of visitors a year, and to some extent the island has suffered from the consequences of over-zealous mass tourism. Some visitors on charter holidays, experience little of the island outside the compound of their all-inclusive resort. But there's much to see if you do, and the compact island is easy to explore whether it be on a guided tour, local *dala-dala* or by hire car.

By criss-crossing the interior via ruined Sultans' palaces or forests that are home to Zanzibar's rare red colobus monkey, you reach the north, northeast or southeast coasts, where there are numerous places to stay from remote rustic thatched cottages to fully-developed holiday resorts with entertainment and activities on tap . Wherever you stay, the undisputed highlight of Zanzibar are the idyllic white-sand beaches, coral reefs and offshore sand bars, which make for dazzling days in the sun.

Stone Town

It may not have a particularly romantic name, but Stone Town is the old city and cultural heart of Zanzibar, where little has changed for hundreds of years. It's a delightfully romantic place of narrow alleys, more than 50 crumbling mosques, two imposing cathedrals and 1700 grand Arab houses with giant brass-studded wooden doors. Most of the buildings were built by the Omani sultans in the 19th century when Zanzibar was one of the most important trading centres in the Indian Ocean. European influences, such as balconies and verandas, were added some years later. Despite its name, the walls of the houses are not, in fact, made of stone but from coralline rock, which is a good building material, but erodes easily.

Since Stone Town was deservedly declared a World Heritage Site by UNESCO in 2000, the Zanzibar Stone Town Heritage Society has been working towards restoring the ancient town before these buildings are lost forever, and many of Stone Town's historical houses have now been beautifully renovated. Most hotel accommodation is in the restored old houses and rooms are decorated with antiques, Persian rugs and the delightful four-poster Zanzibarian beds. At least one night is warranted in Stone Town to soak up the atmosphere by getting lost in the warren of passages, enjoy sleeping in an historical hotel, and a meal or drink in a west-facing spot to watch the sunset.

The original Stone Town is the area west of Benjamin Mkapi Road; formerly and often still referred to as Creek Road (although the creek itself has long gone), which is a major thoroughfare, usually clogged with traffic. In Kiswahili Stone Town is known as Mji Mkongwe ('old town'). The newer part of town, Ng'ambo (literally, 'the other side'), lies to the east of Benjamin Mkapi (Creek) Road and is an unattractive sprawl of buildings most tourists will only pass through on their way to the coast. It is Mji Mkongwe that holds all the important and historical sights. Here the fine buildings were constructed by wealthy Arab slavers and clove traders, British administrators and prosperous Indian businessmen, and these structures were so soundly built that they have survived for the most part. Today wandering around the narrow lanes of coral rag houses with their striking ornate doors and dimly lit curio shops is Stone Town's simplest pleasure.

Darajani Market
Darajani Rd, daily 0600-1800.

A good place to start a walking tour is from the Darajani Market on Benjamin Mkapi (Creek) Road opposite the *dala-dala* terminal. This gable-fronted covered market was opened in 1904 and remains a bustling, colourful and aromatic place, and is known informally in Kiswahili as Marikiti Kuu ('main market'). Here you will see Zanzibarian life carrying on as it has done for so many years – lively, busy and noisy. Outside are long, neat rows of bicycles carefully locked and guarded by their minder while people are buying and selling inside the market. Fruit, vegetables, meat and fish are all for sale here, as well as household implements, many of them locally made, clothing and footwear. This is a good place to get spices (sold to real shoppers as opposed to the ready-packaged ones designed for tourists), packets of delicious *masala* tea and brightly coloured *kikois* and *kangas* at good prices. On Wednesday and Saturday there is also a flea market selling antiques and bric-a-brac. Note that the chicken, fish and meat areas are not for the squeamish – the smell and flies can be somewhat overwhelming.

Tip...
It's best to get here in the morning before it gets too hot. The early morning from 0600 is when the biggest fish auctions take place when you may see huge sailfish or tuna for sale. Things quieten down after 1400.

Anglican Cathedral Christ Church
New Mkunazini Rd, T024-223 5348, www.zanzibaranglican.or.tz, 0900-1800, US$5, children (under 10) free.

Returning to Benjamin Mkapi (Creek) Road, after a further 200 m south there is a large crossroads. To the right is New Mkunazini Road and, after about 50 m, another right leads into the cathedral courtyard. The building to the left of the

Essential Stone Town

Finding your feet

If arriving at the airport (see page 82), which is 7 km southeast of town, you will be badgered by the many taxi drivers. Expect to pay in the region of US$8 to hotels in town. Not all hotels in Stone Town are easily accessible by car right to the front door, but for an extra tip the taxi drivers usually help visitors with their luggage into the hotels. You can also get *dala-dala* No 505 from the airport along Nyerere Road to the Darajani stop on **Benjamin Mkapi (Creek) Road** in Stone Town, which will take around 30 minutes and cost less than US$1. The closest this gets to **Mji Mkongwe** ('old town') is the Mnazi Mmoja Hospital on Kaunda Road, from where it's about 700 m, or less than a 10-minute walk, to Kenyatta Road in Shangani. However, these *dala-dalas* are generally full of people and there'll be little space for luggage, plus you will have to walk the final leg unassisted to your hotel. Some of Stone Town's more upmarket hotels offer free airport pickups, and all of them can prearrange a taxi to meet you – you simply need to look for a sign with your name on it among the mob of taxi drivers outside arrivals.

Tip...

In the towns and villages, it is courteous for women to dress modestly, covering the upper arms and body, with dress or skirt hemlines below the knee. Shorts, bikinis and other revealing clothing cause offence so do cover up. See page 153 for other customs and considerations.

The ferry terminal is in the Malindi area of Stone Town. You can take a taxi directly from the port for little more than US$5 to anywhere in town. Alternatively, you can go to the **Zanzibar Commission for Tourism** (**ZCT**) desk at the port (see page 64) and they will phone the hotels to arrange someone to meet you, walk you to your hotel and help with luggage. The booking offices for the ferries are clustered around the jetty where you will need to reconfirm the date of your return ticket to Dar if you have not already done so when booking the ticket. The dhow harbour is next to the port, but remember it is illegal for foreigners to travel between the mainland and the islands by dhow.

Getting around

Stone Town is compact enough to walk around and, in any case, most of the streets are too narrow for vehicles. However, some *dala-dalas* run around the outskirts for no more than US$0.50 per journey, and taxis are available and a short taxi ride shouldn't cost more than US$5. If you have not pre-booked accommodation, you will need to walk around and find a hotel that suits.

If coming from the airport, the logical option is to get to, and start looking in **Shangani**, from where you can work your way northeast through town If coming off the ferry, just exit the port and turn right, ignoring all the *papasi* (touts), and you'll immediately be in the **Malindi area**, where you can start looking for a hotel and head southwest further into town towards the **Forodhani Gardens**.

Best hotels in Swahili mansions

Beyt Al Salaam, page 65
Emerson on Hurumzi, page 65
Emerson Spice, page 65
Kisiwa House, page 66
Mashariki Palace Hotel, page 66

Time required

A tour of Stone Town will take at least a day, but it is such a fascinating place that you could easily spend a week and still find charming and interesting new places. It is recommended that you spend at night here – watching the sunset from a rooftop in Stone Town is a highlight.

Papasi

In Stone Town you will undoubtedly come into contact with street touts – young men who will tout for business, offering hotels, transfers, spice or other tours in the hope of earning commission. You may well be pounced upon after you get off the ferry; other hotspots include the streets in Shangani around the post office. Some can be very persistent, and most are certainly irritating; in Kiswahili the word means 'tick' (as in the parasite).

One of the most common ploys *papasi* use is to tell visitors that your hotel of choice no longer exists, is full, or not safe or clean etc. Take this with a pinch of salt, as it could well be that they just want to take you somewhere where they know they'll get better commission. Most *papasi* are also hoping that your stay on the island will mean ongoing work for them as your guide, so if you do use one to help you find a hotel, they'll invariably be outside waiting for you later. When arranging tours and transport to the coastal resorts, never make payments on the street; deal directly with a hotel or one of the many tour operators and organize everything in the confines of their office and get a receipt.

A polite 'no thank you' is usually enough to rid yourself of the services of *papasi*, but other strategies include saying that you have already booked hotel accommodation, carrying your own bags to a restaurant first, having a drink and then looking for accommodation later, or saying you have been on all the tours and that you are leaving tomorrow and have already bought the ferry ticket.

Overall, *papasi* are not well tolerated by most licensed companies and locals get annoyed when tourists become distressed by the unwanted attention. In short, some travellers complain bitterly about them, while others actually make firm friends and enjoy their additional helpful local knowledge and services (*dhow* trips for example). It's just a case of your personal preference whether you ignore them or not.

Best sunset views...

The Tea House, page 72
Livingstone Beach (outside tables), page 76
Sunset Lounge, page 76
Tatu (third-floor balcony), page 76
Up North, page 76

Stone Town

Where to stay

Abuso Inn **2** *D2*
Africa House **1** *D2*
Beyt Al Salaam **21** *D1*
Clove **7** *C4*
Dhow Palace **9** *D2*
Emerson on Hurumzi **10** *C4*
Emerson Spice **3** *C4*
Flamingo Guest
  House **11** *E4*
Forodhani Gardens **6** *C3*
House of Spices **4** *C5*
Jafferji House & Spa **22** *D3*
Jambo Guesthouse **24** *D4*
Karibu Inn **17** *D2*
Kholle House **17** *B5*
Kiponda B&B **18** *C4*
Kisiwa House **5** *D2*
Malindi Guest House **20** *A6*
Maru Maru **25** *C3*
Mashariki Palace **8** *C3*
Mazon's **23** *D2*
Mbweni Ruins **12** *E4*
Mizingani Seafront **28** *B4*
Park Hyatt Zanzibar **29** *D1*
Princess Salme Inn **13** *A6*
Pyramid **26** *B5*
Seyyida Hotel & Spa **30** *C4*
St Monica's Hostel
  & Restaurant **27** *D5*
Swahili House **14** *C5*
Tembo House **31** *D2*
Zanzibar **33** *D3*
Zanzibar Coffee
  House **15** *D4*
Zanzibar Grand
  Palace **16** *B5*
Zanzibar Ocean View **19** *E4*
Zanzibar Palace **37** *C4*
Zanzibar Serena Inn **36** *D1*
Zenji **38** *B5*

Restaurants

Archipelago **9** *C2*
Green Garden **2** *D4*
Jaws Corner **7** *D3*
La Taverna **6** *D5*
Lazuli **10** *D2*
Lemongrass Oriental
  Restaurant
  & Café Miwa **8** *D2*
Luckmaan
  Restaurant **12** *D5*
Luis Yoghurt
  Parlour **11** *D3*
Monsoon **3** *C3*
Pagoda **13** *D2*
The Silk Route **14** *C3*
Stone Town Café
  and B&B **15** *D2*
Terrace **16** *D1*
Tradewinds **17** *D2*
Zenji Café &
  Boutique **19** *B6*

Bars & clubs

Livingstone Beach **4** *C2*
Mercury's **1** *B4*
The Sunset Lounge **20** *D2*
Tatu **21** *D2*

To Dar es
Salaam & Pemba

New
Dock

The Big
Tree

Dhow Countries
Music Academy
(Old Customs
House)

Ijunaa
Mosque

KIPONDA

Beit al-Sahel
(People's Palace)

Nyumbaya Moto St

FORODHANI

Aga Khan
Mosque

Doreen
Mashika

Mizingani Rd

Hurumzi St

Beit-el Ajaib
(House of Wonders)

Forodhani
Gardens

Zanzibar
Curio Shop

Forodhani
Market

Changa Bazaar

One Ocean –
The Zanzibar
Dive Centre

Orphanage

Old
Fort

Moto &
Dada

Sasik

Gizenga St

Bahari
Divers

Upendo
Means Love

Hamamni
Persian Baths

Mambo
Msiige

Zanzibar
Gallery

Bohora Mosque

Abeid Curio Shop

Tamim Curio Shop

Mago East Africa

Mrembo Spa

Shangani St

Surti
& Sons

Cathedral St

Memories
of Zanzibar

St Joseph's
Catholic
Cathedral

Ras Shangani

Kelele
Square

SHANGANI

BAGHANI

Kenyatta Rd

Baghani St

Capital Art Studio

Tippu Tip's
House

Suicide Alley

Zanzibar Car Hire Ltd

Former
English
Club

Kanga
Kabisa

Pipalwadi St

Soko muhogo St

Mkunazini St

VUGA

Zanzibar
Medical
Group

Kenyatta Rd

Vuga Rd

Zanzibar
Channel

N

100 metres
100 yards

National Library
& High Court

Kaunda Rd

People's
Gardens
(Victoria
Gardens)

Vuga Rd

To Airport (6 km), Mbweni Ruins & **12** **19**
State House
Mnazi Mmoja Hospital

Beit El-Amani
(House of Peace)

entrance to the courtyard was a hostel for nuns and the **Anglican Missionary Hospital**, which is constructed on top of the old slave chambers. Today it's St Monica's Hostel & Restaurant (see page 70). Construction began on the Anglican Cathedral Christ Church (or Church of Christ) in 1873 on the site of the old slave market to commemorate the end of the slave trade. You can pick up guides here who will, for a small fee, give you a short tour of the slave chambers and cathedral. The altar is on the actual site of the slave market's whipping post. The marble columns at the west end were put in upside down, while the bishop was on leave in the UK. Other points of interest are the stained-glass window dedicated to David Livingstone who was instrumental in the abolition of the slave trade, and the small wooden crucifix said to have been made from the wood of the tree under which Livingstone died in Chitambo in Zambia. If you can, try to go up the staircase of the cathedral to the top of the tower from where you will get an excellent view of the town. It is said that Sultan Barghash donated the clock for the tower on condition that the tower should not exceed the height of the tower at Beit-el-Ajaib (House of Wonders). There are services in Kiswahili and English (check the website for times).

Beit El-Amani

Corner Benjamin Mkapi (Creek) and Kaunda rds.

If you head down to the end of Benjamin Mkapi (Creek) Road, about 400 m south of the cathedral, you will see Beit El-Amani (meaning 'House of Peace'), which was built by the British in 1925 as a memorial to the end of the First World War. Its architecture and domed shape were based on the Aya Sophia Mosque in Istanbul. Sadly it's not open to the public and is presently used as an archive for the Zanzibar Stone Town Heritage Society, but it's recently been restored and is a handsome startlingly white building that sits in a pretty garden.

Tip...
Bishop Edward Steere laid a foundation stone for the cathedral on Christmas Day 1873; it was completed on the same day seven years later in 1880.

Stone Town's western tip

The People's Gardens on Kaunda Road, also known as the Victoria Gardens, were originally laid out by Sultan Barghash for the use of his extensive harem. Many of the plants in the garden were added in the 1880s by naturalist and British Resident Sir John Kirk. Opposite the gardens and behind a white wall is the **State House**. Originally built as the British Residency, it was designed to complement the earlier Arabic buildings such as the People's Palace. Since Independence the building has housed the President's Office. Note that photography is not permitted around the State House.

The **Africa House Hotel** (see Where to stay, below) is on Suicide Alley and was once the **English Club**, opened in 1888 (the oldest such club in East Africa), see box, page 56. One of the great events at the English Club used to be the New Year's Eve fancy dress ball, when great crowds of dumfounded Zanzibaris would gather to stare at the crazy *wazungu* (whites) in their costumes. It has been beautifully restored to its former glory, and the upstairs terrace bar is one of the best places in Zanzibar for a drink at sunset (see also Bars and clubs, page 75). A little further down Suicide Alley is **Tippu Tip's House**, named after the wealthy 19th-century slave trader. Although his real name was Hamed bin Mohammed el Marjebi, everybody called him by his nickname Tippu Tip, which referred to a nervous twitch affecting his eyes. Owner of several plantations on Zanzibar and more than 10,000 slaves by 1895, he was the most notorious of all slavers, making him Livingstone's arch-enemy during his quest for the abolition of the slave trade. The house is not open to the public, and is in an unfortunate state of disrepair, but it has a splendid carved wooden front door.

Also at the western tip of the town off Shangani Street and near Kelele Square is another interesting building known as **Mambo Msiige**, which was built in 1847 and was once owned by a wealthy Arab slave-trader and good friend of Seyyid Said. Its name, meaning 'do not imitate', is a reference to its various architectural styles. The stately main entrance features three Omani style arches with intricately carved wooden doors leading to a cool courtyard. It is said that the owner used to bury slaves alive within the walls of the building and added many thousands of eggs to the mortar to enhance the colour. Since then, the building has been used as the headquarters of the Universities Mission to Central Africa, as the British Consulate and today has been finely restored as part of the five-star **Park Hyatt Zanzibar Hotel** (see page 64).

ON THE ROAD
Zanzibar doors

At last count, there were 560 original carved doors in Zanzibar. When a house was built, the door was traditionally the first part to be erected, with the rest of the house built around it. The tradition originates from the countries around the Persian Gulf and spread through Afghanistan to Punjab in India where such doors were reported in the first half of the 12th century. They started to feature in Zanzibar houses in the 15th century, but most of those surviving today were built in the 18th to 19th centuries. The greater the wealth and social position of the owner of the house, the larger and more elaborately carved his front door. The door was the badge of rank and a matter of great honour among merchant society. British explorer Richard Burton remarked in 1872: "the higher the tenement, the bigger the gateway, the heavier the padlock and the huger the iron studs which nail the door of heavy timber, the greater the owner's dignity." Set in a square frame, the door is a double door opening inwards that can be bolted from the inside and locked from the outside by a chain and padlock. Popular motifs in the carvings on the doors include the frankincense tree, which denotes wealth, and the date palm denoting abundance. Some of them feature brass knockers, and many are studded with brass spikes. This may be a modification of the Indian practice of studding doors with sharp spikes of iron to prevent them being battered in by war elephants. In AD 915, an Arab traveller recorded that Zanzibar island abounded in elephants and, in 1295, Marco Polo wrote that it had "elephants in plenty". These days there are no elephants, and the studs are there merely for decoration. The doors are maintained by the Stone Town Heritage Society (www.zanzibarstonetown.org) who keep a photographic record and a watchful eye that they are not removed and exported. Standout portals include the golden door at the House of Wonders, the entrance to the Old Fort, and the doors on houses along Baghani Street.

Old Fort and around

The Old Fort (also known as the Arab Fort or in Kiswahili *Ngome Kongwe*) is in the west of the town next to the House of Wonders (see below). This huge structure was built in 1700 on the site of a Portuguese church, the remains of which can be seen incorporated into the fabric of the internal walls. Castellated battlements top its tall walls. The fort was built by Omani Arabs to defend against attacks from the Portuguese, who had occupied Zanzibar for almost two centuries. During the 19th century the fort was used as a prison and, in the early 20th century, it was used as a depot for the railway that ran from Stone Town to Bububu. It is possible to reach the top of the battlements on the west side and look at the towers. The central area is now used as an open-air theatre and is a venue during Zanzibar's festivals (see page 76). The fort also houses an art gallery, several small shops selling crafts and spices, and a café with tables in the shade of a couple of large trees.

The English Club

The British in Zanzibar (as everywhere) were profoundly insular and, in general, reluctant to establish social relations with other communities. This was expressed in the formation of the English Club, which subsequently provoked every other significant community to establish its own club, thereby underscoring the religious and racial divisions in the society.

Although the English Club was formed some time before the turn of the 20th century, it was only in 1907 that it began to look seriously for substantial premises. A suitable building, now the Africa House Hotel, was located in Shangani just back from the shore, and, backed by a government loan, the club opened in 1908 on its new site, with a restaurant, a committee room that doubled as a library, a bar and a billiards room.

In 1911 the club proposed taking over two rooms in an adjoining building to provide accommodation for out-of-town members. The government was approached to provide the capital to buy a lease and to refit the rooms. It agreed on condition that the rooms would be made available to the government for officials and their wives and other visitors needing accommodation in Stone Town.

The Secretary, EWP Thurston, reported that the constitution of the club did not allow Americans or Europeans, and that it was a 'Man's Club', and there were the "strongest social and sanitary reasons against ladies occupying rooms." The government reacted vigorously to the proposed exclusions.

Women were allowed in to use the library in the mornings and between 1800 and 2000 in the evenings. They were also admitted to take lunch and dinner in the restaurant. As for the Committee's 'sanitary' objections to women using the accommodation, these were dismissed by the government as the "merest bogies of their perfervid imaginations". In April 1912 the club gave way, and the two rooms were added. Later, some garages were built on the shore side of the building, and more rooms for women were added above them.

In 1916 the club had plans to demolish a warehouse on the shore and build a swimming pool and squash courts. But the war interfered with these plans and they never went ahead. The space was cleared, however, and became known as 'German Forodhani' (Forodhani means 'customs house' – the German Consulate was nearby) or 'Shagani Steps'. Coloured lights were strung from cast-iron telegraph poles (two can still be seen on the site) and, on Tuesday evenings the Sultan's band played a selection of classical and popular music for the benefit of locals who sat around on the grass and those taking sundowners in the club's veranda bar.

On the south side of the fort you can take a walk down Gizenga Street with its busy bazaars. This will lead you to the twin-spired **St Joseph's Catholic Cathedral**, designed by Henri Espérandieu, who designed the Basilica in Marseille and loosely based this work on it. It's a beautiful building but unfortunately it's not's open except for Sunday Mass (0700, 0900 and 1630), which incorporates local elements, including Swahili drumming (be warned, though, it lasts about two hours). On the opposite side of the road is the **Bohora Mosque**.

To the east of the cathedral, and located in its namesake neighbourhood in the centre of Stone Town on Hammani Street, are the **Hammani Persian Baths**, which were built by Sultan Barghash in 1888 for use as public baths and maintained their function until 1920. Today they are a protected monument, and you are permitted to look inside by tipping the caretaker (around US$4). There is no water anymore, but it offers a cool respite from the heat, as well as insight into what life for Stone Town's upper classes must have been like. The baths have been well preserved and there are a number of cubicles, each with a specific function, such as the area where people disrobed and what used to be the warm rooms and hot baths, which were heated by underground hot-water aqueducts.

Beit-el-Ajaib (House of Wonders)
Mizingani Rd.

Close to the fort and opposite the Forodhani Gardens, Zanzibar's tallest building is Beit-el-Ajaib meaning the 'House of Wonders'. In 2001 it became the **Museum of History and Culture or the Museum of Zanzibar**. Sadly however, in 2012 the southeastern corner of the building collapsed, taking with it several of the iron pillars and threatening the building's façade and overall structural integrity. To date it has remained closed (hopefully it will be restored soon and from 2014, the World Monuments Fund has been initiating projects to raise money; www.wmf.org). It's an imposing waterfront building (which can still be admired from the outside) with four storeys surrounded by verandas and some fine examples of door carving. Built in 1883 by a British marine engineer for Sultan Barghash to serve as his palace, the name 'House of Wonders' came about because it was the first building on the island to have electricity and even a lift. At the entrance are two Portuguese cannons, which date from the 16th century. In 1896, in an attempt to persuade the Sultan to abdicate, the British navy subjected the palace to a bombardment. Inside, the floors are of marble and there are various decorations that were imported from Europe.

Forodhani Gardens
In front of the House of Wonders and the Old Fort, the Forodhani Gardens were completely overhauled in 2009 to the tune of more than US$2 million by a grant from the Aga Khan Trust for Culture. It was once the location for the port's customs sheds, before the port was moved in 1936 to the deepwater anchorage. In the middle is a domed bandstand with Arabic arches where the Sultan's band once played for the

> **Tip...**
> By day, a couple of simple garden cafés offer drinks and snacks; by night the park is transformed into the wonderful Forodhani Market (see box, page 59).

public. Nearer the sea is a white concrete arabesque arch, which was built in 1956 for the visit of Princess Margaret, although this was never officially used, as the princess arrived at the dhow harbour instead. She did, however, visit the gardens and planted a tree. Today, the well-kept gardens are a pleasant place to stroll and watch the young boys diving quite spectacularly off the sea wall.

Just to the south of the park, Mizingani Road passes through a tunnel and, if you follow it, the second building on the right has a plaque on the wall that reads: 'This building was the British Consulate from 1841 to 1874. Here at different times lived Burton, Speke, Grant and Kirk. David Livingstone lived here and in this house his body rested on its long journey home.' Livingstone died in Zambia but it was in Zanzibar where the influential abolitionist crusader mounted his anti-slavery campaign. It was also where he started and ended his explorations of Africa. Today, this building houses the **Livingstone Beach**, another good sundowner location with tables on the beach. A few steps along the beach is the seafront façade of the Tembo House Hotel (the main entrance is on Shangani Street), where there is another pleasant terrace café. Both spots (see Bars and clubs and Restaurants, respectively, below) offer a great vantage point to watch the comings and goings on this public beach, where fishing dhows (and sightseeing boats) are pulled up on to the sand and kids play football at dusk. Tembo House itself is a fine Arab-built mansion (and listed building) that served as the American Consulate from 1834 and 1884. It was restored as a hotel in the 1990s.

Beit al-Sahel (People's Palace) and around
Mizingani Rd, north of the House of Wonders, 0830-1800, US$3, children (under 18) US$1.

The Beit al-Sahel (People's Palace), built in the 1890s, is where the sultans, their families and harems lived until their rule was finally overturned by the revolution of 1964. Following the revolution, it was renamed the People's Palace and was used by various political factions until it was turned into the Palace Museum in 1994. There are three floors of exhibits, which are reasonably distracting, although some of the antique furniture is rotting, and the paintings and hanging rugs are fading badly. Additionally the roof is in poor structural condition and, like the House of Wonders, this is another property that has been put on 'watch' alert by the World Monuments Fund. A variety of furniture on show includes the Sultan's huge bed. Look out for the formica wardrobe with handles missing – obviously very fashionable at the time. One room shows memorabilia of Princess Salme, whose father was the first Sultan of Zanzibar and whose mother was a slave (see box41). Another exhibition concentrates on the period between 1870 and 1896 and the changes in Stone Town following the introduction of water pipes and electricity. At the top of the stairs on the first floor are some fine larger-than-life portraits of Sultan Seyyid Said and his two sons Majid and Barghash. There are good views over town from the top floor.

Heading north along Mizingani Road from the Palace Museum is the **Old Customs House**, which was built in 1865 and now houses the **Dhow Countries Music Academy** ① T024-223 4050, www.zanzibarmusic.org. Look for the signboard

ON THE ROAD

Forodhani Market

In Forodhani Gardens between the Old Fort and the sea, this charming nightly food market, which opens at dusk, is a lively, atmospheric place to eat and shouldn't be missed on a visit to Stone Town. There are dozens of stalls selling an extraordinary variety of snacks and seafood cooked on charcoal burners under paraffin lamps, and it's fun to wander around even if you don't feel hungry. It has the best and the cheapest seafood anywhere; you can get prawn and lobster kebabs, giant crab claws, grilled calamari, octopus tentacles and mussels, and fish including kingfish, tuna, barracuda, red snapper and blue marlin. Non-seafood snacks include corn on the cob, cassava, curries, chicken and beef kebabs, falafels and samosas, and keep your eyes peeled for delicious local specialities such as *mantabali* (African pizza), *mishkaki* (skewer-grilled marinated meat), *chipsi mayai* (chip omelette) and *urojo* (a mango and ginger-based soup). You eat your feast on paper plates with small toothpicks and, if you're thirsty, try some fresh coconut milk or freshly squeezed sugar cane juice. You may need to haggle over some of the prices, but you will still come away very full and with change from US$10. Just inspect it carefully in the dim light to ensure everything is cooked well; if it's not, ask the vendor to throw it back on the coals for a little longer.

outside advertising *taarab* music concerts (about US$7) performed regularly by the students on the top floor. There are also occasional performances held in the bandstand in Forodhani Gardens. It was originally a house of one of the Sultan's daughters, Zam Zam Humud bin Ahmed, and from 1928 served as the customs house for the port until it fell into disrepair in 1987. The house was fully restored in 2002 and features many beautifully carved wooden doors, decorated with fish, lotus and anchor chain motifs, an elegant Arab-style interior courtyard, neo-Classical adornments, like columns and stained glass, and there's a fine balcony with four iron pillars supporting the two verandas. The offices of the Zanzibar Stone Town Heritage Society (www.zanzibarstonetown.org) are also here on the ground floor. Just north of here is the **Big Tree**, a giant fig that was planted in 1911 by Sultan Khalifa. Traditionally it sheltered local dhow builders; today it does the same for taxi drivers and is also a good place to organize trips to the islands on boats that leave from the little beach in front.

Ithinasheri Dispensary

Often called the 'Old Dispensary', this very ornate building is on Mizingani Road, north of the Big Tree. It was built in 1887 by Thaira Thopen, Zanzibar's richest man at the time, to commemorate Queen Victoria's Silver Jubilee. It was his intention for the building to be used as a charitable hospital for the poor; but it never was as he died before it was finished. In 1900 the building was bought by another prominent Indian merchant living in Zanzibar, Haji Nasser Nurmohamed, who turned the ground floor into a dispensary, while the upper floors were partitioned into apartments. In 1964 following the Zanzibar Revolution, most Zanzibari Indians, including those who lived in the dispensary, fled abroad. The building was requisitioned by the government, and later fell into disuse and decay. The Aga Khan Trust for Culture obtained it in 1994, and this was one of the first buildings to be successfully restored to its former glory. It's one of the most imposing of Stone Town's buildings, with four grand storeys with wrap-around decorative lattice balconies and a clock tower. Today the dispensary rooms are rented out as offices, but visitors are free to go inside and admire the interior.

Port and dhow harbour

Further up Mizingani Road is the main port and the dhow harbour, which is a lively and bustling part of the Malindi quarter. The deepwater harbour has wharfs piled high with containers, and the landing is most frequently used by boats and hydrofoils from Dar es Salaam and Pemba. Built in 1925, the port remains essentially the 'industrial' end of town, with docks, cargo warehouses and boat-mending sheds. In times gone by ocean-going dhows traditionally followed the monsoon winds across the Indian Ocean, when fleets would arrive carrying goods from Arabia and the Orient, returning loaded with slaves, ivory and the produce of the islands' plantations. These days there is still plenty of smaller dhow traffic between Zanzibar and the mainland, most bringing building materials and flour to Zanzibar, and the dhow harbour is at its busiest in the morning when the fishing boats arrive and unload their catches.

Around Stone Town
slave trade sights and snorkelling spots

Mbweni Ruins
At the Protea Hotel Mbweni Ruins (see Where to stay, below), 6 km south of Stone Town at the end of Mbweni St, off Nyerere Rd to the airport, T024-223 5478/9, free, but you are expected to go for meal or drinks at the hotel (Rain Tree Restruant & Bar, open 0730-2230).

In 1857 Livingstone gave a powerful lecture at Cambridge University about the horrors of slavery. As a result, Anglican members of four universities (Cambridge, Oxford, Durham and Dublin) formed a committee that came to be named the Universities' Mission to Central Africa (UMCA). The aim was to attempt to stop slavery and promote Christianity in Central Africa. The Mbweni Ruins were originally the St Mary's School for Girls, built in 1871 by the UMCA for freed slave girls on 30 acres of land called Mbweni Point Shamba. The girls were trained as teachers so that they could be sent to the mainland to help run mission stations there. Originally there was an old Arab house on the property that was made into the entrance building. Then dormitories and school rooms were added, making the building into a huge square built around an open courtyard, where today two royal palm trees flourish. The construction was overseen by Edward Steere, who also built the Anglican Cathedral Christ Church on the site of the old slave market

ON THE ROAD

Freddie Mercury

The British songwriter, entertainer and powerful lead vocalist of Queen, was born Farrokh Bulsara on 5 September 1946 in Stone Town. His middle-class parents were of Persian descent and Zoroastrian faith, and had moved from the Gujarat region of India to Zanzibar as his father was a cashier at the British Colonial Office. Farrokh spent his very early years here before being sent off to school in India, where, at about the age of 12, he began to call himself Freddie. For a brief spell in 1963 when he was 17, Freddie re-joined his parents in Zanzibar but the whole family left in 1964 as a result of the Zanzibar Revolution, and went to live in Feltham, Middlesex, in England. Although today there's nothing to see except a plaque on the wall ('Mercury House'), which sits above a fine example of a Zanzibari door, the apartment he was born in is now part of the excellent shop, The Zanzibar Gallery, on the corner of Kenyatta Road and Gizenga Street in Shangani (see page 79).

in Stone Town (see page 49). A village of slaves freed by the British was set up around the school, and each family had a plot of land big enough to build a house with a small vegetable garden. St Mary's moved to smaller premises in 1920 and finally closed in 1939 and the buildings slowly fell into a state of ruin. Today the site can be visited from the **Protea Hotel Mbweni Ruins**, and there is a nature walk through the hotel's lovely botanical gardens that meanders around the ruins. The gardens have more than 650 plant species of which 150 are palms. Day visitors are welcome at the hotel's restaurant and you can spend time on the beach and swim in the pool.

Changuu Island

Tour operators run half-day tours for about US$30-40 per person with snorkelling equipment. If you're in a group, it is cheaper to find a boat yourself (about US$40 per boat for up to 6 people); ask around on the beaches in front of the Big Tree or Tembo Hotel. Pay when you have been safely deposited back on the mainland. There is also a US$6 per person landing fee on the island.

Also known as **Prison Island**, Changuu Island is almost 5 km northwest of Stone Town, or a 20-minute boat ride, and is roughly 800 m long and 230 m wide at its broadest point. It lies on a coral reef approximately 6 m above the high-tide mark, and much of the reef is exposed at low tide. All over the island there are disused pits where coral was quarried over the centuries for building in Stone Town. There are some sweet-scented citrus and frangipani trees here interspersed among the indigenous trees. The island was once owned by an Arab who used it for 'rebellious' slaves. Some years later, in 1893, it was sold to General Mathews, a Briton who converted it into a prison. However, it was never actually used as such and was later converted to serve as a quarantine station for yellow fever in colonial times. Sailors were taken off the ships and were monitored here for one or two weeks before being permitted to continue on with their journey. The prison is still relatively intact and a few remains of the hospital can be seen, including the rusting boilers of the laundry. The island is also home to giant tortoises, which were brought over from Aldabra (an atoll off the Seychelles) in 1919 as a gift from the then British governor of the Seychelles. From just four individuals, the population now numbers around 100. They stand up to a rather staggering 1 m high and the older ones have their ages painted on their shells (some are 150 years old). You can buy leaves to feed them (watch out for their snapping beaks) but under no circumstances sit on them. It's possible to snorkel off the island, but it is underwhelming – the reefs are not well protected and jellyfish can sometimes be a problem. Chumbe Island is by far a superior snorkelling destination (see below). There is a simple café serving cold beers and basic meals, such as grilled fish and salad, and the old quarantine buildings on the southwest of the island have now been turned into a smart lodge, the **Changuu Private Island Paradise**, see Where to stay, above.

Chapwani Island
You can only visit if you are staying at the Chapwani Private Island Resort (see page 70).

Also known as **Grave Island**, Chapwani Island is a private island encircled with a coral reef with one exclusive resort on it. It has an interesting cemetery with headstones of British sailors and marines who lost their lives in the fight against slavery and in the First World War. The island itself is 1 km long and 100 m wide, with a perfect swathe of beach on the northern edge. The forested section is home to a number of birds, duikers and a population of colobus monkeys (how they got here is a bit of a mystery).

Chumbe Island
The island is a private conservation project of the same name (see page 71). A day trip can be booked directly, T024-223 1040, www.chumbeisland.com, or through one of the tour operators, US$90, children (3-12) US$45, including boat transfer, snorkelling equipment, nature trail guides and a buffet lunch. Note that they only take day visitors when they're not fully booked with overnight visitors – it's best to book 2 or 3 days in advance.

Approximately 4 km offshore, southwest from the Mbweni Ruins, lies the **Chumbe Island Coral Park**. This is an important marine park with a wonderful reef of coral gardens in a pristine state and is shallow (1-3 m according to tides). If you swim up to the reef ridge, it's possible to spot shoals of barracuda or dolphins.

There are nearly 400 species of fish here: groupers, angelfish, butterfly fish, triggerfish, boxfish, sweetlips, unicornfish, trumpetfish, lionfish, moorish idols, to name but a few. The snorkelling opportunities are excellent but scuba-diving is not permitted in the park. There are nature trails through the forest on the island, which is home to the rare roseate tern and the coconut crab, the largest land crab in the world, which can weigh up to 4 kg. It is also a refuge for the shy Ader's duiker, introduced to the island with the assistance of the World Wide Fund for

ON THE ROAD
Taarab music

The Swahili coast's celebrated music genre, called *taarab*, has been evolving ever since the first seafaring traders arrived. Legend has it that traders travelling by dhow on the monsoon tradewinds grew bored during their long journeys and so started taking musicians on board for entertainment. The musicians were so talented that while the dhows were still anchored in the harbour, people passing were drawn to it, and the music became established on the islands and mainland. By the 1870s, it was so popular on Zanzibar it was played in the sultan's court. It fuses Swahili, Arab, Persian and Indian influences, and the distinctive sound is melodically sung poetry with Kiswahili lyrics accompanied by a full orchestra. One of the key elements of taarab instrumentation is the qanun; a 72-string zither that lies flat and is plucked like a harp. But modern taarab also features drums, tambourines, keyboards and the accordion. The name is derived from the Arabic word tariba, meaning 'to be moved or agitated'.

Nature. For great views across to Zanzibar and a bird's-eye view of the reefs that surround the island, you can climb the 131 steps to the top of the lighthouse that was built by the British in 1904.

Bawe Island
You can only visit if you are staying at Bawe Tropical Island (see page 70).

This tiny island (not much bigger in size than a football pitch) about 6 km from Stone Town was once owned by Cable & Wireless at the end of the 18th century, who used it as an operation station for the underwater telegraph cable connecting Zanzibar to the Seychelles. They built houses on the island to accommodate their personnel. These no longer exist, but today Bawe is the location of one sole lodge, Bawe Tropical Island (see page 70), which is spread out on the gorgeous white-sand beach and is run by the same company as the Chapwani Private Island Resort. The reef around the island is a popular diving spot, and excursions are organized with the dive schools in Stone Town, see page 79.

Tourist information

Zanzibar Commission for Tourism (ZCT)

T024-223 3485, www.zanzibartourism.net.
The official government tourist body with two very helpful desks and both are open 0800-1800; one is at the airport just after baggage reclaim and the other is at the port, just on the left as you disembark from the ferry. Both can organize taxis to town and transport to the coast with their official drivers. They have a list of hotels and can call ahead on your behalf. In the case of the port, they can then organize someone from the hotel to come to the port and walk you to the closer hotels with your luggage. The tour operators (see page 80), which have offices all over Stone Town, also provide comprehensive information for visitors to the islands and can book hotels, transfers and car hire, and arrange excursions.

Tip...
The best maps – *Illustrated Zanzibar Map* and *Illustrated Pemba Map* – are produced by The Zanzibar Gallery (see page 79), which are also available to buy at various other outlets and hotels in Stone Town and Dar es Salaam.

Where to stay

Don't rush off to the beach – there are some simply stunning places to stay in Stone Town that cater for all budgets, and sleeping in an atmospheric historic townhouse is a magical experience.

$$$$ Park Hyatt Zanzibar
Shangani St, Shangani T024-550 1234, www.zanzibar.park.hyatt.com.
Park Hyatt opened this 5-star hotel in 2015 after a wonderful and careful restoration of the 1847 Mambo Msiige mansion (see page 54) and by building the new adjoining Zamani Residence, which is where most of the 67 rooms and suites are. Each of these has all mod-cons, balconies, sea views and contemporary luxurious decor. Like its neighbour, the Serena Inn (below), its location at the western tip of Stone Town overlooking the ocean is unbeatable; especially from the infinity swimming pool and terrace restaurant/bar. There's also a gym and spa.

$$$$ Zanzibar Palace Hotel
Jamatini Rd, Kiponda, T024-223 2230, www.zanzibarpalacehotel.com.
This lovely boutique hotel has 9 a/c rooms individually furnished in stunning Arabian styles. Extras include DSTV, DVD players and Wi-Fi. Tea and coffee is served in the bedrooms before breakfast, and some of the rooms have huge stone baths as their centrepiece. It's worth checking the website to choose a room before booking because all are so different. Bar/lounge, spa and gourmet 5-course dinners in the restaurant.

$$$$ Zanzibar Serena Inn
Kelele Sq, Shangani St, Shangani, T024-223 3051, www.serenahotels.com.
This stunning restoration of 2 historic buildings in Stone Town is in a wonderful location right on the seafront, and has 51 luxury rooms and 10 suites and a swimming pool. Beautifully decorated with antique clocks, Persian rugs, carved staircases, chandeliers and brass-studded doors. The two restaurants and the coffee shop have excellent but pricey menus and **The Terrace** is on the rooftop (see Restaurants, page 72).

$$$ Africa House Hotel
Suicide Alley, Shangani, T024-223 3127, www.africahousehotel.co.tz.
This used to be the English Club in the pre-Independence days and is now restored to its former glory with many archways, studded wooden doors and cool stone floors. The 15 rooms with a/c, DSTV and Wi-Fi, are not luxurious but are tastefully furnished with antiques, original photographs and paintings by local artists. The library houses a rare collection of many 1st editions and antiquarian books, there's a restaurant (see page 73) and the famous **Sunset Bar** (see page 76).

$$$ Beyt Al Salaam
Kelele Sq, Shangani, opposite Serena Inn, T0774-444 111, www.beytalsalaam.com.
This boutique hotel in a traditional Zanzibar house was once a tea house and has 10 individually decorated a/c rooms with 4-poster Zanzibari beds, silks and organza fabrics in an opulent Arabian style. Some of them look out over Kelele Square, and the restaurant is highly recommended (see Restaurants, page 72).

$$$ Dhow Palace Hotel
Just off Kenyatta Rd, Shangani, T024-223 0304, www.dhowpalace-hotel.com.
A good family option and well-priced with old and new wings, 30 a/c rooms with Wi-Fi, fridge, good modern bathrooms and traditional furnishings. There's a lovely interior courtyard with a very attractive swimming pool and a restaurant. Like its sister hotel, the **Tembo House**, it's 'dry', so no alcohol.

$$$ Emerson on Hurumzi
Hurumzi St, T024-223 2784, www. facebook.com/emersononhurumzi.
What originally was the **Emerson & Green Hotel**, Stone Town's original 'boutique' hotel in the 1990s, this charming and quirkily restored 19th-century Omani merchant's house is literally riddled with staircases to get to the 24 individually themed rooms (the Ballroom has soaring ceilings) with old (some would say shabby) Zanzibari furniture and fittings, original stucco decor, ornate carved doors and stone baths, lower rooms have a/c. The highlight here is the rooftop restaurant, **The Tea House** (see Restaurants, page 72). This is the 2nd tallest building in Stone Town so the views over the rooftops are quite spectacular.

$$$ Emerson Spice Hotel
Tharia St, Kiponda, T0775-046 395, www.emersonspice.com.
Of Emerson & Green fame (above) this is late New Yorker Emerson Skeens' painstaking restoration from a near-ruin – he took over 2 years to decorate it and he opened it in 2011. His legacy lives on and the beautiful building with pale blue interior, and wrap-around carved wooden balconies, has 11 stunning rooms named after his favourite opera characters; each features exotic

Zanzibari, art deco and Indian touches and exquisite stained-glass windows. Breakfast is served in bed or on your balcony, and the ground floor tea room offers spiced coffee or delicious iced ginger tea. The gourmet food in the rooftop restaurant is simply outstanding (see Restaurants, page 72).

$$$ Forodhani Gardens Hotel
Mizingani Rd, Baghani, T024-223 4577, www.forodhaniparkhotel.com.
A typical whitewashed house with carved doors and vintage touches including the decorative tiles in the bathrooms in a fantastic location right next to the Old Fort and opposite Forodhani Gardens. 19 fairly spacious mid-range rooms, some triples, all with 4-poster beds, a/c and ceiling fans, fridge and DSTV. Ask for the rooms at the front as these have nice balconies. Friendly staff, rooftop terrace with a small splash pool and the exceptionally filling breakfast will last you through the day.

$$$ Jafferji House & Spa
Gizenga St, Baghani, T024-223 6583, www.jafferjihouse.net.
This lovingly resored boutique hotel is the former family home of renowned East African photographer, Javed Jafferji, who also owns The Zanzibar Gallery (see page 79). It's fitting then that his photographic work fills the walls, providing visual inspiration among the elaborately carved wooden balconies, plush furnishings and antique mirrors. The 10 a/c rooms have DSTV, the **Mistress of Spices Lounge** serves authentic Zanzibari cuisine and spice-infused coffees and teas, and the delightful spa is on the rooftop.

$$$ Kholle House
607-608 Malindi Rd, Malindi, T0772-161 033, www.khollehouse.com.
Built in 1860 by Princess Kholle, the daughter of the first Sultan of Zanzibar, and opened after 3 years of immaculate restoration, with 10 a/c rooms, all different so choose when booking, the larger ones have balconies and gold-painted stone bathtubs Breakfast room, delightful rooftop tea house/bar (but no restaurant) and a swimming pool in a well-tended garden.

$$$ Kisiwa House
572 Baghani St, off Kenyatta Rd, Shangani, T024-223 5654, www. kisiwahouse.com.
Smart offering, with 11 a/c rooms in an Omani merchant's house (1840), with traditional antiques and Persian rugs but very modern bathrooms, DSTV and Wi-Fi. Rooftop restaurant/bar and peaceful courtyard tea salon with palms and fountain. Special touches include perfumed incense.

$$$ Maru Maru Hotel
Gizenga St, T024-223 8516-8, www. marumaruhotelzanzibar.com.
This fairly new and well-located hotel has a 360° view over Stone Town from its rooftop bar, 44 a/c rooms with traditional furnishings and the lovingly restored historic building has nice features like a fountain courtyard, chandeliers and stained-glass windows. The **Fountain Restaurant** serves a buffet breakfast and dinner, while the **Terrace Restaurant** offers Indian cuisine.

$$$ Mashariki Palace Hotel
Nyumba ya Moto, off Hurumzi St, behind Beit al-Sahel (the Palace Museum), T024-223 7232, www. masharikipalacehotel.com.

An exceptionally stylish Italian-run boutique hotel set in a wing of a former palace where the sultan's religious advisor was housed. 18 rooms with balconies or mezzanine floors, thick stone whitewashed walls, lofty ceilings and carved doors, but refreshing contemporary decor and luxurious fixtures and fittings, DSTV, a/c and Wi-Fi. Lovely rooftop sun terrace, massages available, restaurant/bar, and breakfast and afternoon tea and cakes are included.

$$$ Mizingani Seafront Hotel
Mizingani Rd, Malindi, T024-223 5396, www.mizinganiseafront.com.
A good mid-range option, and sensibly priced, in a converted spice merchant's house that has retained all its charm and has lovely lattice and stained-glass balconies at the front. Zanzibari decor in the 33 a/c rooms, rooftop restaurant with great ocean views, and the highlight is the welcoming courtyard swimming pool at the back. A waterfront location near the Dhow Countries Music Academy (Old Customs House) and a short walk from the ferry terminal.

$$$ The Seyyida Hotel & Spa
Nyumba Ya Moto St, by Beit al-Sahel (the Palace Museum), T024-223 8352, www.theseyyida-zanzibar.com.
This elegant boutique hotel is in a good central location and is a marvellous traditional restoration of a house with cool arches, detailed woodwork and a courtyard garden and features antiques, chandeliers Persian carpets and whirring ceiling fans, as well as some interesting modern art on the walls and splashes of contemporary colours. Each of the 17 rooms has a/c, Wi-Fi and DSTV. The spa and rooftop restaurant/bar are open to non-guests.

$$$ The Swahili House
Kiponda St, Kiponda, T0777-510 209, reservations Moivaro Lodges & Tented Camps, Arusha T027-250 6315, www. moivaro.com.
A fine restoration of a 5-storey 19th-century mansion with 20 elegant a/c rooms built around a courtyard, with Swahili furnishings. The larger rooms are higher up, though the staircases are very steep. There's an attractive rooftop terrace with bar, restaurant and sunbathing area with plunge pool and, given its height, excellent views over Stone Town, so it's worth dropping in even if you're not staying.

$$$ Tembo House Hotel
Shangani St, Shangani, T024-223 3005, www.tembohotel.com.
This is a beautifully restored historic building that was the American Consulate in the 19th century (also see page 58). The 37 rooms are decorated with antique furniture and have a/c, satellite TV and balconies overlooking either the ocean or swimming pool courtyard. Great location, and the terrace is good for watching the comings and goings on the public beach. There's an excellent restaurant (no alcohol), and the staff are very friendly.

$$$ Zanzibar Grand Palace
Malindi Rd, Malindi, T024-223 5638, www.zanzibargrandpalace.com.
A mid-range hotel near the port but on a peaceful grassy square. The building is new so doesn't have the old character or atmosphere of other places, but it's built in typical Stone Town style and has 34 well-equipped and smartly decorated rooms with DSTV and Wi-Fi. Rooftop restaurant with views of the harbour, and the ground floor Dock Café

(1000-2200) offers coffees, juices, cakes, pastries and pizzas.

$$$-$$ Zanzibar Coffee House
Market St, T024-223 9379, www.riftvalley-zanzibar.com.
Restored 1885 house with 8 individually decorated a/c rooms, each named after a type of coffee, with floors and walls painted in cool pastel colours, Zanzibari beds, antique lamps and Wi-Fi, some on are en suite, others have private bathrooms in the corridors. Breakfast is served on the rooftop and it adjoins the pleasant café of the same name (see Restaurants, page 75). Doubles from US$95.

$$$-$$ Zanzibar Hotel
Off Bhangani St, at the back of the Dhow Palace Hotel, Shangani, T0778-717 800, www.zanzibarhotel.co.tz.
One of the oldest (if not the first) hotels in Stone Town with a history that goes back to 1923, today this is an elegant hotel with beamed ceilings, Persian rugs, velvet curtains and chandeliers in a 19th-century house. 12 a/c rooms, varying in size and price, restaurant, and all centred around a courtyard with a fountain. The highlight is the surprisingly large and peaceful lawned garden full of palms.

$$ Abuso Inn
Shangani St, opposite Tembo House Hotel, Shangani, T024-223 5886, www.abusoinn.com.
This well located and exceptionally friendly budget hotel is on the site of a building that was first constructed in the 1870s, but was sympathetically rebuilt in 2005 with the same architecture and has been decorated authentically. One of the nicest features is the elaborate woodwork on the arches in the lounge leading to the 20 spacious a/c rooms,

some of which are triples and 2 can accommodate families; some have sea views. No restaurant, but breakfast is taken on the rooftop, and it's an easy stroll to restaurants. Doubles from US$80.

$$ Clove Hotel
Hurumzi St, behind the House of Wonders, T0776-782 001, www.clovehotel.com.
A simple budget option in a nice quiet square with 8 rooms, 2 for families, ceiling fans and hot water. The tall white building itself is quite modern by Stone Town standards, but the interiors include Zanzibari-style elements and traditional beds. Breakfast is taken on the pleasant rooftop terrace, which has sea views and free Wi-Fi. Doubles from US$65.

$$ House of Spices
Kiponda St, Kiponda, T024-223 1264, www.houseofspiceszanzibar.com.
Best known for its excellent restaurant (see page 72) but also has 4 lovely small rooms (originally the owner's living rooms above his spice shop), carefully decorated with rich textiles and antiques, windowless but cool with a/c and whirring fans, and a separate entrance on to the street. A double goes from US$85, or all the rooms can be rented as an apartment for 7 people, and there's a delightful antique Zanzibari baby's cot.

$$ Mazson's Hotel
Kenyatta Rd, Shangani, T024-223 3062, www.mazsonshotel.com.
An imposing whitewashed 1830s merchant's house, but this place gets mixed reviews because of its confusing layout and the difference between the 30-odd rooms; some are tiny cells with no views, while other are spacious and have balconies – try and look at a couple before you decide. They do, however, have a/c, fridge and TV, and it's in a great

central location and offers a decent hot and cold buffet breakfast.

$$-$ Zenji Hotel
Malawi Rd, Malindi, T0774-276 468, www.zenjizanzibar.com.
A consistently well-regarded small hotel near the port, owned by a friendly and helpful Zanzibari/Dutch couple, very community focused, with all locally made furniture and decor and locally sourced food. The 9 individually decorated rooms are reasonably priced; the smallest with a shared bathroom is from US$50, and rates include a generous buffet breakfast served on the roof. The delightful **Zenji Café & Boutique**, is downstairs (see Restaurants, below).

$ Flamingo Guest House
Mkunazini St, just north of junction with Sokomuhogo St, T024-223 2850, www.flamingoguesthouse.com.
A simple option with management well used to backpackers in the heart of the residential twisting alleyways and about a 10-min walk from the Shangani area. 18 spotless rooms, most with shared showers, a small book exchange and DSTV in the lobby, and breakfast is served on an upstairs terrace with views over town. Very good value from US$15 for a dorm bed and US$30 for a double with shared bathroom.

$ Jambo Guesthouse
Just off Mkunazini St, opposite the Green Garden Restaurant (see page 74), T024-223 3779, info@jamboguest.com.
Clean and comfortable, this is a popular budget option where the 9 rooms share 4 bathrooms, and have Zanzibari beds, fans and some with a/c, mosquito nets and reliable hot water. Doubles from US$45, and extra mattresses can be put

in rooms making it less than US$20 per person. Breakfast of bread, eggs, fruit, juice, and tea/coffee included.

$ Karibu Inn
Forodhani St, Shangani, T024-223 3058.
Budget no-frills option in a great location on a narrow street parallel with Kenyatta Rd, tucked away behind the Old Fort, and a 50-m walk to coffee shops, etc. But the rooms are bare to say the least – each has 5-8 dorm beds (from US$15) and there are a couple of doubles, with a fan and mosquito nets, and there's a separate shower and toilet for each room. Bedding has to be requested at reception on arrival and a simple breakfast is included.

$ Kiponda B&B
Nyumba ya Moto St, off Jamatini Rd, Kiponda, T024-223 3052, www.kiponda.com.
Another nicely restored building, with 15 simple clean double/twins, triples and 1 shared room with 5 beds, some have a/c, some ceiling fans. The larger ones are en suite, and the smaller ones have private bathrooms but might be down the hall. Breakfast is served on the breezy open roof with sea views (their fresh avocado and passion fruit juices are renowned), which also has Wi-Fi. Rates are from US$30 per person.

$ Malindi Guest House
Funguni Rd, Malindi, T024-223 0165.
Popular with budget travellers since 1976 and near the port. The 12 rooms sleep 2-4 and are around a central courtyard with plants, some are en suite while others have shared facilities. Breakfast is taken on the rooftop with views of the fishermen landing their catch every morning. The downsides are that this part of

Malindi is a bit rough, it's old-fashioned and there are mixed reports about cleanliness, and the management is either good and helpful, or too pushy about selling tours, etc (it rather depends on what you're looking for). From US$15 per person.

$ Princess Salme Inn
Mizingani Rd, Malindi, T0777-435 303, www.princesssalmeinn.com.
Named after the beautiful princess (see box, page 90), a basic but friendly and good vlaue place near the port in an old Arabic building with Zanzibari beds and decor. Doubles with en suite and a/c from US$45, or there are cheaper rooms with shared bathrooms in the corridors. Good and filling breakfasts are taken in the rooftop lounge, which has sea views, Wi-Fi and comfortable couches.

$ Pyramid Hotel
Kokoni St, between Malindi St and Malawi Rd, Kokoni, T024-223 3000, www.pyramidhotel.co.tz.
Another cheapie hidden in the back streets and not far from the ferry terminal, with charming staff, modest accommodation in 11 rooms, a mixture of self-contained en suite doubles/twins/triples and dorms from US$20 per person but you pay a bit more for a/c. They vary in size (so ask to see a few) and are reached by very steep staircases. A fruit, bread and egg breakfast is served on the roof.

$ St Monica's Hostel & Restaurant
Part of the Anglican Cathedral Christ Church complex (see page 49), New Mkunazini Rd, T024-223 0773, www.zanzibarhostel.com.
An old characterful building next to the cathedral which in the 1890s, was nuns' accommodation and is built on the site of the former slave market. Today it has 16 very clean and comfortable but simple rooms with or without bathrooms and either fans or a/c, some with balconies and views of the cathedral. The restaurant (0700-2100) is next door for breakfast and traditional Swahili dishes. B&B doubles from US$40.

Around Stone Town

$$$$ Bawe Tropical Island
Reservations Arusha T027-254 4595, www.hotelsandlodges-tanzania.com, www.privateislands-zanzibar.com.
A 30-min boat ride from Stone Town, the private lodge on Bawe Island has 15 cottages strung along the beach. There's a thatched dining area, a bar fashioned out of a dhow, and pool area decked with bougainvillea. Suitable for couples (no children under 16) it has a quiet, relaxed atmosphere with massages, snorkelling and boat trips across to nearby Prison Island on offer.

$$$$ Changuu Private Island Paradise
Reservations Arusha T027-254 4595, www.hotelsandlodges-tanzania.com, www.privateislands-zanzibar.com.
On Changuu or 'Prison' Island (see page 60), this smart lodge, a 20-min boat ride from Stone Town, has 15 deluxe thatched cottages on the beach with ocean views, roomy bathtubs and outdoor showers, and 12 rooms in the restored quarantine buildings with views across to Stone Town. Good food, including 4-course seafood dinners, swimming pool and floodlit tennis court, great snorkelling and you can see the giant tortoises.

$$$$ Chapwani Private Island Resort
T0777-433 102, www.chapwani-resort-zanzibar-hotel.com.

Chapwani or 'Grave' Island (see above), about 15 mins from Stone Town by boat, offers super-privacy in only 10 rooms in 5 bandas right on the beach, with 4-poster beds and colourful African fabrics. Seafood is the main feature on the restaurant menu. There's a swimming pool and a relaxing bar with day beds, cushions and lanterns, and fishing and snorkelling can be arranged. At night there are fantastic views of Stone Town.

$$$$ Chumbe Island Coral Park
T024-223 1040, www.chumbeisland.com.
The utmost care has been taken to minimize the environmental impact of this resort; sustainably harvested local materials were used in the construction of the 7 luxury cottages and dining area, there is solar power and composting toilets, and rainwater is collected as the source of fresh water. The emphasis is very much on the wildlife, coral reefs and ecology of the island, and a stay here makes for an interesting alternative to the other beach resorts. All-inclusive rates include forest walks, guided snorkelling and boat transfers.

$$$ Protea Hotel Mbweni Ruins
6 km south of Stone Town off Nyerere Rd, T024-223 5478/9, www.proteahotels.com.
Built in the spacious grounds of the ruins of the first Anglican Christian missionary settlement in East Africa (see page 60), and on a private beach. 13 rooms with a/c and fans, 4-poster beds and balconies, some have extra beds for kids. Stunning tropical gardens full of butterflies, where bushbabies may be seen in the evening, open-air restaurant and bar under thatch, swimming pool, free shuttles to Stone Town 3 times a day, and also offers tranquil kayak trips through the mangroves.

$$$-$$ Zanzibar Ocean View
Kilimani Rd, 2 km south of Stone Town off Nyerere Rd, T024-223 3882, www.zanzibaroceanview.com.
On the beachfront at Kilimani, this is the sister property of the **Amaan Bungalows** in Nungwi (page 98). The 58 simple a/c rooms are comfortable with DSTV, balconies and sea or garden views and there's a restaurant and bar (the pizza's good). However, it's a little dated, and as it's a public beach it gets busy, but it's close enough to Stone Town to use it as a base if you don't want to stay in town itself.

Restaurants

A Stone Town 'must-do' is to eat at the Forodhani Market in the evening (see box, page 59). For breakfast, look out for stalls in the back streets selling *chai tangawizi* (ginger tea) and *mandazi* (fried dough balls), which in Zanzibar are often infused with cardamom. There are some excellent restaurants in Stone Town, most serving fresh seafood, and the hotels have good restaurants and bars, many of which are on rooftops and are open to non-guests. Since this is a Muslim society, not all of the restaurants serve alcohol, so check beforehand if a bottle of wine is an essential part of your dining pleasure. During Ramadan some restaurants do not open during the day (this doesn't apply to those in the tourist hotels).

Tip...
If you are looking for a venue to watch the sunset, remember that, around the equator, sunset is always between 1815 and 1845.

$$$ Beyt Al Salaam
Kelele Sq, Shangani, see Where to stay, above. Open 0700-1000, 1200-1530, 1800-2200.
Popular and romantic Zanzibari-themed restaurant on the ground floor of this boutique hotel with carved wooden ceiling beams and brightly coloured cushions, the sophisticated menu includes seafood casserole poached in lemongrass, mouth-watering crab and coconut soup or giant piri-piri prawns. Good selection of wine too.

$$$ Emerson Spice
Tharia St, see Where to stay, above. Downstairs café daily 1200-1700, one sitting for dinner on the rooftop 1900 (except Thu).
This beautifully resorted and incredibly romantic teahouse with its delicately carved wooden trellises and hanging lanterns is on the rooftop of Emerson Spice. The 5-course degustation menu is considered some of the best Zanzibari seafood on the island, and the experience is magical. A sample menu might be lobster on green papaya salad, squid-ink risotto, coconut kingfish baked in banana leaf, and palate-cleansing sorbets, such as custard apple with saffron or mango with cardamom. Reservations are essential (in fact book before you arrive on the island); cocktails are from 1800 and dinner is served at 1900.

$$$ House of Spices
Kiponda St, Kiponda, see Where to stay, above. Mon-Sat 1000-2200.
Beautifully decorated restaurant and wine bar in a restored 18th-century spice merchant's house, tables are on terraces on the 2nd floor which was once used for drying spices before they were packed for shipment. Delicious food, a mix of seafood (whole lobster is the speciality) and Italian, with good home-made ravioli and thin-crust pizzas. Good choice of Italian and South African wine. The lovely scented shop here sells nicely packaged tea and spice gift boxes.

$$$ The Tea House
At Emerson on Hurumzi, see Where to stay, above. Open for dinner only 1900-2200.
Here you can eat in wonderful surroundings on the rooftop, 81 steps up from the street; if you are not staying here you need to book a day ahead. The semi-fixed dinner menus with an emphasis on seafood have one seating starting at 1900; arrive from 1800 for cocktails, then take all evening to enjoy the excellent food, while sitting on cushions with your shoes off. On Fri-Sun evenings, there's traditional *taarab* entertainment.

$$$ The Terrace
At the Serena Inn, Kelele Sq, Shangani, see Where to stay, above. Open for dinner only 1930-2200.
An expensive but special and romantic place for a treat set on a quiet terrace with ocean views in one of the most beautiful of the restored buildings on Zanzibar – go up there after a drink in the hotel's bar. Famous for its top-class seafood including lobster medallions and giant crab claws and there's a good winelist. The Baharia Restaurant is the less formal option next to the swimming pool.

$$$-$$ 6 Degrees South Grill & Wine Bar
Shangani St, Shangani, T0779-666 050, www.6degreessouth.co.tz. Open 1000-0100.

In a modern building, but still with some typical Zanzibari architectural features, this restaurant is sleek and stylish with a gorgeous, vibey water-front terrace with candle-lit lounge areas. The menu features anything from steaks and sauces and seafood at dinner to breakfast, coffee and home-baked pastries earlier in the day. There's also a west-facing rooftop bar, Up North (see Bars and clubs, below).

$$$-$$ Monsoon
In the tunnel building between Forodhani Gardens and the Old Fort, Shangani, T0777-410 410, www.monsoon-zanzibar.com. Open 1100-2400.
A touristy spot and worth a mention for the location and fun Zanzibari atmosphere, with cushions on the floor indoors, lovely garden terrace outside, fully stocked bar and *taarab* music in the evenings. The menu has a Swahili slant with obviously a good choice of seafood including platters, and there are tasty chicken and vegetarian curries too. Save room for the desserts made from dates and cardamom.

$$$-$$ The Silk Route
Shangani St, Shangani, T024-223 2624. Tue-Sun 1130-1500, daily 1800-2300.
Top-class Indian restaurant with chandeliers, brightly coloured decor and upstairs terrace tables with a sea view (you may need to get there early or book to get these). The long menu includes tandoori chicken and lamb with spinach, Zanzibar fish, such as red snapper, and vegetarian options, such as paneer curry and chickpeas in tamarind sauce. The presentation of dishes and service is excellent, and serves cocktails, some wine and lassis.

$$ Lemongrass Oriental Restaurant & Café Miwa
Above the post office, Kenyatta Rd, Shangani, T0778-933 144, www.lemon grasszanzibar.com, www.cafemiwa.com. Daily except Tue 1200-1500, 1900-2300.
Located above the Shangani Post Office, Lemongrass has a contemporary colourful dining room and breezy open-air balcony with views down the street – great for people-watching – plus there's free Wi-Fi and a long cocktail menu. The food is predominantly Thai, and quite authentic, and the menu features soups, noodles, stir-fries and coconut curries. Café Miwa (opens from 1000 for breakfast) shares some of the balcony, and has a menu of salads, burgers, wraps and pies – plus good spice-infused coffees. You can order from both menus regardless of where you sit.

$$ Tradewinds
At the Africa House Hotel, see Where to stay, above. Open 1900-2200.
As well as the terrace **Sunset Bar** (see Bars and clubs, below), which is perfect for sundowners, the fairly formal restaurant here is on the 2nd floor with a menu of Swahili and Indian dishes and seafood. Nicely decorated with an old map of Africa painted on the ceiling and outside tables with ocean views, but service is notoriously slow and food overpriced.

$$-$ Archipelago
Kenyatta Rd, opposite the National Bank of Commerce, T0778-373 737, www.stone towncafe.com. Open 0800-2200.
Under the same ownership as the Stone Town Café (see below), this long-popular spot offers healthy breakfasts, traditional Swahili dishes, salads, burgers and daily specials of grilled fish – look out for swordfish or marlin. Great coffee, the 'flat

white' is arguably the best in town, and quite delicious desserts, such as sticky date pudding and frangipani tart. Breezy upstairs outdoor terrace overlooking the ocean. No alcohol.

$$-$ La Taverna
New Mkunazini Rd, just south of Darajani Market, T0776-650 301, www.latavernazanzibar.com. Mon-Sat 1100-2300.
Stone Town's most authentic Italian restaurant run by a family from Milan with a pretty street-side terrace decked with bougainvillea. Excellent crispy thin-based pizza, the seafood toppings are not surprisingly the favourite, plus meat dishes, home-made pasta and sandwiches during the day.

$ Green Garden Restaurant
Off Mkunazini St or New Mkunazini Rd, T0779-423 423. Open 1200-2200.
Opposite the Jambo Guesthouse and set in a little square on two tiers with palms and pot-plants and a makuti-thatched roof, this restaurant is quite hard to find. But is worth seeking out and is popular with travellers for its very good pizza and grilled fish or steak with chips and salad and has Wi-Fi. No alcohol but inventive ' mocktails'.

$ Luis Yoghurt Parlour
Gizenga St, near the **Gallery Bookshop**, *T0765-759 579. Mon-Sat 1000-1500, 1800-2100, closes for long periods in low season while the owner goes away.*
A tiny unassuming café bang in the middle of the tourist shops along Gizenga St, which is best known for its unusual Indian-Goan curries with crab, prawns or fish, or lentils for vegetarians, which come with a chapatti and rice. Plus serves excellent lassi, yoghurt drinks, milk shakes, fresh fruit juices, spiced tea and fabulous Italian ice cream.

$ Lukmaan Restaurant
Mkunazini House, New Mkunazini Rd, T0777-482 131. Open 0800-2100.
Traditional Swahili canteen-style restaurant and probably the cheapest sit-down option in Stone Town, with filling dishes from US$4. Tricky to find, but ask, as everyone knows where it is. Try the fish in coconut sauce, spinach and beans, and fish or beef biyriani or pilau rice – cooked in big pots, they may run out of the most popular dishes by 1700. No alcohol.

$ Pagoda Chinese Restaurant
Suicide Alley, behind Africa House Hotel, Shangani, T024-223 4688. Open 1130-1400, 1830-2200.
In the unlikely event that you are craving a Chinese while in Stone Town, this hotchpotch of upstairs brightly lit rooms has an authentic menu, including good hot and sour soups and duck (rare in this part of the world), generous portions and sells beer. However, the ambiance and decor could use a serious boost.

$ Stone Town Café and B&B
Kenyatta Rd just south of the post office, T0778-373 737, www.stonetowncafe.com. Open 0800-2200.
The sister restaurant to the **Archipelago**, with modern a/c interior and outside tables on a palm-shaded patio that is good for people-watching on the street. Popular for breakfasts of fresh fruit, yoghurt and muesli or avocado on toast, lunch includes salads, quiche or falafels, and has more substantial mains for dinner, such as chicken kebabs or pizza. No alcohol. Also now has 5 neat en suite B&B rooms above the café ($$) and rates include breakfast downstairs.

Cafés

Lazuli
Off Kenyatta Rd just south of the post office, Shangani, T0776-266 679.
Mon-Sat 1100-2100.
With a turquoise door, a fresh all-white interior and colourfully painted, this living room-sized restaurant serves great pancakes with fruit, spiced iced coffee, sandwiches, wraps made from chapattis, salads, burgers and some seafood. Look out for the daily specials such as fish stew with cinnamon-infused rice, and the refreshing mango and coconut smoothie is legendary.

Jaws Corner
At the junction of Cathedral and Soko Muhogo Sts. Open dawn-dusk
This friendly and traditional (although inexplicably named) open-air community café is located in the heart of Stone Town and you may well stumble upon it accidentally. You can join the (mostly) men here who while away a few hours sitting on steps or benches in this little square and drink coffee, play board games and discuss politics. The ginger-infused, black Arabica coffee (kahawa) is not that strong (despite its dark appearance), and unusually instead of being sweetened, it's served with a small piece of peanut brittle.

Tamu Gelateria Italiana
Shangani St, Shangani, T0773-234 385.
Open 1030-2230.
Opposite the Park Hyatt Hotel, a small café with tables under whirring ceiling fans and real Italian gelato by the scoop or tub. Quite delicious – try the unusual local flavours like tamarind and masala or the vanilla sorbet made with real vanilla pods. Also sells home-made cakes, biscuits, croissants and savoury snacks which are good to pick up for a picnic.

Zanzibar Coffee House
Market St, see Where to stay, above.
Open 0900-1800.
Great coffee, which is grown on the owner's estate in the Southern Highlands of Tanzania near Mbeya, plus breakfasts of home-made muesli and crêpes, biscuits, muffins and croissants, milkshakes and smoothies. The coffee is roasted in a little back room so the aromas are wonderful, and you can buy coffee beans.

Zenji Café & Boutique
Malwai Rd, Malindi, T0777-247 243, www.zenjicafeboutique.com. 0800-2000.
Lovely a/c café on the ground floor of the Zenji Hotel (see page 69) near the port, with outside terrace and a craft shop where you can watch women make jewellery from beautiful paper beads (you can also buy packets of them). Great coffee and herbal teas, breakfasts, sandwiches using delicious home-made brown bread, and excellent chocolate brownies. Free Wi-Fi. Also runs the Zenji Garden Café in Forodhani Gardens in a kiosk next to the sea wall with pleasant outside tables (0800-2000).

Bars and clubs

Nightlife in conservative Stone Town is restricted to the few licensed restaurants and hotel bars. A highlight of Stone Town is the quintessential sundowner so be sure to be somewhere on the west side for the sunset between 1800 and1845 with a cold drink in hand. Drunken behaviour anywhere on Zanzibar is not tolerated and the police take a stern view.

Livingstone Beach
In the old British Consulate building, on seafront just down from Kenyatta Rd, Shangani, T0779-548 730. Open 1200-1630, 1830-2230, bar open until 0200.

The former home of explorer David Livingstone, this is in a great location with tables in the sand in a roped off area on the edge of the public beach. You can eat and there's a varied menu of continental and Swahili dishes, salads and pastas, but the downside is portions are small for the price and service is slow. Much better for drinks – especially for people-watching on the beach and at sunset – and there are occasional live bands and artwork for sale on the walls.

Mercury's
Mizingani Rd, near The Big Tree, T024-223 3076. Open 0830-2400.

Living rather tenuously off its name, this Freddie Mercury memorabilia-filled bar and restaurant, with its broad wooden deck, is a great place to watch the sunset and the locals playing football on the beach – they have some very skilled players. There's a fully stocked bar with good cocktails, and the Coconut Band plays on weekend nights. It does serve food – pizzas, pasta, seafood and ice cream – but it's very average and overpriced; better to eat elsewhere and drink here.

Sunset Lounge
At Africa House Hotel, see Where to stay, above. Open 1000-2400.

The most popular bar in the town is on a wide marble upstairs terrace that looks out across the ocean – watching the sun set while dhows glide by is a nightly highlight. The beers and cocktails are cold and plentiful, although rather expensive, bar snacks include burgers and calamari and chips, there's free Wi-Fi, and it's a good place to meet people. The adjoining **Shisa Bar** is where you can try traditional fruit-flavoured shisha pipes or black spiced Arabica coffee (kahawa).

Tatu
*Shangani St, opposite **Tippu Tip's House**, T0778-672 772. 1200-2200 for food, bars open until 0100.*

Set on 3 floors ('tatu' means 3 in Kiswahili) in a lovely old house, with lattice wooden balconies overlooking the ocean, a restaurant, lounge and bar, fabulous cocktails and over 85 single malt whiskies (they claim to have the largest collection in East Africa), and the menu features tapas and pub-style grub. Close to **Africa House**, and the rooftop is certainly a competitor for a sunset venue.

Up North
At 6 Degrees South Grill & Wine Bar (see page 72), Shangani St, Shangani, T0779-666 050, www.6degreessouth.co.tz. Open 1000-0100.

Up North is the rooftop bar of this stylish restaurant where there's a long menu of cocktails (the house specialities are the mojitos and slushys made from vodka and fruit juice) plus there are local and imported beers and decent wine by the glass. There's a menu of finger food and complimentary bowls of popcorn. Fantastic ocean views and Happy Hour is 1700-1900. Ideal to watch sunset here and eat downstairs later (reserve a table as soon as you arrive).

Festivals

Feb **Sauti za Busara Swahili Music and Cultural Festival**, usually 2nd week Feb, T024-223 2423, www.busaramusic.org. This 4-day festival attracts talent from all over East Africa, with performances in music, theatre and dance. *Sauti za Busara* means 'songs of wisdom' in Kiswahili. There are concerts (mostly in the Old Fort) of traditional music, from Swahili *taarab* and *ngoma* to more contemporary genres that mix African, Arab and Asian music.

Jul Festival of the Dhow Countries, 2 weeks in the middle of Jul, T0773-411 499, www.ziff.or.tz. Celebrates and promotes the unique culture that grew as a result of Indian Ocean trade and the wooden sailing dhow. All nations around the Indian Ocean known as the dhow countries are included in the celebration, but the Swahili culture is the best represented. Zanzibari *taarab* music and traditional dances are performed by a rich ensemble of cultural troupes, and there are exhibits of arts and crafts, street carnivals, small fairs and canoe races. The highlight is the **Zanzibar International Film Festival**; screenings take place around Stone Town.

Aug-Dec Eid al-Fitr (in Kiswahili also called 'Idi' or 'Sikuku,' which means 'celebration'). The Muslim holiday that signifies the end of the holy month of Ramadan is without doubt the central holiday of Islam, and a major event throughout Tanzania, but especially observed on the coast and Zanzibar. Throughout Ramadan, Muslim men and women fast from sunrise to sunset, only taking meagre food and drink after dark. The dates for Eid al-Fitr vary according to the sighting of the new moon but, as soon as it is observed, the fasting ends and 4 days of feasting and festivities begin. Stone Town is the best place to witness this celebration; the whole town takes to the streets as people go from house to house visiting friends and relatives, and there is live Swahili *taarab* music and much rejoicing.

Shopping

Tourists are advised not to buy any products related to protected species on the islands, such as sea shells and turtles.

For everyday shopping, from freshly caught octopus to mosquito nets, head to the Darajani Market (see page 49). Stone Town also has many shops catering to tourists selling wood carvings, Zanzibari chests, spices, jewellery, paintings, antiques, *kikois* and *kangas* (sarongs), and lovely handmade leather beaded sandals. For most of these it's best just to wander the streets, get the measure of prices and then bargain hard. Most shops are along Kenyatta Rd in Shangani, Gizenga St behind the Old Fort, and on Hurumzi St behind the House of Wonders. Shops in Stone Town are usually open 0900-1400 and 1600-1800 or 1900 but some are open all day.

Abeid Curio Shop, *Cathedral St, opposite St Joseph's Cathedral, T024-223 3832*. Sells antique Zanzibari furniture, including teak canopied beds inlaid with painted glass panels, clocks, and copper and brass, such as Arabic coffee pots. They can arrange international shipping.

Capital Art Studio, *Kenyatta Rd, Shangani, T0777-431 271*. Sells wonderful prints of black-and-white photographs of old Zanzibar, which make great souvenirs and look particularly good when framed in heavy wood. The shop was opened in 1930 by Ranchod Oza who was the royal photographer at the time and today is run by his son. The Zanzibar entrance door is particularly fine.

Doreen Mashika, 268 *Hurumzi St, near Emerson on HurumziHotel, T0786-369 777, www.doreenmashika.com*. Swiss/

Tanzanian designer with a range of top-quality fashionable bags, shoes, jewellery and clothing. She uses some beautiful local fabrics and Maasai beads.

Kanga Kabisa, *off Suicide Alley, near Africa House, Shangani, T024-223 2100, www.kangakabisa.com.* Sells colourful men's, women's and children's clothes and accessories made from *kangas* as well as *kitenga*, which is a heavier batik-patterned cloth.

Mago East Africa, *Cathedral St, T0777-457 795, www.magoeastafrica.com.* Well-respected Italian designer for quality women's shirts, dresses, skirts and accessories using local fabrics which are also sold in Europe. Profits go towards supporting a team of local tailors in starting their own businesses.

Memories of Zanzibar, *Kenyatta Rd, opposite Shangani post office, Shangani, T024-223 9376, www.memories-zanzibar. com.* Upmarket shop on 2 storeys, with quality souvenirs, jewellery, handbags, cloth, cushions, CDs and books. Ideal for those not in the bargaining mood – there are fixed prices on all the souvenirs you could possibly want and you can shop in a/c comfort.

Moto & Dada, *Hurumzi St, near the Clove Hotel, T0777-466 304, www.motozanzibar. wordpress.com, www.dadazanzibar.net.* This is the shop for 2 Zanzibari women's co-operatives. Moto makes beautiful handwoven and lined bags and baskets. Dada makes lovely packaged natural beauty products such as body oils, foot scrubs and soap – orange and green tea, lemongrass and ginger, eucalyptus and sea salt or aloe vera and cinnamon are just some of the more than 60 varieties.

Sasik, *Gizenga St, Shangani, T0777-429 332 www.sasikzanzibar.blogspot. co.za.* Sasik began in 1994, when Saada Adbulla Suleiman taught herself to do appliqué work and encouraged her friends and family to join her. Now a cooperative of more than a dozen women, this shop sells furnishings such as cushion covers, wall hangings and decorated mosquito nets based on Arabic designs with inspiration coming from the patterns on local Zanzibar doors and balconies.

Surti & Sons, *Gizenga St, Shangani, T0777-472 742, www.surtiandsons. wordpress.com.* Stone Town's most famous cobblers have been running this shop for more than 30 years and sell good quality, and super-comfortable hand-stitched leather shoes and sandals (expect to pay from US$25 a pair). There's also a selection of bags and belts.

Tamim Curio Shop, *next door to Abeid's, see above, T024-223 2404.* This is one of the best places to buy carved teak or mahogany Zanzibar chests. These were used by the sultans to transport their belongings and are still used today, typically to hold family heirlooms and other valuables and are often used as decoration in hotels. The ones with brass inlays are less often seen, but this shop is run by a brass artisan whose family brought the skill from Yemen in 1904. Again, shipping can be arranged.

Upendo Means Love, *just off Gizenga St, near Karibu Inn, T0784-300 812, www. upendomeanslove.com.* Sells great clothes for women and children made from *kangas* and *kikois*. All the proceeds go to running a sewing school and workshop where women are trained and employed.

Zanzibar Curio Shop, *Hurumzi St, near the Clove Hotel, T0777-411 501.* This relative treasure-trove run by two friendly brothers sells a good selection of the usual curios, but it's the antiques that it's best known for. These include old Zanzibar doors (yes, you can ship these

for a price), chests, nautical instruments, traditional lamps, stamps and coins.
The Zanzibar Gallery, *Mercury House, corner of Kenyatta Rd and Gizenga St, Shangani, T024-223 2721, www. zanzibargallery.net*. Part of the former home of Freddie Mercury (see page 61), this beautifully decorated shop boasts the most comprehensive range of books in Zanzibar: guidebooks, maps, wildlife guides and the best of contemporary and historical fiction from the whole of Africa. The CD collection focuses on Swahili music such as *taarab*. Authentic artworks, antiques, fabrics and textiles from Zanzibar and mainland Africa, plus clothes and spiced candles and soaps. It also sells excellent postcards, coffee-table books and stunning photographic prints taken by the owner Javed Jafferji (who also owns Jafferji House & Spa; see page 66).

What to do

Cruises
Nakupenda Isles Safari, *T0777-415 460, www.nakupendasafari.com, or book through any hotel or tour operator*. The most popular trip offered by this company is a morning dhow excursion (0900-1300) to Pange Island; a sandbank offshore where a shelter is set up for relaxing with a barbecue lunch, and maybe a massage and snorkelling. US$90 per person for 2, US$70 per person for 3, US$65 per person for 4 plus. Also offers sunset cruises and other dhow trips.
The Original Dhow Safari, *T0772-007 090, www.dhowsafaris.net, or book through any hotel or tour operator*. This outfit has 5 dhows and there are a number of options. The most popular is the 2-hr sunset cruise (630-1830); the views of Stone Town from the water

at sunset are gorgeous, and *taarab* musicians play as you are served soft drinks and snacks. US$35 per person for 2, US$25 per person for 3, US$20 per person for 4+. There are also trips to Prison Island (see page 61), or again a trip out to a sandbank for lunch and some snorkelling.
The Safari Blue, *T0777-423 162, www. safariblue.net, or book through any hotel or tour operator*. This daily cruise (0930-1700) uses a 10-m *jahazi* (ocean-going dhow) and departs from Fumba, a 20-min drive to the southwest of Stone Town; transfers can be arranged. A full day trip explores the sandbanks, small islands and coral reefs in the Menai Bay Conservation Area and includes snorkelling equipment with guides and instructors, sodas, mineral water and beer, and a seafood lunch of grilled fish and lobster (and a vegetarian option), fruit and coffee. Dolphins can be seen most of the time. US$90 per person for 2, US$75 for 3, US$70 per person for 4 plus.

Diving
One Ocean – The Zanzibar Dive Centre, *bottom of Kenyatta Rd, opposite the NBC Bank, Shangani, T0 773-048 828, www.zanzibaroneocean.com*. A professionally run and friendly PADI-affiliated dive school, which also operates from many of the resorts on the east coast (see page 111). Most of the dive sites close to Stone Town are suitable for snorkelling as well as diving as they slope off from 2 m gradually reaching 20-30 m deep; good for beginners or slightly less experienced divers. For advanced divers there are night and wreck dives within striking distance of Stone Town (see Zanzibar dive sites, page 16). Expect to pay in the region of US$45 for a snorkelling trip with lunch, US$85 for a

single dive, and US$500 for a 4-day PADI Open Water course.

Dolphin tour

Humpback and bottlenose dolphins swim in pods off Kizimkazi Beach on the southwest of the island. Dolphin 'tours' or 'swimming with dolphins' is an excursion that has been offered for many years on Zanzibar, but these days the general feeling is that this unregulated activity is deemed not good for the dolphins at all – despite what some of the tour operators tell you. The problem is that several small and noisy motorboats speed around at the same time chasing dolphins, as tourists plop into the sea to snorkel closer to them. Dolphins are wild animals that live in a fragile ecosystem, and have feeding grounds, habitats specific for raising their young and complex social relationship.

If you decide you must go (but bear in mind you'll be encouraging this unethical practice), a half-day trip includes transport by minibus to a boat at Kizimkazi and snorkelling gear, and costs around US$35-65 per person depending on how many in the group. If you arrange the tour independently from Kizimkazi it is best to organize your boat through a local hotel in order to avoid the clans of forceful local touts.

Mrembo Spa

Cathedral St, near St Joseph's Cathedral, T024-223 0004, www.mrembospa.com. Open 1000-1800.
There are many regular spas at resorts and hotels around Zanzibar, but the acclaimed and very enjoyable Mrembo Spa in Stone Town is a little more unique as it specializes in traditional natural treatments using Zanzibari flowers, herbs

and spices. Some of these include the *singo* body scrub with ylang-ylang and jasmine, which is traditionally used by a bride in preparation for her wedding, while the *kidonge* body scrub using clove stems and buds and rosewater is used by men in Pemba to relieve aching muscles. Also try a massage using bags of hot sand (similar to a hot-stone massage) or the scrub using freshly grated coconut to nourish the skin. The cool and tranquil treatment rooms are decorated with *kangas*, scented with incense, and *taarab* music is played in the background. Lotions, scrubs, oils, incenses and soaps are for sale in the shop, along with brass flacons for rosewater and clay pots to burn incense. With notice, workshops can be arranged to learn how to make your own products, which can be combined with a spice tour.

Spice tour

Not only will you see in situ almost all the ingredients of the average kitchen spice rack it is also a good opportunity to see the rural areas in the interior of the island and connect with local people. Pretty much every Stone Town hotel and tour operator will offer some version of the spice tour by a/c minibus. A guide is essential to identify the plant. A half-day tour costs around US$35 per person for two people including lunch leaving from Stone Town at 0900 and returning around 1300-1400. See page 16 for more details of the tour and below for tour operators.

Swahili cooking

Some of the tour operators can arrange a Swahili cooking lesson, and the normal drill is to begin at the **Darajani Market** to buy ingredients, then go to a family home to help prepare and cook lunch or dinner (usually on an outdoor cast-iron stove) before sitting down for a meal in the traditional way. Costs are around US$45 per person for a minimum of 2, the cost goes down for a larger group. Try **Zenji Zanzibar or Zanzibar Different Tours** (see Tour operators, below).

Walking tour
Tour operators can organize a guide for a 3-hr guided walking tour around the streets taking in most of the major sites of Stone Town, such as the Darajani Market, cathedrals, mosques and museums. If you are especially interested in the architecture, this is a good opportunity to learn more about the buildings, but otherwise most of these places can be very easily visited while you are on your own wanderings. Costs are about US$30 per person for 2, US$25 per person for 3 and so on.

Tour operators
All the following operators offer the tours listed above and others, including dhow trips to offshore islands such as **Changuu (or Prison) Island** (page 60) or day trips to **Jozani Chwaka Bay National Park** (see page 112). They also offer transport to the north and east coast beaches, which can be combined with tours. For example, you can be

picked up in Stone Town and taken to the east coast via the Jozani Chwaka Bay National Park, or on the way to the north coast, you have the option of combining a morning spice tour with, perhaps, a visit to the Mangapwani slave caves and ending with a transfer to the hotels in Nungwi. Some are also able to arrange visits to Pemba, domestic flights, and car and motorbike hire. This is certainly not a comprehensive list and there are many tour operators to choose from. The most important things to consider are finding one you like, that doesn't pressurize you and is open to discussing what you would like to do. You can also book all excursions through your hotel, which hopefully will have engaged the services of a good tour operator. It is advised not to make arrangements with people who approach you on the street; for information about Stone Town's *papasi* (touts), see page 52.

Colors of Zanzibar, *just off Mizingani Rd, behind the Old Fort, T024-223 0186, www. colorsofzanzibar.com.*
Discover Zanzibar, *Kiembe Samaki, off Nyerere Rd, near the airport, T024-223 4085, www.discoverzanzibar.net.*
Eco & Culture Tours, *272 Hurumzi St, near Emerson on Hurumzi Hotel, T024-223 3731, www.ecoculture-zanzibar.org.*

Exotic Tours & Safaris, *1st floor, Bombay Bazaar Building, Mlandenge, T024-223 6392, www.exoticzanzibar.com.*

Fisherman Tours & Travel, *Vuga Rd, T024-223 8790, www.fishermantours.com.*

Gallery Tours & Safaris, *off Nyerere Rd, close to Protea Hotel Mbweni Ruins Hotel (page 71), T024-223 2088, www.gallerytours.net.*

Links Tours & Travel, *at the port, Malindi, T024-223 1081, www.linkstours-zanzibar.com.*

Marzouk Tours & Travel, *Hurumzi St, opposite Emerson on Hurumzi Hotel, T024-223 8225, www.marzoukzanzibar.com.*

Mercury Zanzibar Safaris, *Kenyatta Rd, near the junction with Vuga Rd, Shangani, T0777-429 441, www.mercuryzanzibarsafari.com.*

Ocean Tours, *Kelele Sq, Shangani, opposite Serena Inn, T024-223 8280, www.oceantourszanzibar.com.*

Rafiki Tours & Travel, *Shangani St, Shangani, T0716-144 344, www.rafikitoursandtravel.com.*

Sama Tours, *Hurumzi St, near the Clove Hotel, T0 777-430 385, www.samatours.com.*

Sun Tours & Travel, *Kiembe Samaki, off Nyerere Rd, near the airport, T024-223 9695, www.suntoursznz.com.*

Tabasam Tours, *in the Old Dispensary building, Mizingani Rd, T024-550 0193, www.tabasamzanzibar.com.*

Tropical Tours & Safaris, *Kenyatta Rd, opposite Mazson's Hotel, Shangani, T0777-413 454, www.facebook.com/TropicalToursZanzibar.*

Zan Tours, *Migombani St, near the port, Malindi, T024-223 3042, www.zantours.com.*

Zanzibar Different Tours, *Mrembo Spa (see above), Cathedral St, T0 777-430 117, www.zanzibardifferent.com.*

Zenji Zanzibar, *at the Zenji Hotel (see Where to stay, above), Malindi, T0774-276 468, www.zenjizanzibar.com.*

Transport

Air

Renamed in 2010 in honour of Abeid Amani Karume, the island's first president, **Abeid Amani Karume International Airport (ZNZ)** is 7 km southeast of Stone Town *T024-223 3979, www.zaa.go.tz.* Construction of the second terminal started in 2011. When it becomes operational, the old terminal will be used for flights from parts of East Africa and the new one for long-haul flights. Capacity of the new airport will be 1.5 million passengers per year.

Visa requirements are the same as they are for Tanzania, but as the islands are administered semi-autonomously, you may be asked to show your passport to an immigration official on entry and exit. If visitors are arriving on Zanzibar from outside Tanzania they can obtain a visa on entry. The airport has airline desks, a snack bar, souvenir shops, bureaux de change and ATMs. There are numerous daily flights between Dar es Salaam and Zanzibar, which take 20 mins and cost from around US$80 one-way. The airlines that offer these include **Air Excel**, **Air Tanzania**, **Auric Air**, **Coastal Aviation**, **Fast Jet**, **Precision Air**, **Regional Air** and **ZanAir**. There are also a few daily flights from Zanzibar to Pemba, which take 30 mins and cost from US$95 one-way, with **Auric Air**, **Coastal Aviation** and **ZanAir**. The airport is also served by a couple of international airlines and regional flights from Nairobi in Kenya (see page 145), as well as European charter flights.

Airline offices
Air Excel, Arusha, T027-254 8429, www. airexcelonline.com.
Air Tanzania, Ohio St/Garden Av, Dar es Salaam, T0782-737730, www.airtanzania. co.tz.
Auric Air, Julius Nyerere International Airport, Dar es Salaam, T0688-937 165, www.auricair.com.
Coastal Aviation, Zanzibar airport, T024-223 3112, www.coastal.co.tz.
Ethiopian Airlines, opposite the Friday Mosque, off Malawi Rd, Malindi, T024-223 1527, www.flyethiopian.com.
Fast Jet, Julius Nyerere International Airport, Dar es Salaam, T0784-108 900, www.fastjet.com.
Fly 540, Zanzibar airport, T0762-540 540, www.fly540.com.
Kenya Airways, Mlandege Rd, T0786-390 004, www.kenya-airways.com.
Precision Air, Mlandege Rd, T024-223 5126, www.precisionairtz.com.
Regional Air, Arusha, T0784-285 753, www.regionaltanzania.com.
ZanAir, Zanzibar airport, T024-223 3670, www.zanair.com.

Bus, dala-dala and minibuses
The main bus and *dala-dala* terminal is on Benjamin Mkapi (Creek) Road opposite the Darajani Market. All vehicles on routes around Stone Town and across the island have numbers and their destination marked on them. Beware of the touts; there is often someone who pretends to help by showing you the right bus and then asking the fare beforehand – you do NOT pay before boarding the vehicle, and even then on a *dala-dala*, only pay the conductor when you are close to your destination. They generally run from 0600 or 0700 to 1600 or 1800, depending on the destination, and a journey across the island costs no more than US$2. However, they are slow, as they stop in numerous villages and at roadsides along the way. For example a *dala-dala* to Kendwa and Nungwi might take up to 2 hrs, and to Paje and Jambiani up to 3 hrs.

An alternative to the buses and *dala-dalas* is to organize a seat on one of the daily tourist minibuses to the coastal resorts. These usually depart Stone Town around 0800, and again in the early in the afternoon if there is the demand, and cost around US$15 per person and take not much more than 1 hr in any direction. All the hotels and tour operators can organize this and they pick up from most hotels or central areas in town. Likewise they will usually take you right to your hotel door at the other end. If you on a package holiday at an all-inclusive resort, direct transport is normally arranged straight from the airport.

Car hire

> **Tip...**
> If you've hired a vehicle, you may encounter one of the numerous police road blocks around the islands. Standard fines for offences such as speeding are issued on the spot. If the police are not willing to give a receipt, or they claim that your papers are not in order, they may be looking for a small bribe. Insist that you want to go to the police station to deal with it.

Car hire can be arranged through most of the many tour operators in Stone Town or try the companies below. All can arrange pick-ups and drop-offs at the airport. A licence from your own country is permissible, but on Zanzibar (unlike

Zanzibar Island

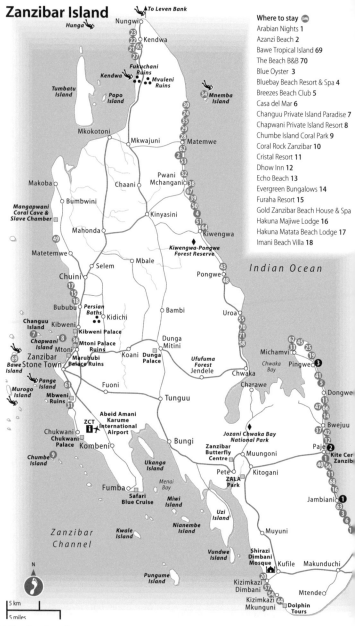

To Leven Bank

Hunga

Nungwi

Kendwa

Fukuchani Ruins

Kendwa

Mvuleni Ruins

Tumbatu Island

Popo Island

Mnemba Island

Mkokotoni

Mkwajuni

Matemwe

Makoba

Chaani

Pwani Mchangani

Mangapwani Coral Cave & Slave Chamber

Bumbwini

Kinyasini

Mahonda

Kiwengwa

Matetemwe

Selem

Mbale

Kiwengwa-Pongwe Forest Reserve

Indian Ocean

Chuini

Pongwe

Bububu

Persian Baths

Kidichi

Bambi

Uroa

Changuu Island

Kibweni

Kibweni Palace

Chapwani Island

Mtoni

Mtoni Palace Ruins

Dunga Mitini

Michamvi

Koani

Dunga Palace

Chwaka Bay

Pingwe

Zanzibar Stone Town

Marahubi Palace Ruins

Ufufuma Forest Jendele

Bawe Island

Pange Island

Fuoni

Chwaka

Dongwe

Murogo Island

Mbweni Ruins

Charawe

Abeid Amani Karume International Airport

Bungi

Tunguu

Bwejuu

ZCT

Jozani Chwaka Bay National Park

Paje

Kite Cer Zanzib

Chukwani

Chukwani Palace

Kombeni

Zanzibar Butterfly Centre

Muungoni

Jambiani

Chumbe Island

Pete

Kitogani

ZALA Park

Fumba

Ukanga Island

Menai Bay

Safari Blue Cruise

Miwi Island

Uzi Island

Nianembe Island

Muyuni

Zanzibar Channel

Kwale Island

Vundwe Island

Shirazi Dimbani Mosque

Kufile

Makunduchi

Pungume Island

Kizimkazi Dimbani

Mtende

N

Kizimkazi Mkunguni

Dolphin Tours

5 km
5 miles

Where to stay

Arabian Nights 1
Azanzi Beach 2
Bawe Tropical Island 69
The Beach B&B 70
Blue Oyster 3
Bluebay Beach Resort & Spa 4
Breezes Beach Club 5
Casa del Mar 6
Changuu Private Island Paradise 7
Chapwani Private Island Resort 8
Chumbe Island Coral Park 9
Coral Rock Zanzibar 10
Cristal Resort 11
Dhow Inn 12
Echo Beach 13
Evergreen Bungalows 14
Furaha Resort 15
Gold Zanzibar Beach House & Spa
Hakuna Majiwe Lodge 16
Hakuna Matata Beach Lodge 17
Imani Beach Villa 18

mainland Tanzania) you also need to get this endorsed locally by the police for a fee of US$10, and you'll get a temporary 15-day driver's permit. Without this permit you may get harassed at the police road blocks on the island, of which there are several. The company that you hire the car from will take care of all of this – either during a 20-min drive around to the respective offices whose stamps and signatures are needed, or before you arrive if you've pre-booked a car (you need to scan and email a copy of your licence). For more information about renting a car and driving on Zanzibar, see Practicalities page 151.

Zanzibar Car Hire Ltd, Kenyatta Rd, Shangani, T024-223 5485, www.zanzibarcarhire.com.

Zanzibar Express Car Hire, Nyerere Rd on the way to the airport, T0777-410 186, www.zanzibar expresscarhire.com.

Zanzibar Rent-A-Car, Nyerere Rd on the way to the airport, T0713-676 033, www.zanzibarrentacar.com.

Ferry

For information for the ferry services between Dar, Zanzibar and Pemba, see Dar es Salaam, page 44. Ferries arrive at the well-organized ferry terminal in the port at Malindi in the north of Stone Town. The booking offices of the ferry companies are at the end of Malawi Rd at the port entrance and are generally open 0600-2000. If at all possible, buy your ticket in advance, as it is easier to then go straight to the departure gate later with your luggage. As in Dar, the companies advise travellers to ignore the touts, and it is easy enough to book a ticket on your own.

North to Nungwi

The stretch of coastline immediately to the north of Stone Town was once an area of villas, recreational beaches and Sultans' out-of-town palaces. This is also the route that was once followed by the Bububu light railway (so named after the noise the train made) and an iron pipeline that carried domestic water supplies to the town during the reign of Sultan Barghash. Today, many of the ruined palaces can be visited, although little of their previous opulence remains and they are fairly overgrown. Nevertheless, they offer an interesting excursion en route to Nungwi.

At the northern end of the island are the villages of Nungwi and Kendwa. Until recently these were sleepy fishing villages hosting a couple of backpackers' lodges, but today the two settlements are almost joined together by a ribbon of hotel development, and this is one of the most popular spots on the island for a beach holiday. The party atmosphere along the Nungwi Strip may not appeal to everyone, but there is no denying that this is a wonderful stretch of palm-lined beach. Days are warm and sunny, the Indian Ocean is a brilliant blue and the snorkelling and diving are excellent.

Maruhubi Palace Ruins
4 km to the north of Stone Town, signposted to just west of the Bububu road. Access is dawn-dusk, free.

The Maruhubi Palace was built in 1882 by Sultan Barghash for his harem of what is said to be one wife and 99 concubines. The Palace was once one of the most impressive residences on the island. Built in the Arabic style, the main house had balustrade balconies, the great supporting columns for which can still be seen. From here you can imagine him looking out over his beautiful walled gardens, which are believed to have been inspired by the Sultan's 1875 visit

Tip...
The sandy beach behind the palace is worth walking along as it is used by local fishermen as a sort of informal shipyard, where they fix their dhows and fishing nets using only hand tools.

Essential North to Nungwi

Getting around

If you are only going to the sites before and around Bububu, then Bus No 502 from Stone Town will get you there; otherwise get off the vehicles that go further north.

Nungwi is 58 km north of Stone Town and 64 km from the airport. Kendwa is off the same road; the turnoff is 3 km south of Nungwi and then the village is 1.5 km to the west. Tourist minibuses (usually with a/c and seven seats) go from Stone Town to both (stopping at Kendwa before/after Nungwi). They usually depart around 0800 (although there are also early afternoon departures if there is the demand) and take approximately 1 hr and cost about US$15 each way; any hotel or tour operator can book these. A private taxi to both from Stone Town, the airport or ferry terminal will cost in the region of US$50-60. There are also local buses and *dala-dalas*; the most useful is *dala-dala* No 116, which goes between the Darajani stop on Benjamin Mkapi (Creek) Road in Stone Town to the end of the tarmac; a short walk from the centre of Nungwi village. You can also get bus No 14 from Stone Town. Both take at about two hours (depending on how many stops they make en route) and should cost about US$1.50 each way; beware though the operators may charge a 'tourist fare' of about US$3. To get to Kendwa, you need to get off the bus or *dala-dala* at the junction for Kendwa, and then walk the1.5-km walk to the coast along a rocky track. Alternatively if you have luggage, get off in Nungwi and get a taxi the 3 km back to Kendwa.

When to go

If you are coming for the diving then the best time to come is between October and April, before the long rains.

to Richmond Park in London. An overhead aqueduct and lily-covered cisterns (or 'pleasure ponds') can also be seen on the site and are evidence of the extensive Persian Baths. On the beach are the remains of a fortified *seble* or reception area, where visiting dignitaries would have been welcomed. The palace was almost completely destroyed by a fire in 1899; the site is now very overgrown, and marble from the baths has long since been stolen.

Mtoni Palace Ruins
2 km after the Marahubi Palace Ruins and next to Mtoni Marine (see Where to stay, below). Open 1000-1800. Free. Every Tue and Fri Mtoni Marine hosts a buffet dinner in the courtyard accompanied by taarab music (contact the hotels or the tour operators for details).

In 1828 and shortly before he relocated his court from Muscat to Zanzibar, Sultan Seyyid constructed the Beit el-Mtoni (the 'Palace by the Stream') as his primary residence, and it is the oldest palace on the island. One of the most famous inhabitants was his daughter Princess Sayyida Salme who was born here (see box, page 90). She recalls in her book, *Memoirs of an Arabian Princess from Zanzibar*, that Mtoni "had a large courtyard where gazelles, peacocks, ostriches and flamingos wandered around, a large bath-house at one end and the sultan's quarters at the other where he lived with his principal wife". The palace was abandoned by 1885, in favour of more modern residences built by Sultan Barghash (see Maruhubi Palace above) and quickly fell into disrepair. Being used as a storage depot in the First World War caused further damage. However, the roofless inner courtyard is fairly intact and it's possible to make out the palace garden and the bathing complex. One row of baths was used by the courtiers, whereas a separate domed aisle was uniquely reserved for the use of the Sultan and his first spouse.

Kibweni Palace
3 km north of Mtoni, to the left-hand side of the road. Not open to the public.

This fine whitewashed building is the only Sultan's Palace on the island to remain in public use, accommodating both the President and state visitors. Constructed in 1915 it was used as a country or 'rest house' for the royal family and was originally named Beit el-Kassrusaada ('Palace of Happiness') but that name fell into disuse and it's now commonly referred to by the name of the nearby village of Kibweni. It was still in use by Sultan Khalifa II until 1960, after which the government took it over during the Zanzibar Revolution.

Persian Baths at Kidichi
1 km north of Kibwenii at Bububu, take a right-hand turn opposite a small filling station, along a rough dirt road. Follow the track for 3 km out through the clove and coconut plantations. Access is dawn-dusk, free.

Built on the highest point of Zanzibar Island by Sultan Seyyid Said in 1850, these baths were for his second wife, who was the grand-daughter of the Shah of Persia,

Fatah Ali, and are decorated in ornamental Persian stucco work. They would come here for hunting excursions and to oversee the work on their plantations, and the bathhouses were built so they could refresh themselves after the journey from town. Persian poetry inscribed inside the baths at Kidichi has been translated (approximately) as "Pleasant is a flower-shaped wine/With mutton chops from game/Given from the hands of a flower-faced server/At the bank of a flowering stream of water". The domed ceiling contains a circle of small windows that used to be stained glass and would cast colourful light patterns over the white walls. Unfortunately though, the site has not been well maintained, and mould grows on much of the beautiful stucco work. The beaches to the west of **Bububu** are good and are the location of several resorts (see Where to stay, below).

Mangapwani Coral Cave and Slave Chamber
Near the village of Mangapwani, about 20 km north of Stone Town. Many of the tour operators stop here on a spice tour. The caves can be reached independently by taking bus No 2 from Benjamin Mkapi (Creek) Rd. It's best to take a torch. Access is dawn-dusk, free.

These were used to hide slaves in the times when the slave trade was illegal but still carried on unofficially. The **Coral Cave** is a natural cavern in the coralline rock with a tapered entrance and a pool of fresh water at its deepest point. The cave itself is said to have been discovered when a young slave boy lost a goat that he was looking after. He followed its bleats, which led to the cave containing the freshwater stream (a blessing for the confined slaves). With care, you can reach the steps that lead down onto the chamber floor. **Mangapwani Slave Chamber** is a couple of kilometres up the coast from the Coral Cave. Although sometimes called the Slave Cave, it is a rectangular cell that has been cut out of the coralline rock, with a roof on top. It was built specifically for storing slaves, and its construction is attributed to one Mohammed bin Nassor Al-Alwi, an important slave trader. Boats from the mainland would unload their human cargo on the nearby beach, and the slaves would be kept here before being taken to Stone Town for resale, or directly to the nearby plantations. After 1873, when Sultan Barghash signed the Anglo–Zanzibari treaty which officially abolished the slave trade, both the caves continued to be used as a place to hide slaves, as an illicit trade continued for many years.

> **Tip...**
> Between the Coral Cave and the Slave Chamber is the Managapwani Serena Beach Club; a day resort for guests at the Serena Inn in Stone Town (see page 65). You can come here for a seafood lunch and to enjoy Managapwani Beach if you pre-arrange it with the hotel first and therefore make use of their transfer service.

BACKGROUND
Princess Salme of Zanzibar

Princess Sayyida Salme was born at Mtoni Palace on Zanzibar in 1844 and was the daughter of Sultan Seyyid Said who ruled from 1804 to 1856. Her mother was one of his concubines and a former Circassian slave from southern Russia, who was tall and strong with startling blue eyes, pale ivory-coloured skin and black hair that came down to her knees (Circassian women were thought to be highly beautiful and spirited which made them desirable as concubines at the time). Salme inherited her mother's great beauty and intelligence and was unusually skilled for a young woman in the royal family; she could swim, ride a horse, shoot, was fluent in both Kiswahili and Arabic and could write. The princess was very keen on learning about Western cultures and she convinced her father to permit her to take English lessons so she could communicate with the wives of Western dignitaries, whose husbands came to greet the Sultan. When her father died in 1856, she was declared of age at 12 years old and received her paternal heritage of a plantation, residence and £5500. Her brother Sayyid Thuwaini bin Said al-Said became Sultan of Muscat and Oman, while her other brother Majid bin Said became the Sultan of Zanzibar. (She was also the half-sister of Barghash bin Said who took the throne after Majid.)

The princess fell in love with a young German businessman from Hamburg, Rudolph Heinrich Ruete, whom she met across the balconies on the rooftops of Stone Town. (It is reputed that the courtship took place on the second-floor balcony of today's People's Bank of Zanzibar on Cathedral Street behind the Old Fort.) But because of her strict Islamic upbringing, Salme was restricted from coming into contact with men, let alone Western men. Nevertheless, they had a secret love affair and she became pregnant. As it was impossible for the princess to conceal her pregnancy from her family, she eloped to Germany with Ruete in 1866. En route to Hamburg she converted to Christianity and was baptized in a small English church in Aden in Yemen. (She also gave birth to their son while they were in Yemen.) Once in Germany, she married Ruete in 1867 and adopted the name Frau Emily Ruete. She learned to speak and write German, she dressed beautifully in the cumbersome Western

---

Listings Stone Town to Mangapwani *map p84*

Where to stay

$$$$ Sea Cliff Resort & Spa
Mangapwani, 20 km north of Stone Town, T0767-702 241-9, www. seacliffzanzibar.com.

A quality resort on Mangapwani Beach and sister property to the **Hotel Sea Cliff** in Dar (page 39), built in mock-Arabic style architecture with makuti thatched roofs. There are 120 rooms, 2 very large rim-flow swimming pools, tennis courts, spa, gym, water sports centre, bike

dress, ran a household herself and had three more children. Sadly, her marriage was not to last long, as her husband was tragically killed in a tram accident in 1870.

His death left Salme in difficult financial circumstances and she tried to get some support from her estranged family in Zanzibar. However, Majid had died two months after her husband, and her half-brother Barghash, who was now on the throne, refused to have anything to do with her. After all, she had eloped with a foreigner and broken Islamic law and, having converted to Christianity, had given up the faith of her birth. Nevertheless, Salme tried repeatedly to get some kind of settlement of her claims and to become reunited with her family and childhood friends in Zanzibar, but her brothers, first Barghash then Khalifa, refused to meet with her and, in October 1888, bitterly disappointed, Emily Ruete left Zanzibar for the last time.

During this period, and partly to alleviate her economic problems, she wrote *Memoirs of an Arabian Princess from Zanzibar*, which was first published in the German Empire in 1886, later in the United States and Britain. It was the first known autobiography of an Arab woman. The book presents an extraordinary and intimate picture of life in Zanzibar between 1850 and 1865. It covers Salme's life in Mtoni Palace and describes both her privileged and inferior position as a woman in the royal family. She writes about the dress, jewellery and customs of the concubines at the palace, and also provides a fascinating inside portrait of her powerful father, whom she speaks of with great affection, as well as her brothers Majid and Barghash.

After 25 years living in Beirut in Lebanon, Emily moved back to Germany in 1917. By this time the generation which had known her in Zanzibar had died and, with them, the animosity towards her; so, in 1922 Sultan Seyyid Khalifa bin Harub finally bestowed a pension upon her. Emily Ruete, née Princess Salme of Zanzibar, died in Germany in 1924 at the age of 79. Ironically, she was the longest survivor of all Said's children and perhaps today her name is better known than those of Said, Majid and Barghash themselves. She was laid to rest in the grave of her husband at a cemetery in Hamburg. With her ashes was buried a small bag of sand from a Zanzibar beach which was found in her possessions, and which she had carried with her since her last visit to the island in 1888.

hire, walking trails through a coconut plantation, a jetty into the sea, a bar and restaurants. An excellent all-round option.

$$$$-$$$ Hakuna Matata Beach Lodge
Chuini, 12 km north of Stone Town, T0777-454 892, www.hakuna-matata-beach-lodge.com.
German-run lodge built around the ruins of Chuini Palace built in 1873 but mostly destroyed in fire in 1914. There are 13 secluded a/c bungalows with terraces and ocean views set in leafy gardens around a small cove, some with sleeper couches for children. An excellent restaurant serves the usual seafood and there are fairly formal 3-course set dinners, the bar is built on stilts in the sea, and there's a spa.

$$$ Imani Beach Villa
Bububu Beach, 9 km north of Stone Town, T024-225 0050, www.imani-zanzibar.com.

Fairly secluded, with only 7 clean, comfortable a/c rooms and traditional-style furniture. The quality and presentation of food is very high, with fresh fish and organic vegetables from their gardens, and you eat Swahili-style, seated on cushions around low tables. The restaurant is open to non-guests, and there's a barbecue on Thu nights. From US$180 double B&B or US$600-900 (depending on season) for private use of the whole house for up to 17 people.

$$$-$$ Mtoni Marine
Between the Maruhubi and Mtoni ruins to the north, 6 km north of Stone Town, T024-225 0140, www.mtoni.com.

Set in an attractive palm tree garden with large swimming pool, this old-fashioned but reasonably good-value place is somewhere between a traditional resort and a large hotel complex. It has 41 rooms, plus 4 family apartments with kitchenettes, the open-air restaurant has barbecue buffets, plus there's a sports bar. NOTE: at the time of writing this was going under a major refurbishment by new owners; check the Facebook page for progress (www.facebook.com/mtoni.marine.92). It still, however, organizes a buffet dinner and entertainment on Tue and Fri at the Mtoni Palace Ruins for about US$45 per person (can book with the hotel or tour operators).

$$ Furaha Resort
Bububu Beach, 9 km north of Stone Town, T024-225 0010, www.furahazanzibar.com.

Fairly simple but very friendly option set on a quiet part of the beach, with 13 large, comfortable a/c rooms and Zanzibari beds; most of the rooms are set around the swimming pool. There's a terrace restaurant and bar with ocean views offering a decent continental breakfast and grilled seafood for dinner. Doubles from US$75.

Kendwa and Nungwi

resort heaven

Kendwa

About 3 km by road south of and before Nungwi is the resort of Kendwa. At most times it is the quieter alternative to Nungwi, although these days the string of resorts effectively joins the two up. The gorgeous white-sand beach is a little broader than Nungwi and if you walk south you'll find some isolated spots. It takes about 30 to 40 minutes to walk along the beach between Kendwa and Nungwi but you can only do this at low tide. Alternatively you can negotiate a ride (about US$3-5) on an *ngalawa*; much smaller than a dhow, these are essentially dugout canoes with outriggers and little sails used by local fisherman. There is also more organized two-hour sunset cruises by dhow between the two (see page 79). Kendwa is famous for the 'full moon' parties on the beach hosted by the Kendwa Rocks Beach Hotel (see below). With DJs, acrobats and fire-eaters, these are normally held on the Saturday night nearest to full moon each month (the hotel publishes a calendar online). The parties can be tremendous fun; but avoid Kendwa on these weekends if this is not your thing.

Nungwi

At the north tip of the island Nungwi is traditionally a fishing village and dhow-building centre surrounded by banana palms, mangroves and coconut trees, with a local population of around 6000. However, tourism has rapidly expanded in this area and today it is the most popular beach resort on the island. It has a string of large self-contained

Tip...
Unlike the east coast beaches, because the tide only retreats about 6 m at low tide along the beaches around Kendwa and Nungwi, you can swim at any time of day without walking out too far to reach the sea.

resorts, a number of good budget beach-side bungalows, a short line of lively outdoor bars and restaurants, known as the 'Nungwi Strip', and a clutch of dive schools and water sports centres. In short, Nungwi has everything tourists expect of a sun-sea-and-sand holiday, but it also has its negatives: aggressive touts selling

Nungwi

Mnarani Marine Turtle Conservation Pond & Zanzibar Cycling Adventures

Ras Nungwi Lighthouse

Dhow Boatyard

Fish Market

East Africa Diving

Kiteboarding Zanzibar

Football Pitches

Dala-Dala Stand

Zanzibar Parasailing

Taxis

School

Nungwi Supermarket & Chef's Baking Shop

Zanzibar Watersports

Bottle Shop

Bottle Shop

Spanish Dancer Divers

To Kendwa (3 km) & Stone Town

To 17 18

N

500 metres
500 yards

Where to stay
Amaan Bungalows 1
Baraka Bungalows 2
Double Tree Hilton Nungwi 8
Essque Zalu Zanzibar 7
Flame Tree Cottages 12
Hideaway of Nungwi
  Resort & Spa 17
Jambo Brothers
  Bungalows 14

Langi Langi 3
Mnarani Beach
  Cottages 6
Nungwi Inn 13
Paradise Beach 9
Ras Nungwi Beach 10
The Royal Zanzibar
  Beach Resort 18
Sazani Beach Lodge 11
Smiles Beach 16
Union Beach Bungalows 15
The Z 5

Bars & clubs
Cholo's Bar 19
Mangi's Bar 20

sunset cruises, young men posing as Maasai warriors and talking Italian while they hawk wooden carvings, loud bars playing dance music, and a little reproachfulness from the local community – their traditional attitudes do not sit easily with swimsuits, drinking and partying. Nevertheless, the beach really is lovely and is lined with palm, mangrove and casuarina trees, and because the tide doesn't retreat far, you can swim at any time of the day. The accommodation is of a good standard and most of Nungwi's cottages are built in a traditional African style with makuti thatched roofs to blend in with the natural surroundings. Some of the bars are fantastically rustic and you'll find beautifully carved Zanzibari furniture sitting on the beach. The more reserved restaurants offer top quality seafood with impeccable service and ocean views. And, when tourists cover up and are respectful and polite when visiting Nungwi village, the local people are extremely welcoming (see box, page 153).

There are few sights per say – Nungwi is a beach resort after all – but you can admire the **Ras Nungwi Lighthouse**, adjacent to the Mnarani

Beach Cottages, which was first constructed in 1881 with its present 14-m square tower built in 1926. It is still in use but not open to the public. At the dhow boatyard you'll often see local men working in groups to build dhows with hand tools and boat building here has been a traditional skill for generations. Upon completion a big ceremony is organized and all the villagers are invited. Before the launch the boat builder hammers the boat three times in a naming ceremony. The local fishermen leave for their night of fishing around 1600 everyday – the sight of the fleet of dhows all with white sails at the same angle is a great photo opportunity. They return around 0630, after which the fish auctions at the village's Fish Market are a lively affair.

Every day from about 1600 to sunset, there are informal beach volleyball matches on the sand in front of the Nungwi Inn and Spanish Dancer Divers; tourists, villagers and hotel staff all join in.

Mnarani Marine Turtle Conservation Pond ⓘ *near the lighthouse, T0773 204 320, www.mnarani.com, open 0900-1800, US$10*, is a protected natural coral rock pool behind the beach, in a stunning spot, with beautiful crystal-clear water, which is replenished by the high tide as the ocean seeps. Hawksbill turtles have traditionally been hunted around Zanzibar for their attractive shells, and green turtles for their meat, and as such they are both endangered. Many of these turtles frequently nest on Nungwi Beach or are caught up in fishermen's nets, and the locals bring them to this laudable community-driven conservation centre and natural aquarium in the village. The team at Mnarani Marine Turtle Conservation Pond nurture newly hatched babies to adolescence and nurse rescued adults to good health, and then they are rereleased back into the sea. You can look down on the turtles from a wooden boardwalk, and also quite uniquely (and harmlessly) swim with them – they are in fact very curious and nudge you in the water to request a handful of seaweed to nibble on. Check the Mnarani Marine Turtle Conservation Pond's Facebook page (www.facebook.com/turtleconservation) for details of their annual turtle release day in February; it's of great celebration for the village and many Nungwi people get involved to help release the turtles on the beach and from boats.

Tumbatu Island

Northwest of Zanzibar, the mysterious island of Tumbatu is the third largest island in the archipelago and, despite being only 8 km long by 3 km wide, it has a very individual (if not muddled) history. The island's people, the **Watumbatu**, are distinct from the people of Unguja and claim to be descended from Shirazi kings who left Persia in the 10th century. The sultan is said to have ruled all Zanzibar from Tumbatu until rebel groups terminated the monarchy in the mid-13th century. The Watumbatu have since had understandably tense relations with the people of Unguja, and have gained a reputation as an aloof and unfriendly population. They are also strictly Muslim, speak their own dialect of Kiswahili, are fiercely independent, and have always resisted the booming tourism industry that swept Zanzibar. They also have the reputation of being the best sailors on the East Coast of Africa. The island contains Shirazi ruins of a large ancient town dating from the 12th century; about 40 of the stone houses remain, while the Mvuleni ruins in the north of the island are the remnants of the Portuguese attempt to colonize Zanzibar. Visitors are not generally welcome; however, some hotels in Kendwa or Nungwi can arrange informal boat trips to the island with a translator or Tumbatu guide, but it's only advised if you can show that you are genuinely interested in their culture. The island's coral reefs are spectacular, and are often visited on snorkelling and diving trips from Kendwa and Nungwi.

Listings Kendwa and Nungwi *maps pp 84 and 93*

Where to stay

Kendwa

$$$$ Kilindi Zanzibar
Reservations Elewana Collection, Arusha
T027-250 0630, www.elewana.com,
www.kilindi.com.
Stunning luxury resort with beautiful architecture and 15 very spacious and private brilliant white villas with domed roofs to keep them cool (makes a change from makuti thatch), each with its own plunge pool, some have 2 bedrooms and 3 have rooftop gardens. There's an open restaurant, bar with waterfall feature, beautiful spa with its own walled garden, and unique T-shaped infinity swimming pool next to the ocean. A useful/useless fact is that this was originally built as a holiday retreat for Benny Andersson of ABBA.

$$$$-$$$ Gold Zanzibar
Beach House & Spa
T0779-700 005, www.goldzanzibar.com
Located in a good position on Kendwa Beach, this resort has good standards and service and 67 individually and contemporarily decorated a/c rooms with terraces overlooking the ocean or tropical gardens in vaguely Moorish-style units. The 5 luxury suites have their own tented gazebos on the beach. Both a buffet restaurant for breakfast and an elegant a la carte restaurant with tables in the sand, 2 bars, large swimming pool, water sports centre and spa.

$$$ PalumboKendwa
T0776-001 300,
www.palumbokendwa.com.
An Italian-run mid-range resort with nice stone architecture, good facilities and service, but not on the beach – although it's only a short 3-min drive on the complementary shuttle service to get there (which runs until 2300 for the nightlife too). The advantage is it makes its quiet and the palm-shaded large swimming pool is some compensation. The 30 a/c rooms have Zanzibari beds and terraces, and there's a choice of restaurant/bars.

$$$-$$ Sunset Kendwa Beach Hotel
T0777-413 818, www.sunsetkendwa.com.
One of the cheaper places to stay in Kendwa, perched on top of a small cliff above the beach, with a reasonably organized feel to it, friendly staff and a choice of 50 bright traditionally decorated rooms ranging from simple thatched beach bungalows to cliff-side apartments – all are reasonably priced from US$85 for a double, extra beds can be added, and most rooms have a/c. The good bar and restaurant does great fresh fish and pizzas, and the **Scuba-Do** dive centre is here (see page 101).

$$$-$ Kendwa Rocks Beach Hotel
T024-294 1113, www.kendwarocks.com.
The original Kendwa backpackers' lodge, this had a much-needed overhaul and renovation in 2014 and now sits at somewhere between a party palace and a typical north coast resort. The accommodation suits most budgets with 34 rooms in brick cottages, wooden bungalows and basic thatched bandas on the beach. Rates vary from US$20 per person in a quad room with shared bathroom, to US$145 for an en suite double with balcony and sea views. The restaurant/bar is in a huge double-storey thatched building with tables in the sand and serves pizza, seafood, sushi, veggie and Indian food. The Rocks Lounge is a legendary bar and club (open Mon-Sat dusk-dawn), which is famous for hosting 'full moon' parties once a month on the beach (see above). Zanzibar Watersports has a centre here (see page 101).

Nungwi
There are more than 1000 hotel beds in and around Nungwi and rates vary from US$30 to US$500 plus, so the resort appeals to all budgets. In recent years, new hotels, including large, soulless package resorts, have been built here and they effectively join up Nungwi with Kendwa to the south. These rarely accept walk-ins and offer all-inclusive packages with transfers straight from the airport in Stone Town and may or may not appeal; although like many of the other beach resorts in Zanzibar they can be good value especially if you look for early-bird or last minute deals. Of these, a couple of recommended places because they are popular with a cross-section of nationalities, are well-managed and have excellent facilities are: **Hideaway of**

Nungwi Resort & Spa (T0758-818 281, www.hideawaynungwi.com); and **The Royal Zanzibar Beach Resort** (T0783-345 345, www.royalzanzibar.com). The accommodation below is run on a non-all-inclusive basis, athough there is always the option of organizing half- or full-board rates.

$$$$ Essque Zalu Zanzibar
T0778-683 960, www.essquehotels.com.
Opened in 2011, this large resort, with its enormous thatched main building (the roof is more than 40 m high), now dominates a previously low-key part of east Nungwi. Italian-owned but popular with a mixture of international holidaymakers, it has 40 slick rooms and 9 super-luxury villas, a stylish restaurant and bar, expansive spa, stunning infinity swimming pool and pier into the ocean. East Africa Diving has a base here.

$$$$-$$$ Ras Nungwi Beach Hotel
T024-223 3767, www.rasnungwi.com.
This attractive, quality and well-run place was one of the first resorts in Nungwi and it has a refreshing personable small-hotel atmosphere. The 32 rooms, some in the lodge, some beach chalets and 1 suite that is a huge detached house with a plunge pool, are all are linked to the beach by pathways and have ocean views, 4-poster beds, carved doors, a/c and balconies. Restaurant, bar and lounge area are under thatched roofs, there's a large pool, spa, and water sports centre.

$$$$-$$$ The Z Hotel
T0732-266 266, www.theZhotel.com.
An excellent boutique hotel with 35 elegant sea-view rooms boasting a classy mix of Zanzibari and contemporary decor and special touches like the TVs built within the mosquito

nets over the beds. The 2 rooftop suites and 2 oceanside cottages are especially nice. The relaxing infinity pool overlooks the beach, and there's an open-air restaurant serving African-continental fusion food built up on stilts over the sea. The **Cinnamon Bar** is a perfect spot for sundowners, there's a spa, they have their own 'Z' dhow for sunsets cruises, and **East Africa Diving** has a base here.

$$$ Double Tree Hilton Nungwi
T024-224 0476,
www.doubletree3.hilton.com.
A modern resort, with 96 neat a/c rooms with DSTV and balconies overlooking the ocean or pool in whitewashed blocks with thatched roofs, pool with swim-up bar, 2 restaurants with themed nights and live entertainment, gym and spa, and East Africa Diving has a base just in front of the hotel. A little impersonal but good standards and service from Hilton's mid-range brand. There are good views of the dhows moored off the village to the north of here.

$$$ Flame Tree Cottages
T0737-202 161,
www.flametreecottages.com.
Set in colourful gardens with coconut palms, frangipane and bougainvillea just off the beach, the 16 immaculate a/c cottages with terraces are all named after trees or plants that are common to Zanzibar. The 3 family cottages have 2 bedrooms and kitchenettes. Candle-lit restaurant specializing in seafood, swimming pool, and can organize yoga on the rooftop, as well as specific yoga retreat-style holidays (www.yogazanzibar.com). Centrally located but the whole place has a charming air of tranquillity about it. Doubles from US$140.

Tip...
The beach party crowds tend to hang out around the Nungwi strip in the southern part of the village. If you want to avoid the crowds, the northeast of the peninsula is generally quieter and has some smaller, more intimate places to stay.

$$$ Langi Langi
T024-224 0470/1,
www.langilangizanzibar.com.
Pleasant thatched bungalows with 34 a/c rooms with verandas just across the track from the beach, some in 2-storey buildings next to the pool and cheaper units in garden cottages, plus a good-value 2-bedroom family house. Swimming pool in peaceful garden, very good restaurant on a pleasant deck over the beach with reasonably priced food, including octopus and lobster, and unusual spicy Indonesian dishes. Doubles from US$125.

$$$ Mnarani Beach Cottages
T024-224 0494,
www.mnarani-beach-cottages.com.
A quiet and secluded spot near the lighthouse, and a 20-min walk from the main strip, with friendly management and a good atmosphere. 37 rooms ranging from simple cottages in the garden, to spacious family apartments with balconies and sea views in the main building, all with a/c and Zanzibari beds. Great seafront bar with hammocks, restaurant that focuses on seafood and international cuisine, massages available and has its own dhow for excursions. Rates vary from US$140 to US$290.

$$$ Sazani Beach Lodge
T0776-668 681, www.sazanibeach.com.
A quiet option near Ras Nungwi about a 20-min walk from the 'strip', with 10

thatched bungalows with fans set in tropical gardens dotted with day-beds and hammocks and linked to the beach by sandy paths. Morning tea is brought to your veranda, the Pweza Juma bar and restaurant serves original dishes with local flavour, specializing in 3-course set dinners of seafood and barbecues. The secluded beach is good for kiteboarding and **Kiteboarding Zanzibar** is here (see page 101).

$$$ Smiles Beach Hotel
T0714-444 105,
www.smilesbeachhotel.com.
This friendly family-run place has 16 spacious a/c rooms, the triples represent very good value, terraces or balconies in 2-storey pagoda-style houses with wide spiral staircases to the upper floors. It's a little bit exposed next to the beach track, but the attractive tropical gardens and the swimming pool compensate. The restaurant, just off the beach, serves traditional Swahili food; it's Muslim owned so no alcohol but the fresh fruit 'mocktails' are good and it's an easy stroll to bars. Doubles from US$135.

$$$-$$ Amaan Bungalows
T024-501 152, www.ocean.co.tz.
This, the original Nungwi resort, was established in the 1990s and is really the centre of the whole Nungwi strip. Today it's a sprawling place set in tropical gardens with 86 rooms of varying standards but all very well maintained and have recently been refurbished – the best are those with balconies right over the beach or the ones in the new blocks next to the swimming pool. The 2 restaurants and bars serve good quality food and are deservedly popular, plus there's a curio/coffee shop. Doubles with fan start from US$80, with a/c US$120.

$$ Nungwi Inn
T024-224 0091,
www.nungwiinnhotel.co.tz.
A neat and friendly set-up with 24 quieter-than-most bungalows in a pretty garden behind **Spanish Dancer Divers**, with spacious tiled bathrooms, terraces, a/c and Zanzibari beds. The beach restaurant and bar, with a relaxed atmosphere and chilled music, has a pizza oven, occasional seafood barbecues, and it's worth making a detour for the chocolate, banana and honey pancakes and coconut-based cocktails. Doubles from US$65.

$$-$ Baraka Bungalows
T0777-422 901, www.barakabungalow.atspace.com.
The 16 rooms here are in thatched cottages scattered around a beautiful little garden oasis set just back from the beach. They are simply furnished with quiet terraces, fans or a/c and nets, good tiled bathrooms, and some have 3 beds. The restaurant, which is on the beach, serves generous portions and good juices such as avocado and cucumber. You can organize bicycle rental from here. From US$60 for a double, and sharing a triple or quad room brings it down to around US$25 per person.

$$-$ Paradise Beach Bungalows
T0777-416 308,
www.nungwiparadisebungalows.com.
It is totally misleading to call this 'bungalows' when the 20 basic rooms are in a tired-looking block facing the sea. They have fans, nets and chairs outside on the terrace/balcony and can be cheap – from US$40 for a double in quiet times; but if being charged around US$90 in high season then you are paying too much – there are better alternatives. It is right in the heart

of things on the Nungwi strip, has a popular restaurant serving pizza and curries and a lively beach bar. Difficult to pre-book but you should be able to get a room. **Zanzibar Watersports** is on the beach here (see page 101).

$ Jambo Brothers Bungalows
T0777-492 355.
A slightly simpler concern than some of its neighbours and almost on the beach just north of Cholo's Bar & Grill (see below), but it's exposed as people walk right by on the public beach track. The 15 rooms in large cottages with terraces have nets, fans and hot water, but it's a little scruffy and not as well maintained as some. Doubles from US$35 with breakfast, no restaurant but an easy stroll to the other places. Again, not easy to pre-book but it's easy to organize a room when you get off the minibuses in the centre of the village.

$ Union Beach Bungalows
T0777-354 927, www.facebook.com/ unionbeachbungalows.
Low budget option with 10 bungalows on the beach but again dotted around the main track so very exposed – people passing by can look straight in the door. Each has its own bathroom, nets and fans, some have fridges and small porches. Questionable plumbing and cleanliness but probably the cheapest accommodation in Nungwi with doubles from US$30 including a breakfast of eggs, fruit and bread.

Restaurants

Nungwi
Almost all the restaurants are in the hotels and resorts. The densest crop is the string along the Nungwi strip and you can take your pick as you walk along the beachside track between the hotels. Most kitchens are open 0700-2130, but the bars open until at least 2300. Menus are very similar and offer seafood, pizza and pasta; expect to pay in the region of US$8-12 for a main course rising to US$15 or more for lobster or a seafood platter. The best of the more formal restaurants are at **Langi Langi**, **The Z Hotel** and **Double Tree**. In the village itself, look out for the friendly **Chef's Baking Shop** next to Nungwi's only supermarket; here you can pick up cheap and tasty eat-in or takeaway local food – meat stews, chicken or fish curry, whole fried fish and the like.

Bars and clubs

Kendwa and Nungwi
For late night music and partying, head to **Mangi's Bar** (on the beach just south of The Z Hotel), **Cholo's Bar** (on the beach near Kiteboarding Zanzibar's office), or get a taxi to **Kendwa** and **The Rocks Lounge** at the Kendwa Rocks Beach Hotel (see page 96).

Shopping

Nungwi
Remember there is no ATM or bank in Nungwi – ensure you bring enough TSh cash from Stone Town. The only formal supermarket is in the centre of the village and is usually open daily from early in the morning until about 2000. It's small, but sells soft drinks, carton juice and bottled water, toothpaste, soap and shampoo, chocolate, biscuits and Pringles and the like. You can also buy basics at other small shops. Remember to cover up if you go into the village. There are a couple of unnamed bottle shops for alcohol on the tracks behind the beach (one is near Langi Langi, the

Henna tattoos

The art of henna body-painting has been used for centuries as a woman's adornment in Asian and Middle East countries and it was imported to Zanzibar during the establishment of the Swahili culture. Known as hina in Kiswahili, the dye is obtained after pounding the dried leaves of the plant, then mixing them with water to form a paste. Lemon or lime juice is added to make the dye more reddish, and the colour can be further enhanced by adding cloves, tea, coffee or indigo. Sugar and oil are added to make it last longer. Today, henna occupies a special place in both rural and urban Zanzibar and Pemba in marriages and occasions such as births, naming and circumcision ceremonies and the Muslim holiday of Eid-al-Ftir (end of Ramadan). It is applied on the soles of the feet, ankles, palms and nails, and patterns represent good health, fertility, wisdom, protection and spiritual enlightenment; the more complex the design is, the more attractive the woman becomes. Rather delightfully, wives also paint themselves to gladden and welcome home their spouses who have been away for days, and men return the compliment by buying their wives new *kangas* (pieces of cloth worn by local women), shoes or jewellery.

Many visitors to Zanzibar (both male and female) get henna 'tattoos'. (For men a trailing vine or geometrical pattern around the upper arm that's popular for normal tattoos is the norm). Ladies or *wachoraji* (henna painters) offer this service at most of the beach resorts on the island, and you can also get tattoos done in the small art galleries in Stone Town, especially around Hurumzi Street behind the Old Fort, and they may be offered on a Spice Tour. Because henna is a natural dye (it's permanent on fabric or wood), and the skin reacts and absorbs the powder, it stains the skin and cannot be scrubbed off with soap and water. The tattoos usually last around two weeks, although they do fade and disappear over that time.

other near The Z Hotel). There are curio and souvenir stalls dotted around, and several places for massages, manicures and pedicures, hair-braiding and henna tattoos (see box, above) along the beach track or at the resorts.

What to do

Cycling

Zanzibar Cycling Adventures, *at Mnarani Marine Turtle Conservation Pond, near the lighthouse, T0772-292 566, www. zanzibarcyclingadventures.com.* This local

enterprise offers fun and easy half-day guided cycling excursions around Nungwi to visit farms, beaches and caves. Bike and helmet included; US$30.

Diving and snorkelling

There are more than 20 dive sites around the top of Zanzibar between Tumbatu Island in the west and Mnemba Island in the east. There is an abundance of tropical reef fish as well as large pelagic fish and, if lucky, you will encounter barracuda, manta rays, whale and reef sharks; hawksbill and green turtles, and schools of dolphins are often seen. The average water temperature is 27°C and visibility sometimes exceeds 40 m, with the average all year at 20 m. For more information on Zanzibar's dive sites, see box, page 16. The most popular trip from Nungwi is to **Mnemba Island Marine Conservation Area**, see page 105.

Several dive schools operate on the north coast. Single dives start from US$60-95, US$90 to Mnemba with the conservation fee, night dives from US$75, and deals can be done for 2 plus dives. A 1-day PADI Discover Scuba Diving course is from US$85, a 4-day PADI Open Water course around US$500, and other advanced courses are on offer. They can also organize snorkelling boat trips for around US$45 to Tumbatu and US$55 to Mnemba. Snorkelling equipment for use from the beach can also be hired at the resorts or from some of the shops in Nungwi village.
East Africa Diving, at **Double Tree, The Z Hotel**, **Essque Zalu Zanzibar**, and **Royal Zanzibar Beach Resort**, Nungwi, *T0777-416 425, www.diving-zanzibar.com.*
Scuba-Do, at **Sunset Kendwa Beach Hotel**, Kendwa, **La Gemma Dell' Est** and **My Blue Hotel**, Nungwi, *T0777-417 157, www.scuba-do-zanzibar.com.*
Spanish Dancer Divers, in front of **Nungwi Inn**, Nungwi, *T0777-417 717, www.divinginzanzibar.com.*
Zanzibar Watersports, at **Kendwa Rocks Beach Hotel**, Kendwa, and **Paradise Beach Bungalows**, Nungwi, *T0773-235 030, www.zanzibarwatersports.com.*

Fishing
Fishing trips go to the Pemba Channel just north of Nungwi. The yellowfish tuna season is Aug-Nov and the billfish season for blue, black and striped marlin Nov-Mar. A 5-hr trip, including tackle and bait and refreshments, costs in the region of US$500-600 for 4-6 fishermen.
FishingZanzibar.com, at **The Z Hotel**, *T0773-875 231, www.fishingzanzibar.com.*
Zanzibar Big Game Fishing, based at the **Zanzibar Watersports Centre** at Kendwa Rocks Beach Hotel, Kendwa, *T0773-235 030, www.zanzibarfishing.com.*

Kiteboarding
Nungwi has reliable winds, white powdery beaches and shallow turquoise water, which make perfect conditions for kiteboarding. The best winds for experienced boarders are Jan-Apr, but beginners can learn at any time of year.
Kiteboarding Zanzibar, office near **Jambo Brothers** and at **Sazani Beach Lodge**, Nungwi, *T0779-720 259, www.kiteboardingzanzibar.com.* Offers lessons from 3 hrs (from US$80) to a 3-day course and rents out equipment to experienced boarders. Also Stand Up Paddling (SUP); board rental is US$20/1 hr and lessons are from US$40/1-hr.

Sightseeing tours
In the event that you have arrived in Kendwa/Nungwi straight from the airport, its' possible to visit Stone Town, Jozani Chwaka Bay National Park, and go on a Spice Tour on day trips. Again all the hotels/resorts can organize this, most of which are affiliated with a local tour operator. Also try:
Mrembo Tours, at **The Z Hotel**, Nungwi, *T0732-266 266, www.mrembotours.com.*
Nungwi Tours, close to **Double Tree**, Nungwi, *T 0777-461 517, www.nungwitours.com.*

Sunset cruises
Given that Kendwa and Nungwi face west, a must-do is go on a sunset

cruise by dhow. All the hotels/resorts, tour operators and touts on the beach can organize this and costs are from US$15-40 per person. What you pay rather depends on what you get; ideally you want to be on the ocean for at least 2-hrs, perhaps there will be some snorkelling gear on board so you can plop over the side, and there is something decent to drink that preferably comes out of a cooler box full of ice.

Water sports

A range of water sports can be arranged from either the resorts or at centres on the beach at Nungwi and Kendwa. Expect to pay around the following; **Parasailing** takes around 1 hr for the boat ride with about 15 mins in the air and is best at sunset when you can see the other side of the peninsula; US$90, tandem US$150. **Waterskiing/ wake-boarding**, US$40 for 15 mins or US$80 for a 30-min lesson. **Banana boat/rubber rings**, US$15 for 15 mins. Jet-ski hire, US$50 for 15 min, or guided **jet-skiing** trips last 1 hr 30 min and go approximately 15-20 km to the tip of Tumbatu Island and back, US$220 for 1 rider or US$250 for 2.

ZP Ocean Sports & Parasailing, *Kendwa Beach, T0779-073 078, www.zpoceansports.com.*

Zanzibar Watersports, at **Kendwa Rocks Beach Hotel**, Kendwa, and **Paradise Beach Bungalows**, Nungwi, *T0773-235 030,* www.zanzibarwatersports.com.

Northeast
coast

The very northeast part of the island seems miles away
from the party scene of the Nungwi area and has a
more remote, 'get away from it all' feel. Villages such as
Matemwe stretch right up the coast, fringed with shady
palms. The local people live a peaceful existence making
a living from farming seaweed or octopus fishing. An
extensive coral reef runs down the whole east coast of
the island, protecting a long, idyllic white sandy beach
that runs for miles and is one of Africa's most beautiful.
The only problem here is that the ocean is tidal and,
during some parts of the day, it's a very long walk over
the tidal flats to reach the sea (look out for sea urchins
when walking). Further south, particularly around
Kiwengwa and Pongwe, there has been a mushrooming
of fully inclusive resort properties along the coast,
which are quite characterless and could quite frankly
be anywhere in the world, many of them frequented by
European package holidaymakers.

Chwaka

The road from Stone Town travels due east and after 32 km reaches the village of Chwaka. Chwaka is a quiet fishing village overlooking a broad bay of shallow water and mangrove swamps. Its history is evident from a line of fine but decayed villas, standing above the shoreline on the coral ridge, and it was once popular as a holiday resort with slave traders and their families in the 19th century. There is a lively open-air fish market but little accommodation, and most visitors head north along the coast to the hotels.

The **Chwaka Bay** itself is a large indentation in the central east coast of the island and contains several small islands, and the southwest corner of forms part of the Jozani-Chwaka Bay National Park (see page 112); usually visited on the way to the southeast coast. On the way to Chwaka (about 5 km before) you will pass the tiny **Ufufuma Forest**, which covers not much more than one square kilometre. It is, however, a home for Zanzibar red colobus monkey and many bird and butterfly species, and also the site of several caves. **Ufufuma Forest** is also where the last evidence of the Zanzibar leopard was encountered. Although not seen since 1970, prints and droppings were found in 1994, but it's presumed extinct now. The forest has been actively conserved since 1995 and, although it's not a very well-known attraction, tourists are welcome to walk along the narrow paths here. You may be able to pick up a guide for a tip in Jendele village if you get off the buses there; ask around.

North of Chwaka

The road from Chwaka heads north through the coastal fishing villages where there are several accommodation options and water sports centres on what is a fantastic beach. **Uroa** is a lovely small fishing village 8½ km north of Chwaka, and is close to an accessible reef, which offers suitable diving for novices. **Pongwe** is

Essential Northeast coast

Finding your feet

Chwaka is 32 km west of Stone Town, and like the north coast, tourist minibus transfers to the resorts along the northeast coast can be arranged in Stone Town and cost around US$15. They usually depart around 0800 (although there are also early afternoon departures if there is the demand) and take approximately 40 minutes. A private taxi from Stone Town, the airport or ferry terminal will cost in the region of US$40-50. There are also local buses and

dala-dalas; bus Nos 206, 214 and 217 go from the Darajani stop on Benjamin Mkapi (Creek) Road in Stone Town to Chwaka (taking roughly 1½ hours depending on how many stops they make en route), and then No 214 continues north to Uroa and Pongwe, while No 217 also goes as far north as Kiwengwa. Bus No 118 goes from Stone Town up the westerly north–south road and then cuts across to Matemwe (46 km/roughly 1½ hrs). Each journey costs approximately US$1.50.

ON THE ROAD

Mnemba Island and reef

About 3 km off the coast of Matemwe lies the small island of Mnemba. About 500 m in diameter and a stunning teardrop-shaped oasis of white sand, the island is surrounded by an oval coral reef, which is the Mnemba Marine Conservation Area. This is renowned for its diving and snorkelling, and trips go here from Nungwi on the north coast as well as from the northeast coast. Mnemba Island and its reef are sometimes called Mnemba Atoll, which is incorrect because an atoll is an island that encircles a lagoon, which is not the case for Mnemba Island. Diving here is the best on Zanzibar; on the inside of the reef it's like being in a giant aquarium, and the outside offers excellent wall and drift dives. The water is home to approximately 600 species of coral reef fish, as well as three species of dolphin, Hawksbill and green turtles, and even whale sharks and humpback whales may be seen between July and September. Migratory and resident shore birds feed and roost on the island itself, and quite remarkably, in the tiny forest in the middle of the island, there is a population of suni antelope. While many dive and snorkelling boats visit the reef every day, the island is privately leased and to go ashore it is necessary to stay in the exclusive Mnemba Island Lodge (see page 111).

6.5 km north of Uroa, and **Kiwengwa** another 9 km north of Pongwe. From the main road between Kiwengwa and Pongwe, there are sections where there seems to be one gated tourist package hotel after another (predominantly occupied by Italians). This is one of the most heavily developed stretches of coastline on Zanzibar and, in some respects, locals have taken badly to many of the largest and least considerate resorts at which many guests show flagrant disregard for Zanzibari culture (topless sunbathing is illegal on the island although in parts of Italian-Kiwengwa you would be forgiven for not believing so). Nevertheless, Kiwengwa is popular on account of its beautiful beach and the 'all-inclusive' appeal of a holiday here – although guests rarely leave the resort compounds. The large barricaded resorts diminish as you head further up the coast road through **Pwani Mchangani**, 8 km north of Kiwengwa, to the small village **Matemwe**, 6 km north of Pwani Mchangani. Inland from Matemwe is some of the most fertile land on the island, a centre for rice, sugar and cassava production. Matemwe beach itself makes few concessions to tourists in that it's a centre for gathering seaweed and fishing. Depending on the position of the tide, you'll either see scores of women wading fully dressed into the sea to collect their daily crop or fleets of dhows sailing away to fish. It's one of the most interesting stretches of coast on the island and beautiful in the sense that it's very much a place where the locals carry on their traditional way of life.

Kiwengwa-Pongwe Forest Reserve

Open 0800-1700; guides can be picked up at the gate for a tip of roughly US$10. About a 2-km walk west from Kiwengwa on the road to Kinyasini; the small sign on the left is difficult to spot; from here it is another 500 m on a dirt road to the entrance. If you don't want to walk, get off a dala-dala going towards Kinyasini. Most of the Kiwengwa-Pongwe hotels/resorts can organize visits.

This infrequently visited conservation area covers about 3000 ha of scrubland, mixed thickets and coral rag forest where there is the option of 200-m, 400-m or 2-km nature trails. Wildlife is varied, and you might catch sight of the endangered red colobus monkey, Sykes and blue monkeys, although they are much shyer and less used to visitors here than at the Jozani Chwaka Bay National Park (page 112). The forest is also home to Aders duiker, several species of snake, clouds of butterflies and some 40 species of bird, including ones indigenous to Zanzibar, such as the Zanzibar sombre greenbul, crowned hornbill, collard sunbird and white-browed coucal. Many of the 100 or so plant species are used by local people for medicinal purposes.

You can also explore the interesting coral caves here, which have impressive stalactites formed by water dissolving from the calcium carbonate of the coral stone. Another curious feature are the roots that have forced their way through the ground and look like electric wires connecting the ceiling to the bottom of the caves. The cave system is divided into three parts: the north and south caves are over 200 m long, sometimes 200 m deep, are accessible by stairs and walkways (although they are a bit of a scramble) and have naturally formed holes in the ceilings to let sunlight in. The east cave is 50 m long, darker, has a lot of bats, and can only be entered by crawling. Although the caves were only re-discovered in 2002, it was thought that they were traditionally used by villagers to make sacrifices in order to gain assistance with earthly matters such as harvests and fertility. The caves were also used as hiding places in the First and Second World Wars, when young men hid to avoid being drafted, and their parents would sneak down in the dead of night to bring them food. When leopards were still present on the island (there were still some alive in the mid-1990s but they are now thought to be extinct), it is said that witchdoctors would sometimes keep them tethered in the caves, as they conferred status on the owners and induced terrible fear among the local people.

Where to stay

For the most part, it is necessary to book accommodation in the tourist resorts of Kiwengwa and Pongwe through a tour operator in Stone Town, Dar es Salaam or Europe (many are Italian- or Swiss-owned) – or take a chance on getting a room when you arrive, although several do not take 'walk-in' guests. This is particularly risky in high season from June to September and over the Christmas and New Year period.

North of Chwaka
Uroa

$$$ Samaki Lodge & The Beach B&B
T0772-633 063, www.samakilodge.com.
In a good location on Uroa Beach, two separate properties and Italian-owned with a 'boutique' feel and popular with a number of nationalities. Samaki has 18 rooms in an attractive thatched building with terraces/balconies, Zanzibari furnishings and rustic 4-poster beds, and there's an open restaurant/bar, sandy garden with hammocks, small spa and swimming pool. The Beach B&B has only 4 very peaceful rooms, which can also be booked by a group, and is a short stroll to facilities at the lodge. Doubles from US$150.

$$$ Uroa Bay Beach Lodge
T0778-672 809, www.uroabay.com.
A fairly good value resort with 61 rooms in low, thatched buildings surrounded by pretty flowerbeds, either sea- or garden-facing, some for families, with DSTV and a/c. Buffet meals are included but you have the option of paying more for the likes of lobster. There are 2 bars,

> **Tip...**
> There is very little choice of budget accommodation along the stretch of coast around Pongwe or Kiwengwa, although Matemwe has more options.

2 swimming pools and at low tide a sandbar appears off the beach that you can swim to. From US$115 for a double.

$$ Tamarind Beach Hotel
T0777-411 191, www.tamarindhotelzanzibar.com.
One of the older options on the east coast and fixtures and fittings could do with a spruce up and the rooms are a bit dark, but it's very affordable and has a relaxed and informal atmosphere. 18 simple bungalows near the beach with nets, ceiling fans and Wi-Fi, a pleasant restaurant, open-air bar, swimming pool, and they can arrange diving at Mnemba Island Marine Conservation Area, as well as snorkelling, bike hire and massages. Doubles from US$60, triples from US$75.

Pongwe

$$$ Pongwe Beach Hotel
T0784-336 181, www.pongwe.com.
A deservedly popular small hotel that has retained its peacefulness, with 16 nice stone and thatch beach bungalows and Zanzibari beds set in lovely relaxing gardens with hammocks strung between the palms. Attractive swimming pool area with decking overlooking the beach. The food is excellent, including inventive 3-course set dinners, and there's a cocktail bar. They can arrange all the usual activities, such as snorkelling and game fishing, and also rent out jeeps.

$$$-$$ Santa Maria Coral Park
T0777-432 655,
www.santamaria-zanzibar.com.
A relaxed spot on the beach near the village, with rustic thatched bungalows and double-storey reed huts with basic twin/doubles/triples with fans and nets, a generator provides electricity and hot water in the evenings, thatched restaurant/bar serving seafood meals, can organize a local boat for fishing and snorkelling. A new addition is the swimming pool and they also have similar rooms in the nearby Queen of Sheba Beach Lodge. Doubles from US$90.

Kiwengwa
Bear in mind there's a string of back-to-back mostly Italian resorts along Kiwenga Beach. The ones below cater to visitors of mixed nationalities.

$$$$ Bluebay Beach Resort & Spa
T0774-413 321,
www.bluebayzanzibar.com.
One of the better all-round family resorts on the east coast set on 12 ha of palm-filled grounds and on a lovely stretch of beach, with 112 a/c rooms ranging from ultra-luxurious Sultan's Suites to pretty garden rooms with sea views, 4-poster beds, DSTV and minibar. There are several restaurants and bars, disco, swimming pool, opulent spa, tennis court, children's club, water sports. **One Ocean – The Zanzibar Dive Centre** have a base here (see page111). **Sultan Sands Island Resort** is the sister resort (same contact details) next door with 76 rooms and similar facilities (many are shared).

$$$$ Ocean Paradise Resort
T0774-440 990-5,
www.oceanparadisezanzibar.com.
Another good all-inclusive option with 100 a/c rooms in round thatched bungalows in 6 ha of pretty gardens sloping gently towards the beach, with DSTV and terraces. A full range of facilities is on offer, including 3 restaurants, several bars, water sports and one of the largest swimming pools on the island. **One Ocean – The Zanzibar Dive Centre** have a base here (see page 111).

$$$$-$$$ Shooting Star Lodge
T0777-414 166,
www.shootingstarlodge.com.
Still owned by the charismatic Elly, who opened this lodge more than 20 years ago as the first in Kiwengwa. It's a beautiful, intimate place to stay, with 16 rooms furnished in Zanzibari style, ranging from pretty garden rooms to two top-class luxury private villas with private pools and roof terraces. The open-air bar and restaurant on sand with *makuti* roof serves seafood, grills and traditional Zanzibari cuisine – some of the best food to be had on the east coast. There are bicycles for hire and a lovely infinity swimming pool 10 m above the beach. Out of season rates start from a not unreasonable US$150 for a double.

$$$ Mvuvi Resort
T0777-425 669,
www.zanzibar-mvuvi-resort.com.
This Italian-run place is close to the large resorts, but is nothing like them given that it only has 6 rooms and has a charming intimate feel more akin to a friendly European B&B, although delicious Mediterranean-style meals are served in the double-storey thatched restaurant/bar. The affordable rooms can sleep up to 4 and are decorated in bright colours, have a/c, 4-poster beds, and terraces and there's a small pool set in pretty flowering gardens.

Pwani Mchangani

$$$ Mchanga Beach Resort
T0776-590 016,
www.mchangazanzibar.com.
A small, low-key lodge with 8 sea-view
lodge rooms and 2 garden suites that
can sleep up to 4 on the couches/
day beds, with a/c and locally crafted
Zanzibari furniture set in pretty gardens
opening on to the beach – morning tea
is brought to your terrace. Swimming
pool right by the beach, open-air
restaurant specializing in Swahili cuisine
and seafood, snorkelling and diving can
be arranged. Low season rates start from
US$100 for a double.

$$$ Next Paradise Boutique Resort
T0773-822 206, www.next-paradise.com.
A boutique hotel with 16 a/c rooms
and suites, very spacious and stylish
with decor of hand-carved dark wood
furniture and bright organza fabrics.
There's DSTV and terraces overlooking
the beach or swimming pool. Day-beds
are scattered around the flowering
gardens, there's an open-air bar and
good restaurant with well-presented
Mediterranean and Swahili food.
Intimate and peaceful and a popular
spot for honeymooners.

$$$-$$ Waikiki Zanzibar Resort
T0777-877 329, www.waikikiafrica.com.
This attracts a mixture of nationalities
for its youthful, lively and sporty
atmosphere and as it specializes in
kiteboarding (courses on offer), people
visit here for the day from the string
of large Italian resorts to the south.
There are 12 simple rooms in thatched
cottages, the restaurant serves Italian
and Swahili food, and the bar offers
acrobats and an open-air disco on Fri
nights. Doubles start form US$100, but

the cheaper quad rooms bring the price
right down.

Matemwe

$$$$ Matemwe Lodge
Reservations through Asilia
Africa, Arusha, T0736-500 515,
www.asiliaafrica.com.
Along with the Retreat, this is the most
secluded spot on Matemwe beach and
a fair distance from the closest resort
to the south (and out of the 'beach-
boy' zone). 12 upmarket thatched a/c
bungalows, terraces with couches and
hammocks, an open-air restaurant and
bar serving good buffet lunches and set
seafood dinners, swimming pool and,
again, spa treatments and water sports
can be arranged. Asilia run a number
of upmarket safari lodges in Tanzania
and Kenya, so a visit to Zanzibar can be
combined with those properties.

$$$$ Matemwe Retreat
Reservations through Asilia Africa
(above).
A luxury lodge with 4 stunning
whitewashed stone and thatched private
villas, each with rooftop terrace, private
plunge pool, a fully stocked bar, bathtub
with ocean views, stylish rustic- chic
decor, a personal butler and guests can
choose whether to have dinner in their
private gardens or go to the restaurant
at **Matemwe Lodge** (above). There's
an infinity pool, spa treatments and all
water sports can be arranged. Privacy
comes at a price and rates are from
US$570 per person.

$$$$-$$$ Azanzi Beach Hotel
T0775- 044 171,
www.azanzibeachhotel.com.
Classy hotel with 35 a/c rooms linked
by wooden walkways through lush

gardens, furnished in a contemporary style with lovely Zanzibari touches, such as carved wood furniture and doors, some have outdoor showers and free-standing baths. Swimming pool, spa, and the **Mnemba View** bar and **Bridge** restaurant on the 1st floor of the main building have great ocean views.

$$$ Matemwe Beach Village
T024-223 8374,
www.matemwebeach.com.
One of the nicest mid-range places to stay in Matemwe, with 20 pretty rooms, some of which sleep 3, and great wholesome food. The swimming pool cascades into another pool below, the thatched restaurant, bar and lounge is scattered with cushions and low tables, and its strongest point is its chilled atmosphere and friendly staff. **One Ocean – The Zanzibar Dive Centre** has a base here (see page 111) and this is a good spot to base yourself on a learn-to-dive package.

$$$ Sunshine Hotel
T0774-388 662,
www.sunshinezanzibar.com.
A similar setup to **Matemwe Beach Village** next door, this equally friendly mid-range place has 15 comfortable and brightly decorated rooms with fans in 2-storey Swahili-style houses with balcony. The well-designed central thatched area has a restaurant, bar and lounge on a mezzanine floor, all with lovely views over the 2 swimming pools or beach. There's a good menu that changes daily.

$$$ Zanzibar Retreat Hotel
T0776-108 379,
www.zanzibarretreat.com.
Charming, hospitable and Finnish-owned hotel with just 12 double/twin

a/c rooms which can be converted into triple or family accommodation, with elegant and sleek hardwood furniture and floorings, good-sized pool near the beach, relaxing bar, well above-average cuisine, arranges water sports, and staff can take you on village walkabouts. Out of season doubles from US$120, but the hotel is closed in May.

$$ Matemwe Baharini Villas
T0756-780 468,
www.matemwebaharinivilla.com.
Simple place with 7 stone bungalows sleeping 2-3 with makuti roofs, a/c, fans and nets. There's a decent-sized swimming pool overlooking the beach and a cavernous open-air restaurant with some chill out areas with cushions. It's a little old-fashioned but it's economical and the friendly new management are making some improvements. Out of season doubles from US$70.

$$-$ Keys Bungalows
T0777-411 797,
www.keysbungalows.com.
A low-budget local guesthouse/backpackers place with plenty of character and chilled atmosphere and usefully the buses and *dala-dalas* from Stone Town stop right outside the front door. The 9 rustic bungalows are simply but nicely furnished, set back from the beach in lush gardens. There's a cool seating area outside with hammocks and loungers, and the bar right on the beach plays reggae music, serves fresh fish and uses old dhows for furniture. Run by the affable Ali who can arrange bike and jeep hire too. Doubles from US$60, triples from US$75.

**$$-$ Mohammed's
Restaurant & Bungalows**
*T0777-431 881, www.
mohammedsbungalows.wordpress.com.*
The cheapest option in these parts
run by Mohammed (obviously) and
his extended family in the middle of
the village, with just 4 clean and basic
bungalows in a garden right next to the
beach with nets, fans tiled bathrooms
but cold showers. The small restaurant
here serves surprisingly good meals,
such as chicken and fresh fish, and the
prawns in coconut are delicious. Can
arrange snorkelling and fishing with the
local boatmen. Doubles from US$50,
triples from US$60.

Mnemba Island

$$$$ Mnemba Island Lodge
*15 mins by boat from Matemwe,
reservations Johannesburg, South
Africa, T+27-(0)11-809 4300,
www.andbeyond.com.*
This very stylish, very discreet and
very expensive beautiful lodge is the
only way to experience the wonderful
Mnemba Island and it has a reputation
for being one of the world's finest beach
retreats and is very romantic, with 10
stunning cottages well-spaced along
the beach and gourmet food. It has its
own PADI dive school, and snorkelling,
kayaking and massages can be arranged.
If you can afford it, enjoy; fully inclusive
rates are from US$1150 per person.

Restaurants

Like the north coast, most of the
restaurants are in the resorts and
hotels. Many welcome walk-ins
and you don't have to be staying.
However, the large all-inclusive places
do not – and at some non-guests may
not even be permitted into the gated
complexes. This part of the coast
is 'Italian Zanzibar; you can expect
excellent pasta and pizza as well as
Swahili dishes and seafood.

What to do

Diving
**One Ocean – The Zanzibar Dive
Centre**, *T0777-414 332, www.
zanzibaroneocean.com.* On the east
coast One Ocean have dive centres at
Bluebay Beach Resort & Spa, Meliá
Zanzibar, **Matemwe Beach Village and
Ocean Paradise Resort & Spa**, and most
of the other resorts can arrange diving
with them at these. Expect to pay in
the region of US$60 for a single dive,
US$90 to the Mnemba Island Marine
Conservation Area (see page 105) with
the conservation fee, night dives from
US$75, and US$500 for a PADI Open
Water Course.

Southeast
Zanzibar

The route to the southeast of the island leaves Stone Town's Benjamin Mkapi (Creek) Road at the junction that leads out through the newer part of town, Ng'ambo. Eventually the houses begin to peter out and are replaced by small fields of cassava, maize, banana and papaya. The road continues via Tunguu and Bungi to the Jozani Chwaka Bay National Park near Pete, before joining the coastal road linking the resorts of Jambiani, Paje and Bwejuu, a little more than 50 km southeast of Stone Town. There is a magnificent beach here that runs for nearly 20 km from Bwejuu to Jambiani, with white sand backed for its whole length by palm trees, laced with incredibly picturesque lagoons. You will see the fishermen go out in their dhows, while the women sit in the shade and plait coconut fibre, which they then make into everything from fishing nets to beds.

To the coast
a run of wildlife attractions

Jozani Chwaka Bay National Park
0730-1700, US$8, children (2-12) US$4, which includes a guide for the 45-min nature trail. It is 35 km southeast of Stone Town and 14 km before Paje; an easy stop-off en route to the southeast coast beaches. Dala-dalas and buses from the Darajani stop on Benjamin Mkapi (Creek) Road in Stone Town going to Paje and beyond pass the entrance (if you are returning to Stone Town from here, make sure you're on the main road again well before 1700).

Most of Zanzibar's indigenous forests have been lost to agriculture or construction, but the Jozani Forest in the centre of Zanzibar has been declared a protected national park (the only one on the islands). The park also incorporates the sea grass beds of Chwaka Bay to the north, the shores of which are fringed with mangrove forests. It covers 50 sq km, roughly 3% of the whole island. Because of human interference and the introduction of some alien plants and trees in the past, Jozani is not entirely an 'authentic' indigenous forest, but it is almost natural and most of the species seen here once existed throughout Zanzibar. (Kiwengwa-Pongwe Forest Reserve on the northeast of the island is considered to be the islands' last tract of completely virgin coral rag forest; see page 104).

Jozani is home to roughly one third of the remaining endemic Zanzibar red colobus monkeys, one of Africa's rarest primates. The present population is believed to be about 2000. In Zanzibar the Kiswahili name for the red colobus monkey is *Kima Punju* – 'Poison Monkey'. It has associations with the kind of poisons used by evil doers. Local people believe that when the monkeys have fed in an area, the trees and crops die, and dogs will lose their hair if they eat the colobus. The monkeys appear oblivious to tourists, swinging above the trees in troops of about 40, babies to adults. They are endearing, naughty and totally absorbing.

> **Tip...**
> You can visit Jozani Chwaka Bay National Park as part of a one-day tour from Stone Town, often combined with the Butterfly Centre and ZALA Park (below) and/or a dolphin tour.

The forest is completely managed by the local people, who operate tree nurseries and act as rangers and guides. Visitors can go on the guided forest walk, which takes about 45 minutes. Something more substantial than sandals are recommended as there are some venomous snakes. Lizards, civets, mongooses and Ader's duiker are plentiful and easy to see, and there are also Sykes' monkey, bush babies, hyraxes and over 50 species of butterfly and 40 species of birds. From the visitor centre there's also a short walk that takes you through coral forest to an old tamarind tree, which marks the beginning of the **Pete-Jozani Mangrove Boardwalk**. The transition from coral forest to mangroves is abrupt, and the boardwalk, which is

Essential Southeast Zanzibar

Finding your feet

The gateway to the southeast coast, Paje, is 57 km southwest of Stone Town. Tourist minibuses serve most of the coast and usually depart around 0800 (although there are also early afternoon departures if there is the demand) and take just over one hour to Paje, longer if going north or south. A private taxi from Stone Town, the airport or ferry terminal will cost in the region of US$50-60. There are also local buses and *dala-dalas*; bus No 309 from the Darajani stop on Benjamin Mkapi (Creek) Road in Stone Town serves Paje and continues south to Jambiani; bus No 310 goes via Paje and Jambiani to Makunduchi, and Bus 326 all the way to Kizimkazi. Bus No 324 also goes to Paje and then continues north to Bwejuu. Each journey costs approximately US$1.50.

horseshoe-shaped, takes you through the mangrove swamp. Mangroves anchor the shifting mud and sands of the shore and help prevent coastal erosion. When the tide is out, the stilt-like roots are visible. Crabs and fish are plentiful and easily seen from the boardwalk.

Zanzibar Butterfly Centre

Just beyond the village of Pete, 1 km on the left before the entrance to the Jozani Chwaka Bay National Park; again you can get here by dala-dala *and bus, T0774-224 472, www.zanzibarbutterflies.com. Open 0900-1700, US$6, children (2-12) US$3.*

This enclosed tropical garden is teaming with clouds of around 50 species of colourful Tanzanian butterflies – some endemic to the Jozani Forest area – and is a community-driven enterprise where the funds generated help local butterfly farming projects and conservation in the forests. Tours last around half an hour and guides explain the project and the butterflies' life cycle from pupae to pesky caterpillars (you can see how destructive these can be from the passion fruit vines at the top of the enclosure), to beautiful harmless butterflies with names such as the 'floating handkerchief'. The butterflies are most active 1030-1530.

ZALA (Zanzibar Land Animal) Park

Open 0830-1730, US$5, children (under 16) free. Just south of Kitogani, about 4 km beyond the Jozani Chwaka Bay National Park; get here by dala-dala *and bus but you'll need to get off/on in Kitogani. At Kitogani, the road splits and goes either due west to Paje or south via an inland road to Kizimkazi (see page 115).*

Just south of the junction at Kitogani, ZALA Park is primarily a small educational facility set up by an enthusiastic teacher from the nearby village of Muungoni for Zanzibari children to help them learn about and conserve the island's flora and fauna (many school buses bring classes here from around the island). You can see a number of reptiles here, including monitor lizards, chameleons and indolent rock pythons weighing up to 40 kg, Eastern tree hyrax, as well as Suni antelopes, an endemic Zanzabari subspecies. There's also a short nature trail through some mangroves and fruit trees, along which guides point out and explain the medicinal uses of plants and leaves. Further donations to support this worthwhile enterprise are appreciated.

Coastal resorts

trom kiteboarding to snorkelling

Paje

Paje is the coastal village at the end of the direct road from Stone Town (57 km). It has its share of resorts spreading both north and south, while the centre of the village is centred on a roundabout at the road junction and a convenient little supermarket, the **SupaDuka**, which has a post office and a small café that does takeaway cooked food and can even provide car and bike hire. Paje offers a stunning strand of white sand and, with no rocks or sea urchins, this is one of the better places on the east coast to swim. Paje is also one of the island's favourite kiteboarding destinations thanks to a gentle but consistent side-onshore wind blowing most of the year.

Bwejuu and Dongwe

Only 3 km north of the road junction in Paje, Bwejuu is best known for its proximity to the Chwaka Bay mangrove swamps, which can be reached by a small road leading inland from the back of Bwejuu Village. It is possible to find a guide locally who can navigate the way through the maze of channels and rivers in the swamps. Here you can stroll through the shallow rivers looking at this uniquely adapted plant and its ecosystem; there is also a good chance of seeing a wide variety of crabs, which live in the mudbanks among the tangle of roots. The best snorkelling in the area is to be found at 'the lagoon', about 3 km to the north of Bwejuu, just past the pier at **Dongwe**. Bicycles and snorkels can usually be hired from any of the children on the beach.

> **Tip...**
> Local *dala-dalas* and buses only go as far as Bwejuu, from where you'll need to arrange a taxi to go further north.

Pingwe and Michamvi

Roughly 6 km north of Dongwe, these are the twin villages located on either side of the northern tip of the Michamvi Peninsula, which are linked by a 2-km track. The 10-km-long Michamvi Peninsula is a headland that lies between the sea and the picturesque Chwaka Bay. On the ocean side, there is a long barrier reef approximately 1 km offshore, which at low tide can be walked to for snorkelling. On the bay side, the area is not quite as tidal as much of the east coast so swimming is possible most of the day. Also, the resorts facing west over the bay have the added benefit of seeing the sunset. Although there's a handful of hotels and lodges here (mostly in the luxury bracket), the area still has an 'off-the-beaten-track' feel to it.

Jambiani

The name Jambiani comes from an Arabic word for dagger, and legend has it that early settlers found a dagger here in the sand – evidence of previous visitors. These days the village, some 6 km south of Paje, extends for several kilometres along the coast road and is home to about 6000 people, although it's so spread out and quiet, this is hard to believe. You will, however, notice the women attending to their seaweed farms at low tide, and the fishermen returning their *ngalawas* from the reef on high tide. There are a number of resorts on Jambiani's especially white stretch of sand, and the village has a post office and several small shops where it is possible to get most of what you need.

Kizimkazi

Most people visit here as part of the controversial tour to 'swim' with the large resident pods of humpback and bottlenose dolphins (see page 80 for details of this activity). The village is split into two parts: Kizimkazi Dimbani in the north, and

Kizimkazi Mkunguni in the south. It is 24 km southwest of Jambiani, so the most direct approach from Stone Town is by taking the inland road from Kitogani, 20 km to the north of Kizimkazi Dimbani. The coastline here is very different from the classic palm-backed lagoons of the east coast. Here a coral rag cliff elevates above the ocean and the beaches take the form of small coves rather than broad expanses of sand. The **Kizimkazi (or Shirazi Dimbani) Mosque** ruins are 2 km to the northeast of Kizimkazi Dimbani and contain the oldest inscription found in East Africa – from AD 1107. The mosque has been given a tin roof and is still used. Its significance should not be underestimated for it may well mark the beginnings of the Muslim religion in East Africa. It was built by Sheikh Abu bin Mussa Lon Mohammed and archaeologists believe that it stands on the site of an even older mosque.

> **Tip...**
> Other than when the dolphin-trippers come in the mornings, Kizimkazi is a fairly quiet and conservative area, so if you're after a lively night scene, this wouldn't be your best option.

Listings Coastal resorts *map p84*

Where to stay

Paje

$$$$ Zanzibar White Sand Luxury Villas & Spa
T0776-263 451,
www.whitesandvillas.com.
The most luxurious option on this section of the coast with both classic Zanzibari and contemporary decor, and with a good environmental ethos which includes using grey water, solar and wind power. Accommodation is in 3 villas with 2-5 bedrooms, private plunge pool, kitchen, outdoor bathtub and shower, plus there are 11 spacious garden rooms with patios. Excellent and varied food in the restaurant, spa, swimming pool, beach bar, rooftop champagne bar, and a seasonal kiteboarding centre.

$$$ Dhow Inn
T0777-525 828, www.dhowinn.com.
Once a small informal place of only 5 rooms, the 28 new a/c rooms here are in attractive brilliantly white thatched chalets, stylishly decorated with terraces and palm-filled gardens overlooking one of the 3 swimming pools. There are 2 restaurant/bars, a coffee shop, comfortable lounge areas and a kite-boarding centre. It's not quite on the beach (a 50-m walk along a sandy path), but a section of the beach is reserved exclusively for the hotel.

$$$ Hakuna Majiwe Lodge
T0777-454 505,
www.hakunamajiwe.com.
Set on the southern end of the beach towards Jambiani with 20 individual and very attractively decorated rooms in stone and thatch, extra beds can be supplied for children, surrounded by palms and shrubs and sand (the name means 'place without stones'). The swimming pool is set back from the beach, and there's a huge open dining area with big sofas at the bar. Snorkelling and bike hire can be arranged.

$$$-$$ Arabian Nights Hotel
T0777-854 041,
www.zanzibararabiannights.com.
A slightly dated but good value hotel with 11 a/c rooms in stone cottages either facing the beach or around the garden or pool with spacious bathrooms, private terraces, DSTV and a/c. There's a bar, restaurant and a lounge area in an Arabian tent. There's also a nearby block with its own small pool and cheaper guesthouse rooms, and yet another block of self-catering apartments, which are a bit plain in a holiday-flat sort of way but having a kitchen is rare in Zanzibar and may appeal to some. It's a base for **Buccaneer Diving** (see page 123) and **Adventure Fishing** (see page 123) will pick up from here.

$$$-$$ Cristal Resort
T0672-147 993, www.cristalresort.net.
In a pretty location surrounded by palm trees and pines, with 32 rooms in total in either free-standing deluxe bungalows with a/c and spacious bathrooms, or a row of adjoining a/c rooms on the beach with terraces which can be shared by families, or attractively rustic 'eco' bungalows, which are cheaper but nicer with fans, home-made furniture and terraces with sea views. Swimming pool, chilled bar/restaurant on the beach, and the excellent Maua Spa has a surprisingly long menu of treatments and is open to day visitors. Doubles from US$90 and economical triples from US$100.

$$ Paje by Night
T0777-460 710, www.pajebynight.net.
Very rustic verging on ethnic, with a vibey atmosphere, and run by affable Italian Marco. 20 self-contained thatched bungalows, each one colourful and individually decorated, the 2-storey one sleeps 4, with ceiling fans and nets set

about 50 m back from the beach around the swimming pool. Bar and restaurant with very good local and international food, including Swahili dishes, seafood and pizzas. An unashamed party place and the bar stays open until the last person leaves (hence the name). **Paje by Kite** is also here.

$$-$ Paje Beach Guesthouse
T0777-461 917,
www.pajebeachguesthouse.com.
This small local guesthouse is about a 4-min walk to the beach and is run by helpful Rashid (aka 'Mr Polite'). The 6 rooms are simple but neatly kept in a house just off the main drag and have large beds, nets, ceiling fans and their own bathrooms. A bread, eggs, fruit breakfast is available and you can eat/drink at the other places around and use the swimming pool at the nearby Dhow Inn. Rates are US$30-60 per room.

$ Teddy's Place
T0776-110 850, www.teddys-place.com.
A well-run and popular backpackers' spot right on the beach and built entirely on the sand. Basic thatched bandas with nets and fans, shared bathrooms, chilled bar and restaurant, with hammocks and furniture made from dhows, good music and a tasty choice of food, such as grilled fish and Swahili curries. Simple, friendly and affordable with dorms for US$20 and doubles from US$45 including breakfast of fruit pancakes or omelette and chapati.

Bwejuu and Dongwe

$$$$ Breezes Beach Club
3.5 km north of the village, T0720-538 148, www.breezes-zanzibar.com.
An established favourite on Zanzibar and a good mid-range all-inclusive choice

popular with a number of nationalities with high standards, 70 smart rooms with either balconies or terraces, shopping arcade, spa, restaurants, bars, large swimming pool, gym, water sports centre, tennis courts and disco. The **Rising Sun Dive Centre** is based here.

$$$$ The Palms
Adjoining **Breezes**, *T0720-538 148, www.palms-zanzibar.com.*
A stunning super-luxurious resort and the sister property to Breezes with just 6 very private villas, colonial decor, DSTV, DVD player, private terrace with plunge pool, living room and bar. Facilities in sumptuous surroundings include tiered swimming pool, spa, gym, tennis court, elegant dining room, bars and lounge areas. Activities are organized at **Breezes**.

$$$ Echo Beach
Just south of Breezes, T0773-593 260, www.echobeachhotel.com.
Owned by a British couple, one a French-trained chef and the other an interior designer, this place is very stylish with an excellent restaurant menu. The 9 rooms in local stone and makuti thatch are individually designed with African antiques, silk fabrics and locally crafted wooden furniture, with spacious verandas, and the swimming pool and jacuzzi are near the beach.

$$ Evergreen Bungalows
3 km north of the village, T024-224 0273, www.evergreen-bungalows.com.
Reed-and-thatch bungalows set in a palm grove directly on the beach with 14 rooms, each with a different touch and decorated using local materials and a balcony. The double-storey ones are the nicest and have sea views; cheaper bandas are set further back and have no hot water but some sleep 4. Relaxing bar and restaurant with a good choice of Swahili dishes, and there's a dive school. Doubles from US$70.

$$-$ Twisted Palms Lodge
Just north of Evergreen Bungalows T0776-130 275, www.twisted-palms-lodge.com.
Rustic backpackers' favourite and deservedly so for the youthful vibe and its prime location on the beach. 10 basic en suite rooms in thatched bandas with 2-4 beds, fans, nets and some with verandas. The restaurant/bar is on stilts (worth coming for a meal or a party even if not staying) and serves a good mix of local seafood and Italian dishes, spiced Zanzibar coffees and a huge range of local and imported booze. Hammocks and day beds on the sand, bike hire, snorkelling boat trips and massages. Doubles from US$45 in the garden, US$60 on the beach.

$ Mustapha's Place
In the village, T0772-099 422, www.mustaphasplace.com.
A chilled, low-budget place run by Mustapha, a friendly Rastafarian. The 12 rooms are fun and bright, with paintings on the walls, and vary from smaller bandas with shared bathrooms to larger bungalows with their own bathrooms; the 1 called Treetops is on huge stilts. Very relaxing, with lovely gardens with hammocks, reggae music, bar where you can play drums, good seafood, and it's across the road from the beach, reached via a pretty pathway. Rates start from US$17 per person per night, depending on the number of people and type of room. Buses from Stone Town drop outside.

$ Robinson's Place

2 km north of the village just past **Evergreen**, *T0777-413 479, www.robinsonsplace.net.*

A simple place in a similar vein to **Mustapha's**, with accommodation in 5 reed and thatch cottages that sleep 2-6, and run by the charming Rastafarian Edi and his wife Ann. All rooms have nets and some have bathrooms. There's no electricity here, just solar power and a generator, and they serve local Zanzibari dinners cooked over coals and eaten on cushions on the floor. Rents out bikes and snorkelling gear. Doubles from US$40, extra person US$10.

Pingwe and Michamvi

$$$$ Konokono Beach Resort

North of Michamvi, T0772-265 431, www.konokonozanzibar.com.

This luxurious, secluded and contemporary resort is almost at the very top of the Michamvi Peninsula and faces Chwaka Bay. It has a vast main thatched building perched on top of a small cliff above the beach for fantastic views from the bar, lounge areas, restaurant, and lovely infinity swimming pool. The 24 massive a/c villas are either sea view, garden view or family-sized and all have plunge pools and private gardens.

$$$$-$$$ Michamvi Sunset Bay

Michamvi Village, T0772-138 579, www.michamvi.com.

A well-run, friendly and out-of-the-way resort overlooking Chwaka Bay, with 20 attractive a/c rooms in 4 blocks facing the sea and the swimming pool, all with a balcony or terrace, contemporary decor and very spacious modern bathrooms, some with double showers. The bar and restaurant serves quality international cuisine and, since the bay

is calm, as well as the usual activities, the sunset cruises by *ngalawa* to see the mangroves are very pleasant.

$$$ Karafuu Hotel Beach Resort

North of Pingwe, T0777-413 647/8, www.karafuuzanzibar.com.

The name means 'cloves' in Swahili. A large but peaceful and professionally run mid-range resort popular with a cross-section of European holiday-makers, with almost 100 a/c rooms with thatched roofs in spacious gardens. There are 3 restaurants, numerous bars, water sports, swimming pool, tennis courts, nightclub and diving. The beach is good, although watch out for the very sharp coral close offshore.

$$$ Kichanga Lodge

North of Pingwe, T0777-835 515, www.kichanga.com.

Sleepy and mid-priced place in a secluded cove with a half-moon beach, the 23 pretty bungalows are spread out in gardens, with fans, nets and private terraces; the spacious **Ocean Villas** are the best and have a mezzanine floor for extra beds. There's a bar and dining area in a breezy makuti-roofed building. Swimming pool, dive centre, bikes and canoes are for hire, and the gift shop makes up dresses to order out of traditional *kangas*.

$$$ Ras Michamvi Beach Resort

North of Pingwe, T0777-413 434, www.rasmichamvi.com.

This discreet and very pretty lodge right at the tip of the peninsula is built on low coral cliffs overlooking the beach. 15 a/c rooms in 4 stone bungalows with cool tiled flooring and big Zanzibari beds. There are 3 small beaches here, 1 of which – Coconut Beach – is backed by forest and has resident red colobus monkeys. The nice swimming pool and the restaurant are set above the beach with wide ocean views.

Jambiani

$$$ Blue Oyster Hotel
T0783-045 796,
www.blueoysterhotel.com.
Deservedly popular and well managed and priced, the 15 rooms have fans, neat tiled bathrooms and beautiful carved beds and are arranged around a serene ornamental pool and garden or in 2-storey buildings with balconies and sea views. Good food is served in the rooftop restaurant, there's a beach bar, bike hire, and they have their own dhow for fishing and snorkelling. Rates start from US$60 per person depending on how many in a room.

$$$ Casa del Mar Hotel
T0777-455 446,
www.casa-delmar-zanzibar.com.
A rustic resort with 14 rooms arranged in 2 blocks with sea views, the ones on the 1st floor are bigger with a sleeping gallery for extra beds on the mezzanine. The swimming pool is set in tropical gardens, there's an excellent restaurant and bar in a circular-shaped, open thatched building serving generous portions of Zanzibari and Mediterranean dishes and fresh fruit cocktails (highly recommended).

$$$ Coral Rock Zanzibar
T0776-031 955, www.coral-rock.com.
As the name suggests on a coral rock above the sea, a popular, friendly option with 14 a/c rooms in bungalows, nice Zanzibari beds and pleasant patios, some sleeping 3-4, which make them good value for friends or a family. The food is exceptionally good with a nod

at African fusion cooking and great seafood platters (worth coming to eat even if you're not staying). There's a pleasant swimming pool on the edge of the beach, and free 'toys' to use include windsurfing and snorkelling gear, kayaks and bikes. Doubles from US$110.

$$$ Mamamapambo Boutique Hotel
T0773-862 059,
www.mamamapambo.com.
Italian-owned by a friendly young couple, Paolo and Cristina, this is a quite beautiful quirky little place with stunning views and superb gourmet food and fine wines that will especially appeal to honeymooners. It only has 6 individually decorated rooms and the large makuti main building with its flowing fabric walls is full of ethnic objets d'art collected from around the world. Can organize *ngalawas* for snorkelling trips.

$$ Red Monkey Beach Lodge
T0777-713 366,
www.redmonkeylodge.com.
At the southern end of the string of resorts and about 2 km from the village in a lovely location on a gentle slope above the beach and popular with kiteboarders. It's named after the red colobus monkeys that can sometimes be spotted in the gardens. The 13 simple rooms with fans and nets are in whitewashed stone cottages with makuti roofs and there's 1 sleeping 4. Evening meals change daily and there's a choice of 4 courses including seafood and sometimes barbecues. The relaxing bar can sometimes be in the party mood. Doubles from US$90.

$$ Zanzest Beach Bungalows
T0778-765 591, www.zanzest.co.tz.
Just after Red Monkey Beach Lodge, a

simple friendly budget resort and the last place at the southern end of the beach so very peaceful, with 10 double/triple rooms in thatched wooden bandas set in neatly tended gardens with bathrooms and fans, 2 with balconies on the 2nd floor with sea views. The restaurant/bar has a good choice of food (the wood-fired seafood pizza is delicious). From US$70 for a double.

Kizimkazi

$$$$ Unguja Lodge
Kizimkazi Mikunguni, T0774-477 477, www.ungujalodgezanzibar.com
A very atmospheric, discreet resort set in tropical gardens with huge baobab trees and palms. 12 stunningly designed a/c villas with makuti roofs, curved walls and private terraces; the 3 that don't have sea views have their own plunge pools as compensation. There's a large swimming pool, dive centre, comfortable bar and restaurant and a coral beach.

$$$ Karamba Zanzibar
Kizimkazi Dimbani, T0773-166 406, www.karambazanzibar.com.
This lovely and laid-back lodge is popular with Spanish tourists and has 19 pleasantly decorated rooms with fans and sea-facing terraces on a small cliff above the sea (if lucky you can spot dolphins). It has its own yoga teacher, plus massages, snorkelling and sunset dhow trips can be arranged. The extensive restaurant menu offers Swahili and Italian dishes and tapas. There's an infinity swimming pool, and at high tide steps go down the cliff straight into the sea.

$$$ Swahili Beach Resort
Kizimkazi Mkunguni, T0777-844 442, www.swahilibeachresort.com.

On one of the better beaches in this area, with 19 a/c rooms in stone and red-tiled roofed bungalows with veranda and DSTV, most with sea views. There's a swimming pool, restaurant and pool bar, and **Adventure Fishing** (page 123) is based here. The hotel will cook your fish for dinner. There are more charismatic places to stay, perhaps, but it's good value from US$110 for a double.

$$-$ Promised Land Lodge
1 km south of Kizimkazi Mkunguni, past Swahili Beach Resort, T0779-909 168, www.promisedlandlodge-zanzibar.com.
A bit out of the way and a 20-min walk from the village, but a very chilled place, with 12 rooms in the main house or attractive whitewashed reed-and-thatch bungalows, each with bathrooms, fans and nets. There's a beach bar, restaurant serving good Swahili dishes, hammocks and day beds dotted around the sand for hanging out, a bonfire is lit on the beach in the evening, and bikes can be hired. Doubles from US$50.

Restaurants

As elsewhere on the island, restaurants are at the hotels and resorts and most are open to non-guests so you don't necessarily have to eat where you are staying. There are, however, a couple of standout individual spots on the southeast coast.

Paje

$ Mr Kahawa
Paje Beach (next to Kite Centre Zanzibar), T0776-531 535, www.facebook.com/mr.kahawa. Open 0800-1700.
This café on the sand is the hub among the kite schools on Paje Beach and serves fantastic freshly brewed

Tanzanian coffee, chilled tropical juices, cakes, salads and wraps (try the delicious mango chicken one). There's free Wi-Fi, patio tables and bean bags and hammocks on the beach where kite-boarders relax while waiting for the wind to pick up.

Michamvi

$$$ The Rock Restaurant
Pingwe, just south of where the road turns inland west to Michamvi, T0776-591 360, www.therockrestaurantzanzibar. com. Open for lunch and dinner but only has 14 tables so reservations are essential.
This really has to be seen to believed. The thatched whitewashed restaurant with wrap-around balcony is remarkably built on a tiny coral islet about 50 m off the shore that actually becomes 'beached' at low tide when you can walk across (at other times you can wade or there is a boat). Naturally the menu focuses on seafood, most of it grilled on an open fire, but there are also inventive salads and pastas, and a superb international wine list including Moët & Chandon and Dom Perignon champagne. Expensive but very special, particularly if the moon rises above the ocean. Expect to pay in the region of US$100 for 2 for a 5-course meal with wine.

Jambiani

$$$-$ Alibi's Well
About 200 m north of the Blue Oyster Hotel, T0786-231 988, www.jtti.org/ restaurant-allibis-well. Mon-Fri 1130-1800, dinner Fri only from 1830.
This is run by the Jambiani Tourism Training Institute, which works to provide people in Jambiani with skills to work in Zanzibar's hospitality industry, and is well worth seeking out for its amazing food and beachside setting. Lunches are simple and include freshly made sandwiches, tacos and pizzas, juices, coffees and herbal teas, and amazing puddings – date, beetroot or carrot cake, or coconut and chocolate ganache. Dinner is only served on Fri and should be booked in advance – each week showcases a different cooking style, and previous menus have included Indonesian, Lebanese, Thai and Japanese. A 3-course dinner costs in the region of US$25, which is excellent value for the very high standard. There's also a good choice of wines and cocktails.

Festivals

Jul/Aug Mwaka Kogwa. This is the traditional Shirazi New Year on Zanzibar and it's celebrated with traditional Swahili food, *taarab* music, drumming and dancing on the beach all night. Although the festival is celebrated around the island, the village of Makunduchi is the heart of the celebration. The men of the village have a play fight and beat each other with banana fronds to vent their aggressions from the past year. Then, the *mganga*, or traditional healer, sets fire to a ritual hut and reads which way the smoke is burning to determine the village's prosperity in the coming year. Makunduchi is on the southeastern tip of the island, 13 km south of Jambiani. If you are around at this time, ask the local hotels for information on the village's celebration plans.

What to do

Cycling
Bike Zanzibar, *based at Red Monkey Lodge, Jambiani, T0 777-122 461, www.bikezanzibar.com*. Run by Juma Lukondya, Zanzibar's only professional cyclist, who can organize fairly challenging day rides (of up to 80 km) to Kizimkazi, Jozani Chwaka Bay National Park and other places and also multi-day cycling holidays around the island. Discuss with him what you would like to do.

Diving
As with other dive centres around the island, expect to pay in the region of US$60 for a single dive and US$500 for a PADI Open Water Course.
Buccaneer Diving, *Arabian Nights Hotel, Paje, T0777-853 403, www.buccaneerdiving.com.*
Paje Dive Centre, *T0777-853 403, www.pajedivecentre.com*. Despite its name this centre is now in Kizimkazi, on the main road in Kizimkazi Mkunguni.
Rising Sun Dive Centre, *Breezes Beach Club, Bwejju, T0774-440 885, www.risingsun-zanzibar.com.*

Fishing
Adventure Fishing, *Swahili Beach Resort, Kizimkazi, and can also arrange trips from Arabian Nights Hotel, Paje, T0777-416 614, www.zanzibaradventurefishing.com*. Half-and full-day fishing trips go along the coast between Kizimkazi and Paje for both experienced anglers and beginners with tuition. The above hotels will cook whatever you catch. A half-day trip, including tackle and bait and refreshments, costs in the region of US$300 for 4 in a boat.

Kiteboarding
With its wide flat sand beach, shallow waves and virtually no obstructions, Paje is one of the best beaches for kiteboarding on the island. Conditions are good throughout the year, but the best months are Jun-Oct, when the Kusini winds blow, and Dec-Mar during the Kaskasi winds. These centres rent out equipment to experienced boarders for about US$50 for a half-day, and can arrange introductory 3-hr lessons for US$120.
Kite Centre Zanzibar, *Paje Beach in the centre of the village, Paje, T0776-531 535, www.kitecentrezanzibar.com.*
Paje by Kite, *Paji by Night Hotel, Paje, T0777-460 710, www.pajebykite.net.*

Pemba

Unlike Zanzibar Island, which is flat and sandy, Pemba's terrain is hilly, fertile and heavily vegetated, and, because of higher rainfall, is always green – early Arab sailors called it 'Al Jazeera Al Khadra', meaning 'The Green Island'. Pemba does not enjoy the easy accessibility to the external world. The turbulence of the Pemba Channel has discouraged light sea vessels from making regular visits and with just a few roads and scanty public transport, the island is also infinitely more difficult to get around.

But it is well known to the scuba-diving fraternity, and the sea around Pemba is the location of some of the best diving in the Indian Ocean. The Pemba Channel drops off steeply just off the west coast, and, protected by coral reefs, the diverse variety and quantity of marine life is exceptional. While much of the coast is lined with mangroves, there are also a few good stretches of shoreline and attractive offshore islands with pure, clean beaches and interesting birdlife.

Although the tourism industry is still in its infancy there is a clutch of lodges and a few more foreigners visiting than before. For those who do cross between the two very different islands, they will find a mosaic of forests, swamps, gentle hills covered in fruit and spice trees, charming Swahili villages and hidden beaches. Pemba is truly a Robinson Crusoe experience and during the clove-blooming season, visitors are welcomed by the scent of cloves and the buzz of honey bees looking for nectar.

Essential Pemba

Finding your feet

Pemba Island lies approximately 80 km northeast of Zanzibar Island (Unguja) and is about the same distance from the Tanzanian mainland, situated directly east of Tanga. The island is most easily reached by air, and the views of the uninhabited islands and reefs from a small low-flying plane are quite incredible. The ferries between Zanzibar and Pemba arrive at Mkoani on the southwestern end of Pemba Island. Pemba is about 70 km long and 22 km wide. There is one tarred but bumpy main road running from Msuka in the north to Mkoani in the south, which is served by public transport.

Tip...

The schedules to Pemba can change regularly, and flights will be cancelled if there are not enough takers, so it's essential to continually check with the airlines even on the day of departure.

Getting there

Air Flights are either from Zanzibar (30 minutes), or from Dar es Salaam (1¼ hours), with a touchdown in Zanzibar, or there is the odd flight from Tanga on the northern mainland (25 minutes). The airlines that serve Pemba are **Auric Air**, **Coastal Aviation** and **ZanAir**. Flights cost from US$95 from Zanzibar and US$130 from Dar es Salaam. The small Karume Airport on Pemba is 7 km to the southeast of Chake Chake. There is just a simple semi-open waiting area with a snack bar. You can take a *dala-dala* to Chake Chake or else taxis meet the flights; the more reliable option is to organize an airport pickup with your hotel, and these transfers cost US$40-60 depending on the location.

Ferries For details of the ferries, see Dar page 44; note though there are only presently two weekly services on Wednesday and Saturday. Fares between Zanzibar and Pemba, are: economy class US$35, children (under 12) US$25, first class US$40 per person. An immigration officer may or may not check a foreigner's passport on arrival (it doesn't seem very important given that everyone comes from Zanzibar in any case). *Dala-dalas* and buses run from in front of the port at Mkoani; and to Chake Chake it takes around 1½ hours, Wete (two hours) and Konde (2½ hours). Again there are taxis and transfers can be arranged by the hotels and lodges and cost US$40-60 depending on the location.

Getting around

There are buses or *dala-dalas* along the main roads, which cost around US$1.50 per journey, but these tend to operate in the mornings and early afternoons only and there are very few vehicles after 1500. Useful services are *dala-dala* No 603 between Mkoani and Chake Chake, No 606 between Chake Chake and Wete, and No 24 between Wete and Konde (for the Ngezi Forest Reserve). Besides this, it is very difficult to get around on public transport, and budget travellers will need to walk to get to the more out-of-the-way places.

It's possible to hire a car with a

driver at around US$70-80 per day, which is effectively hiring a taxi for the day, but it is good value (especially if there are four in a car). Although not common, you may also be able to hire a self-drive car for about US$60 per day. You can rent out motorbikes for around US$40 and bicycles for around US$10. All the hotels organize these and remember that negotiation is necessary, as ever. Motorbikes are the most common form of transport on the island, more so than cars, as potholes are more readily avoided, and it's a little too hilly in most places for cycling. But they could also be considered dangerous due to erratic local driving practices; remember you won't have insurance if your motorbike is hired. The alternative is to jump on the back of a motorbike *boda-boda* (taxi), which are plentiful.

When to go

During September and March the visibility around Pemba has been known to extend to a depth of 60 m, and there are great game fish, such as sharks, tuna, marlin and barracuda.

Tip...

There are branches of the People's Bank of Zanzibar, in the three towns: Mkoani, Chake Chake and Wete, but none of them have ATMs currently and must not be relied upon to change foreign currency. You need to bring TSh cash from Zanzibar or Dar as only the couple of top-end lodges take credit cards, and these attract a surcharge of 6-9%. At a push some places will accept US$ and Euro cash for payments.

Pemba Island

Where to stay
The Aiyana 10
Emerald Bay Resort 3
Fundu Lagoon 2
Hifadhi 12
Kervan Saray Beach
  Lodge 4

Manta Resort 1
Pemba Crown 5
Pemba Lodge 6
Pemba Misali Sunset
  Beach Resort 9
Sharook Guest House 7
Sharook Riviera
  Grand Lodge 8
Zanzibar Ocean
  Panorama 11

5 km
5 miles

Mkoani

With a population of around 11,000, Mkoani is 30 km southwest of Chake Chake and is Pemba's third largest town and the port of entry for ferries from Zanzibar and Dar es Salaam. It is set on a hill overlooking a wide bay and comprises a mix of palm-thatch huts and rundown multi-storey apartment buildings. The landing stage is a modern jetty that projects out from the shallow beach on either side, where fishermen load their daily catch into donkey carts for the short trip to market. The main road runs directly from the port up the hill and most of this distance is rather surprisingly covered by a dual carriageway, complete with tall street lights on the central reservation. This, along with the ugly apartment blocks around town, is evidence of the East German influence in Tanzania during the 1970s, which is also present at Chake Chake and Wete, and in the concrete estates on the edge of Stone Town on Zanzibar Island. Following the winding road up the hill from the port, the old colonial **District Commissioners Office** is on the right, where there is a bandstand in front of the compound. On the left is **Ibazi Mosque**, with a fine carved door. Most people around the tiny town derive their livelihood from agriculture, but there are some who work at the wharf and at the Chinese-built **Abdalla Mzee Hospital**; the main hospital on the island.

Chake Chake

This, Pemba's main town, is about halfway up the west coast of the island and 30 km northeast of Mkoani and 28 km south of Wete. It is also the closest settlement to the Karume Airport. The town sits on a small hill overlooking a creek and with a view to the west on a bay and the tiny Misali Island and is fairly small, with a population of around 22,000. It is the unofficial capital of Pemba and there are several government offices, a post office and it has the most shops on the island. However, it has a dearth of other facilities including accommodation and even the Barclay's Bank has recently shut down. The bus stand is in the centre close to the mosque and next to the market, which is particularly pleasant to wander around with its spices, fresh fruit and fish on display, and some of the local stores stock some interesting *kikois* and *kangas* (sarongs) in patterns and colours not seen on Zanzibar Island. Chake Chake is also an excellent place to buy *halua*, a sticky sweet made of wheat gluten, sugar, nuts and spices that is wrapped in woven palm fronds.

The oldest surviving building in the town is the **Nanzim Fort**, which is thought to date back at least to the 18th century and possibly as far back as the Portuguese occupation (1499-1698). Records dating back to the early 19th century describe the fortress as being rectangular, with two square and two round towers at the corners, topped by thatched roofs. Round towers are typical of the Arab and Swahili architecture of the time, but the square towers are unusual and indicate possible Portuguese influence. Construction of the old hospital destroyed all but the eastern corner and tower, which now houses part of the hospital. A battery, dating from the same period, overlooked the bay to the west, but only two cannons remain to mark the site. There are some handsome Moorish-style administrative buildings near the fort, with verandas, and a **clock tower**.

Pemba Essential Oil Distillery

On the outskirts of town towards Wete, there is the Essential Oil Distillery, which, in addition to cloves, produces essential oils from sweet basil, cinnamon leaf, lemongrass and eucalyptus. The distillation process involves the spices being dropped into a large metal vat, then bombarded with steam until their aromatic oils are released upwards into a pipe and then into smaller containers for collection and bottling. From July to February you can see local farmers deliver their sacks of clove stems here. It is possible to visit the factory on week days and you can organize a taxi in Chaka Chaka or get off at the factory from a *dala-dala* heading north of town; ask at the office and someone will show you around for a tip.

> **Tip...**
> The island's clove oil can be bought at a number of places and it has a strong, warm and spicy smell. It works on the skin as an antiseptic and to repel insects, while gargling with it as a mouthwash, sweetens the breath and is a pain relief for toothache and mouth ulcers.

Mkame Ndume Ruins

About 10 km southeast of Chake Chake and also known as the Pujini Ruins, the original settlement is thought to date back to the 15th century. There was a fortified enclosure and rampart surrounded by a moat, the only known early fortification on the East Africa coast. It is believed to have been built by a particularly unpleasant character, nicknamed Mkame Ndume, which means 'a milker of men', because he worked his subjects so hard. He was known to order his servants to carry the large stones used to build the fortress whilst shuffling along on their buttocks. The memory remains and local people believe that the ruins are haunted. The Portuguese destroyed the settlement and the palace of Mkame Ndume when they arrived on the island in about 1520. Today, the site is largely overgrown, and there is little left of the fortifications except for a crumbling staircase and some remains of 1-m thick walls. There are also the remnants of a two-chambered well that reputedly was used by the two wives of Ndume who lived in separate parts of the palace and never met.

> **Tip...**
> The site is near the village of Pujini and you can get here from Chaka Chaka by infrequent *dala-dala*, by hiring a bicycle, or by taxi and asking it to wait.

Ruins at Ras Mkumbuu and Misali Island

About 20 km west of Chake Chake, **Ras Mkumbuu** is probably Pemba's most important archaeological site, and is above the beach at the head of the peninsula

ON THE ROAD

Dive Pemba

Pemba has some of the most spectacular diving in the world. The Pemba Channel separates Shimoni in Kenya from Pemba Island. The channel runs deep until it approaches the Pemba coastline and then begins a dramatic rise creating a sheer wall off the coast. Diving is characterized by crystal-clear blue-water drop-offs, along with pristine shallow reefs and hard and soft coral gardens. These offer glimpses of sharks and turtles, and encounters with eagle rays, manta rays, Napoleon wrasse, great barracuda, tuna and kingfish are the norm. Visibility can range from 6 m in a plankton bloom to 60 m, though 20 m is classed as a bad day and 40 m is average. The average sea temperature is a pleasant 26°C.

Here are a few of the more famous dive sites with their descriptions, although there are many more spectacular sites around Pemba's smaller offshore islands.

Fundu Reef The visibility ranges from 20 to 40 m and there is a large sheer wall with overhangs and caverns. The coral is remarkable, especially the large rose coral and red and yellow sea fans. You can see many types of fish here including kingfish, triggerfish and wrasse. The reef is relatively shallow and therefore Fundu is a good spot for a first dive.

Kokota Reef Ideal for night diving, the waters are shallow and generally calmer, ranging from 8 to 20 m. Of all the creatures that come out after dark, the Spanish dancer is a particular attraction.

to the north of Chake Chake's creek. It is believed to date back about 1200 years, making it the oldest settlement south of Lamu Island in Kenya, and is the site of a settlement originating in the Shirazi period. The ruins include stone houses and pillar tombs and the remains of a 14th-century mosque. Of interest are the tombs decorated with pieces of porcelain that suggest an early connection with the Chinese.

Most people visit by boat on the way to teardrop-shaped **Misali Island**, where the marine life on the reef make it excellent for diving and snorkelling and there is a fine beach. Divers will be interested to know there are more than 40 types of coral and over 300 species of fish, and given that dragnet (and dynamite) fishing has been banned around the reef since the late 1990s, it is in pristine condition. There are pleasant trails through the forest in the middle of the island, which is rich in birdlife and is also home to vervet monkeys and the Pemba flying fox (a large bat that is endemic to the island). Legend has it that the notorious 17th-century pirate, Captain Kidd, once had a hideout here and perhaps even buried some treasure during his stay.

There is no road to the end of the peninsula and most people visit by boat from Chake Chake landing at the nearby fishing village and strolling up through the

Manta Point Visibility averages from 20 to 40 m. Manta Point is one of the best sites in the world for close encounters with the giant manta rays that inhabit this area. The rays can be seen in groups of up to 15 and rise to depths as shallow as 9 m. The enormous variety of coral, fish and other marine life is so concentrated here that you should try and include at least two dives. This is truly one of the finest dive sites in the region.

Misali Island Visibility averages between 40 and 50 m. This is a wall dotted with small caves and ridges. Large rivers of sand run off the top of the reef to form wide canyons that enter the wall at approximately 25 m. Gorgonian fans are in abundance below 20 m and, on a turning tide, the marine life is exceptional and the currents strong. Giant grouper drift lazily through the reef and hundreds of surgeonfish cruise below divers.

Njao Gap Njao Gap is well known for its amazing wall diving. Mantas can be seen here in season and the coral is spectacular, but what distinguishes this particular location is the profusion of titan trigger-fish. Visibility varies from day to day, but is usually good to 30 m.

The following places to stay have dive centres: **Fundu Lagoon, The Manta Resort, Pemba Misali Sunset Beach Resort** and **Kervan Saray Beach Lodge**. In the event you are not staying at these, they can also organize dives for non-guests but you have to get there and back, which can be tricky just for the day. Nonetheless it can be done. Expect to pay in the region of US$80 for a single dive, US$165 for double dives, and US$600 for a 5-day NAUI or PADI learn to dive course.

fields and palm trees to the ruins. Dive schools regularly visit the area, and most of the lodges and guesthouses can arrange boat excursions for non-divers.

North from Wete

luxury lodges, ancient forest, sublime beaches

Wete

This town of around 27,000 people on the northwest coast of Pemba, 28 km north of Chake Chake, once served as a port for the clove trade; today the port has been surpassed by the more modern wharf at Mkoani, where the cloves are exported either on the ferries or special boats arranged by the government after harvest time. Wete is now a laid-back place on a hill overlooking the ocean, with houses and small shops lining the main road down to the dhow harbour. Clustered close to the dock area is a pleasant group of colonial buildings. The town has a post office and police station, and the market and *dala-dala* stand are about halfway up the hill.

Mtambwe Mkuu is the small peninsula opposite Wete, connected to the main island by a causeway that is submerged at high tide, and the name means in Kiswahili 'great arm of the sea'. It was once home to an 11th-century town, and a

ON THE ROAD

Clove production

The Zanzibar archipelago is sometimes known as the Spice Islands, and was once the world's largest producer of cloves. Cloves were at one time only grown in the Far East and they were greatly prized. On his first trip back from the East, Vasco da Gama took a cargo back to Portugal and they were later introduced by the French to Mauritius and then to Zanzibar by Sayyid Said. At this time all the work was done by slaves, who enabled the plantations to be established and clove production to become so important to the economy, and Zanzibar became the leader in the world's clove production. However, when the slaves were released and labour was no longer free, some of the plantations found it impossible to survive. And then in 1872 a great hurricane destroyed many of the trees on Zanzibar Island and it was after this that Pemba took over as the largest producer.

Today the income for many Pemba small-scale farmers is from cloves; the trees cover about one-tenth of the island and there are three government-run collection points from where the cloves are sorted and exported to buyers. Most of the trees have been in the family for generations, and clove production is very much a family affair, especially during the harvest when everyone joins in the picking. Harvest occurs about every five months and everything is worked around it – even the schools close.

Cloves are actually the unopened buds of the clove tree. They grow and are collected in clusters (or 'sprays') and must be picked when the buds are full but before they actually open. Clove trees grow to a height of 10 to 15 m and can produce crops for over 50 years. Harvesting is strenuous work: the clusters can be tucked away in dense foliage where they are difficult to get at. They are then spread out on mats made from woven coconut palm fronds for about five days, turned over regularly so that they dry out evenly – the quicker they dry the better the product. As they dry, they release a sweet, heady aroma, which wafts throughout the island. As a whole or ground product, cloves are used as a spice in cooking, to flavour drinks, in perfumes and fragrances, and in medicine.

number of silver coins have been discovered at the site, although there is nothing to see today except rubble and is the location of a small fishing village.

Konde and Tumbe

The agricultural settlement of **Konde** is in the northeast of the island at the end of the tarmac road, about 15 km north of Wete, and is the furthestmost point of the *dala-dala* network. It is at the junction of the sandy road to Ras Kigomasha, the northern-most tip of Pemba via the Ngezi forest and you will pass through here to get to the lodges. An excursion from Konde might be to **Tumbe**, 7 km to the east. This is a surprisingly busy fishing village with a market where people from all around buy their fish in the mornings. Local fishermen contract to provide catches for firms, which chill the fish and export it to Tanzania's mainland. At the end of the cool season in October, there is a boat race here. Teams of men compete, paddling dug-out canoes, and the day is completed with a feast provided for contestants and onlookers. There is no accommodation in Konde or Tumbe but both can be reached by *dala-dala* from Wete.

Ngezi Forest Reserve
4 km west of Konde on the road to Ras Kigomasha, open 0730-1530, entry US$5 includes a guided walk along the sandy nature trail which is about 2 km long and takes about 1 hr.

The reserve covers 1440 ha and compromises ancient coastal forest that once covered all of Pemba. The area was declared a reserve in the 1950s, after much of the island had been cleared for clove production. This is a thick blanket of forest, with vines and creepers and a dense undergrowth that supports a variety of plants and wildlife. It has its own plant species and subspecies that are unique to this area. Most of the 27 species of bird recorded on Pemba have been spotted in the forest including the African goshawk, palm-nut vulture, Scops owl, malachite kingfisher and the endemic Pemba white eye. Much of the ground is ancient coral rag, often sharp-edged, containing pockets of soil. Mangrove forests grow on the tidal coastal creeks, and the incoming tide sees seawater running deep upstream, forming brackish swampy areas. The central area contains heather-dominated heathland where the soil is leached sand. The heather, *Philippia mafiensis*, is only found on Pemba and Mafia Islands. The Pemba flying fox, a large fruit-eating bat endemic to the island, is found in Ngezi, as are vervet Zanzibar red colobus monkeys. Indolent-looking tree hyrax can also be seen climbing and eating leaves. The Pemba blue duiker, an antelope about the size of a hare, is also here, though it is very shy and is rarely spotted, as is the endemic marsh mongoose, which normally lives by ponds and streams.

Kigomasha Peninsula
To the north of Ngezi, the Kigomasha Peninsula is at the far northwestern tip of the island. This is where Pemba's most secluded and idyllic white-sand and forest-fringed beaches are located – Makangale Beach and Panga ya Watoro Beach on the west side and Vumawinbi Beach on the east – and as such is the location of a couple of 'barefoot luxury' resorts. At the end of the peninsula is the lighthouse at Ras Kigomasha (an easy walk from the Manta Resort). It's an odd-looking 38-m-high prefabricated iron structure that was built and shipped out to Pemba by the British in 1904. A concrete cover was added in the 1970s to prevent corrosion. It is still functioning today, using kerosene lamps that are lit every evening. For a tip of about US$5, the lighthouse keeper will allow you to climb to the top (not for the faint-hearted as the 95 steps are on the outside), which is well worthwhile for the views over the ocean and south across the island.

Where to stay

Accommodation on Pemba is very limited and there are just a handful of places to stay – consequently it's recommended to make reservations before you arrive on the island. Even Mkoani, the arrival point of the ferry from Zanzibar, only has one local guest house. The reasons why there are so few hotels or lodges are that there's no real local market for accommodation and very few international visitors to Pemba (which of course is part of the attraction). As such places open and then close quite frequently – simply because of economics. All can organize pick-ups from the ferry or airport by taxi; transfers cost US$40-60 depending on the location.

Tip...
It is a bit tricky getting food in the small towns – most of the street vendors close by 1700 and you need to pre-order meals at the few places to stay.

Mkoani and around

$$$$ Fundu Lagoon
North of Mkoani across Kingoji Bay near the village of Wambaa and reached on a 10-min speedboat ride organized by the resort, T0777-438 668, www. fundulagoon.com.
This luxury British-owned development is the top place to stay on Pemba, with 18 very stylish tented rooms on stilts, overlooking a beautiful mangrove-fringed beach, and furnished with locally crafted hardwood furniture. 4 suites have private plunge pools and decks and are perfect for honeymooners. There's

a restaurant, 3 bars, an infinity pool and spa, and all water sports are available, including diving and windsurfing. It supports local communities through its Village Fund and has built a school for 500 children and installed several water wells. Rates are between US$375 and US$900 per person, depending on room and season.

$$$$ Pemba Lodge
Shamiani Island, approximately 20 km southeast of Mkoani, T0777-415 551, www.pembalodge.com.
This remote eco-lodge on Shamiani is a 15-min boat ride from the southern tip of Pemba and is under the same ownership as Mnarani Beach Cottages in Nungwi (page 97). The 5 reed-and-makuti thatch bungalows are built on stilts 1 m above the ground and discreetly spaced at least 30 m apart along the beach. Each has showers using collected rainwater, solar power and furniture made from old dhows. Excellent food and views from the elevated bar and restaurant, activities include snorkelling and kayaking around the island and in the mangrove forests. There's no dive school but they can arrange transport to other places for diving, though this needs to be organized when booking. It's not luxury but a genuine Robison Crusoe experience. Doubles from US$330.

$$$ Emerald Bay Resort
In Chokocho village, 14 km south of Mkoani on the southern coast, T0777-979 667, www.emeraldbay.co.tz.
A friendly setup with 7 simple but spacious self-contained rooms with Zanzibari beds, private verandas and sea

views, the lounge/bar is in an attractive thatched building with vaguely Arabic whitewashed walls, and the creative chef produces good seafood meals. One of the highlights here are the boat rides (with a picnic) out to the sandbanks that appear at low tide, from where you can sunbathe and snorkel. From US$230 for a double.

$$-$ Zanzibar Ocean Panorama
Mkoani, T024-245 6166, T0773-545 418, www.zanzibaroceanpanorama.com.
Up the hill in Mkoani with great ocean views and a 15-min walk from the ferry, this budget local guest house has 4 basic but clean rooms, 1 has dorm beds, with nets and fans, in a fairly new bungalow with broad thatched terrace. Good meals are served, especially the crab and grilled tuna, and they can organize activities and pickups from the airport. It faces west so the sunsets over the bay are quite special. Doubles from US$50, dorm beds US$20, including breakfast.

Chake Chake and around

$$$ Pemba Misali Sunset Beach Resort
Near Wesha, about 3 km west of Chake Chake and a 15-min drive from the airport, T0775-044 713, www. pembamisalibeach.com.
Under the same ownership as **Amaan Bungalows** in Nungwi, this is a mid-range to high-budget option on Pemba set on a beautiful beach on a little peninsula that is completely surrounded at high tide creating a little island. 39 a/c bungalows with either sea-facing or garden terraces, thatched restaurant and bar serving seafood and Swahili dishes. However, it's in need of a little refurbishment and some of the rooms are small; look at them first. Activities

include snorkelling, fishing on local dhows, kayaking, trips to the ruins at Ras Mkumbuu and Misali Island and **Pemba Misali Divers** is based here. Doubles from US$100.

$$ Hifadhi Hotel
Tibirinzi St, Chake Chake, T0777-418 023, www.hifadhihotel.com.
The only hotel in Chake Chake, which also serves as a local conference centre, with 14 clean and comfortable a/c rooms, decent choice of meals (especially the fish and vegetable curries), and there's a nice swimming pool in the compound. It's a fairly modern glassy block, though the plumbing and quality of furnishings is a little hit and miss (and it's not on the coast) but the management and staff are super friendly and polite. Doubles from a negotiable US$90.

Wete and around

$ Pemba Crown Hotel
Wete Main Rd, T0777-493667, www.pembacrown.com.
A cheap local place and in a handy location for the market and *dala-dala* stand in an imposing and reasonably maintained white 4-storey block, with 15 en suite a/c clean rooms with balconies, nets, TV and fairly reliable hot water. There's no restaurant as such, but dinner can be pre-ordered. They can help arrange taxi drivers for day trips to Ngezi Forest Reserve and Vumawinbi Beach on the Kigomasha Peninsula. Highly negotiable doubles from US$35 which includes a bread/eggs/coffee breakfast.

$ Sharook Guest House
Near the market and dala-dala stand, down the track that leads to the harbour, T024-245 4076, www.pembaliving.com.

Run by friendly Mr Sharook and his brother who are somewhat local celebrities and obviously take great pride in showing visitors Pemba – they may well arrive at the airport to pick you up themselves and arrange tours to just about everywhere including snorkelling trips to local islands and bicycle hire. Accommodation is in 4 very simple but clean 2- or 3-bed rooms for US$20 per person regardless of how many in a room. There's no restaurant but excellent pre-ordered meals can be eaten in the lounge with DSTV.

$ Sharook Riviera Grand Lodge
On the road to the port, take the road opposite the Pemba Crown Hotel, and it's on the left about 10 m up a small track, same contacts as above.
Mr Sharook's second and rather importantly named property is slightly more comfortable, as it's in a fairly new purpose-built house. 8 en suite rooms sleeping 2-4 with gleaming black-and-white floor tiles, a/c and ceiling fans, Zanzibari beds, fans and nets; again US$20 per bed. Good meals can be pre-ordered and you can go up to the rooftop for views of Fundu Island.

Kigomasha Peninsula

$$$$ The Aiyana
Makangale Beach, T0772-409 017, www.theaiyana.com.
Opened in late 2015, this Mauritian-managed, stylish, all-inclusive resort has 30 rooms in whitewashed villas – from 80 to 160 sqm – all on the beachfront, with gorgeous contemporary pale cream interiors and nice features like outdoors showers. Dining is in the restaurant, outdoors under makuti umbrellas or on a sandbank (tide allowing). Although it's newly opened, it has taken a few years to build, so the tropical gardens have matured already. Organizes dhow excursions and visits to Ngezi Forest Reserve. It doesn't have its own dive centre yet, but is expected to and diving can be arranged at **Swahili Divers** at the Kervan Saray Beach Lodge (below). Doubles from US$390.

$$$$ The Manta Resort
Panga ya Watoro Beach, T0777-718 852, www.themantaresort.com.
Considered one of the East Africa's finest beach lodges, this place is quiet and wonderfully remote set on a cliff overlooking Panga ya Watoro Beach. There's a large central area with terrace, lounge, restaurant and spa, and 20 attractively decorated rooms in individual cottages with sea or garden rooms. As well as a swimming pool and beach bar, snorkelling, kayaking and game fishing can be arranged, and there's a dive centre. All-inclusive doubles from US$460. The highlight here is the underwater room – which has had much worldwide press exposure and is truly magical and unique. It's a private floating wooden structure 250 m from the shore and accessed by boat, and guests are left there totally alone. You can either sleep on top on the roof deck or in the bedroom 4 m below the surface where you simply fall asleep watching the fish swim by. This wonderful experience, however, comes with a cool price tag of US$1500 per night.

$$$-$$ Kervan Saray Beach Lodge
Makangale Beach, T0773-176 737, www.kervansaraybeach.com.
A very chilled lodge and the home of **Swahili Divers** (www.swahilidivers.com). It's primarily a diving centre with accommodation, although there's plenty here for non-divers too, such as

kayaking, fishing and walks in the forest. Set in lovely gardens, the 11 clean and spacious rooms are in 6 bungalows and have traditional *barazza* beds, nets, fans and private bathrooms. There are also 2 rooms with 6 bunks in each – either dorms for backpackers or families/ groups. There's an open restaurant and bar/lounge area and good 3-course set dinners. Full board rates are from US$90 per person in a room, US$45 per person in a dorm, and there are some good value 5- to 10-day packages that include accommodation, meals and diving.

Background

Zanzibar

The word Zanzibar is of Persian or Arabic origin, although there is some dispute over the origin of the name. The Persians may have derived it from **Zangh Bar**, meaning 'the Negro Coast'; while it could have also been from the Arabic *Zayn Z'al Barr*, which means 'Fair is this land'. The earliest visitors were Arab traders in the eighth century who brought with them Islam, which has remained the dominant religion on the Zanzibar Archipelago. The earliest remaining building is the mosque at Kizimkazi, which dates from about 1100. For centuries the Arabs had sailed with the monsoons down from Muscat and Oman in the Gulf to trade in ivory, slaves, spices, hides and wrought-iron. The two main islands, both of roughly similar size, Unguja (known as Zanzibar Island) and Pemba, provided an ideal base, being relatively small islands and thus easy to defend. From here it was possible to control 1500 km of the mainland coast from present day Mozambique up to Somalia. A consequence of their being the first arrivals was that the Arabs became the main landowners.

In 1832 Sultan Seyyid Said, of the Al Busaid dynasty that had emerged in Oman in 1744, moved his palace from Muscat to Zanzibar. Said and his descendants were to rule there for 134 years. In 1822, the Omanis signed the Moresby Treaty, which made it illegal for them to sell slaves to Christian powers in their dominions. To monitor this agreement, the United States in 1836 and the British in 1840 established diplomatic relations with Zanzibar and sent resident consuls to the islands. The slaving restrictions were not effective and the trade continued to flourish. Caravans set out from Bagamoyo on the mainland coast, travelling up to 1500 km on foot as far as Lake Tanganyika, purchasing slaves from local rulers on the way, or, more cheaply, simply capturing them. The slaves, chained together, carried ivory back to Bagamoyo. The name Bagamoyo means 'lay down your heart' for it was here that the slaves would abandon hope of ever seeing their homeland again. They were shipped to the slave market in Zanzibar's Stone Town, bought by intermediary traders, who in turn sold them on without any restrictions.

All the main racial groups were involved in the slave trade. Europeans used slaves in the plantations in the Indian Ocean islands, Arabs were the main capturers and traders, and African rulers sold the prisoners taken in battle to the traders. Nevertheless, it is the perception of the African population that the Arabs were mainly responsible.

Cloves had been introduced from Southeast Asia, probably Indonesia, prior to the advent of Sultan Seyyid Said. They flourished in the tropical climate on the fertile and well-watered soils on the western areas of both Zanzibar and Pemba. Slaves did the cultivation and harvesting, and the Sultan owned the plots: by his death in 1856 he had 45 plantations. Other plantations were acquired by his many children, as well as by numerous concubines and eunuchs from the royal harem. In due course, cinnamon, nutmeg, black pepper, cumin, ginger and cardamom were all established, their fragrance was everywhere and the Zanzibar Archipelago became known as the 'Spice Islands'. Slaves, spices and ivory provided the basis of considerable prosperity, mostly in the hands of the Arab community, who were the main landowners and who kept themselves to themselves and did not intermarry with the Africans.

This was not true of the Shirazis who came from the Middle East to settle on the East African coast. Intermarriage between Shirazis and Africans gave rise to a coastal community with distinctive features and a language derived in part from Arabic. This became known as Kiswahili, the first language of the Swahili people. In Zanzibar the descendants of this group were known as the Afro-Shirazis. They were not greatly involved in the lucrative slave, spice and ivory trades, and instead cultivated coconuts, fished and became agricultural labourers. Those Shirazis who did not intermarry retained their identity as a separate group.

Two smaller communities were also established. Indian traders arrived in connection with the spice and ivory trade and, as elsewhere, settled as shopkeepers, traders, skilled artisans, money-lenders, lawyers, doctors and accountants. The British became involved in missionary and trading activities in East Africa while attempting to suppress the slave trade. And, when Germans began trading on the mainland opposite Zanzibar, things needed to be sorted out with the Sultan of Zanzibar, who controlled the 10-mile coastal strip that ran for 1500 km from Mozambique to Somalia. The Germans bought their strip of the coast from the Sultan for £200,000. The British East African Company had been paying the Sultan £11,000 a year for operating in the Kenyan portion. In 1890, Germany allowed Britain to establish a protectorate over Zanzibar in return for Heligoland, a tiny barren island occupied by the British, but strategically placed opposite the mouth of the River Elbe, 50 km from the German coast. In 1895 Britain took over responsibility for its section of the mainland from the British East African Company and agreed to continue to pay the £11,000 a year to the Sultan. The British mainland territory (later Kenya) was administered by a Governor, to whom the British representative in Zanzibar, the Resident, was accountable.

The distinctive feature of Zanzibar as a protectorate (Kenya had become a colony in 1920) was recognized in 1926 when the British Resident was made directly responsible to the Colonial Secretary in London. Germany had by this stage lost control of its section of the mainland when, as a result of its defeat in the First World War, the territory was transferred to British control and became Tanganyika.

The colonial period

Further legislation in 1873 had made the slave trade illegal, the slave market in Zanzibar was closed and the Anglican cathedral erected on the site. But slavery lingered on. The trade was illegal, but the institution of slavery existed openly until Britain took over the mainland from the Germans in 1918, and covertly, it is argued, for many years thereafter. Many former slaves found that their conditions had changed little, and they were now employed as labourers at low wage rates in the plantations.

Zanzibar continued to prosper with the expansion of trade in cloves and other spices, and the wealth of the successive Sultans was considerable. They built palaces in Stone Town and around Zanzibar. Islamic law allowed them to have up to four wives, and their wealth enabled them to exercise this privilege and raise numerous children. Until 1911 it was the practice of the Sultan to maintain a harem of around 100 concubines, with attendant eunuchs. The routine was established whereby the Sultan slept with five concubines a night, in strict rotation. The concubines had children, which were supported by the Sultan.

Social practices changed with the succession of Khalifa bin Harab, at the age of 32, as Sultan in 1911. He was to reign until his death, in 1960, at the age of 81. The harem and concubines were discontinued – apart from anything else, this proved a sensible economy measure. Gradual political reforms were introduced and the practice of Islam was tolerant and relaxed. Social pressures on non-Muslims were minimal. But the office of the Sultan was held in considerable awe. As the Sultan drove each day to spend the afternoon a few kilometres away at his palace on the shore, his subjects would prostrate themselves as he passed. In 1959, when it was suggested that there should be elected members of the Legislative Councils and Ministers appointed to deal with day-to-day matters of state, the Sultan received numerous delegations saying change was unnecessary and the Sultan should retain absolute power.

However, there were significant tensions. Several small Arab Associations combined to form the Zanzibar National Party (ZNP) in 1955 and their main objective was to press for Independence from the British without delay, while two African associations, active with small landless farmers and agricultural labourers, formed the Afro-Shirazi Party (ASP) in 1957.

Although the ZNP tried to embrace all races, the fact was that they were seen as an Arab party, while the ASP represented African interests. Arabs comprised 20% of the population, Africans over 75%. Elections to the Legislative Council in 1955 were organized on the basis of communal rolls – that is, so many seats were allocated to Arabs, so many to Africans, and so on. This infuriated the ZNP who wanted a common electoral roll so that they could contest all seats. They boycotted the Legislative Council, but the next elections, in 1957, were held on the basis of a common roll, and the ZNP did not win a single one of the six seats that were contested. ASP took five and the Muslim League one. But in the next four years, the ZNP greatly increased its efforts, and wealthy Arab landowners and employers flexed their economic muscles to encourage support for ZNP among Africans. ZNP was greatly assisted in 1959 by a split in the ASP. Sheikh Muhammed Shamte, a Shirazi with a large clove plantation in Pemba, formed the Zanzibar and Pemba People's Party (ZPPP). In the run-up to Independence, the ZNP, ASP and ZPPP contested the next three elections, which were on the most part deadlocked between the ZNP and ASP which formed a coalition.

In 1962 a Constitutional Conference was held at Lancaster House in London, attended by the main figures of the three political parties. A framework was duly thrashed out and agreed, with the Sultan as the constitutional Head of State. The number of seats was increased and women were given the vote. Elections in 1963 resulted in a ZNP/ZPPP coalition government under the leadership of Shamte of ZPPP, and Independence was set for later that year, on 10 December.

Meanwhile, the old Sultan had died in 1960 and was succeeded by his son Abdullah bin Khalifa, who was to reign for less than three years, dying of cancer in July 1963. His son, Jamshid Bin Abdullah, became Sultan at the age of 34.

The revolution

It has been described as 'the most unnecessary revolution in history'. At 0300 on the night of 12 January 1964, a motley group of Africans, armed with clubs, pangas (similar to machetes), car springs and bows and arrows, converged on the Police Headquarters at Ziwani on the edge of Stone Town. John Okello, a labourer and leader of the attacking force, had campaigned for the ASP in the three elections in the run-up to Independence. Highly religious, Okello was convinced he had been given orders in his dreams by god to break the powerful position of the Arabs and to found the revolutionary state on Zanzibar and Pemba, and to do this he had built up a small army of determined African nationalists. The attackers stormed the building and, in a matter of moments, the police had fled and the mob had broken into the armoury. Thus armed, they moved on to support other attacks that had been planned to take place simultaneously at other key installations – the radio station, the army barracks and the gaol. By midday, most of the town was in the hands of Okello's forces.

As the skirmishes raged through the narrow cobbled streets of Stone Town, the Sultan, his family and entourage (about 50 in all) were advised to flee by the Prime Minister and his Cabinet. A government boat was at anchor offshore, and the Sultan's party was ferried to Mombasa in Kenya. The government there, having gained Independence itself only a month earlier, had no desire to get involved; the Sultan was refused permission to land, and the boat went south to Dar es Salaam in Tanganyika. From there the party was flown to Manchester and exile in Britain.

Okello began the business of government by proclaiming himself Field-Marshal and Leader of the Revolutionary Government, and members of the ASP were allocated ministries, with Abeid Karume as Prime Minister. But as a semblance of order was restored, it was clear that Okello was an embarrassment to the ASP government and, by 11 March, he was expelled from Zanzibar, resuming his former career of wandering the mainland, taking casual employment and languishing for spells in prison. Meanwhile there was considerable mayhem throughout the islands, as old scores were settled and the African and Arab communities took revenge upon one another. Initial figures suggest that 12,000 Arabs and 1000 Africans were killed before the violence ran its course.

The union

Instability on the islands, army mutinies in Kenya, Tanganyika and Uganda earlier in the year, the presence of British troops in the region and some ominous remarks by the US Ambassador in Nairobi about Communist threats to the mainland from Zanzibar, all served to make Karume anxious. He felt vulnerable with no army he could count on and what he saw as hostile developments all around. He needed some support to secure his position.

On 23 April 1964, Karume and Julius Nyerere signed an Act of Union between Zanzibar and Tanganyika to form Tanzania. Zanzibar became semi-autonomous and retained its own president and House of Assembly, with a full set of ministries and the control of its own foreign exchange earnings. In 1977, the mainland party and ASP merged to form Chama Cha Mapinduzi (CCM), which remains in power on both the mainland and the islands today. Separatist movements have emerged, most notably the Civic United Front (CUF), which was a party formed in 1992 when Tanzania's constitution was changed to allow for a multi-party system. At the time, the CUF called for greater autonomy, and some members wanted complete Independence. But under the ruling pro-union CCM, Zanzibar remained, and still is, part of Tanzania.

In recent years, internal political conflicts have been more pointed in Zanzibar than on the mainland, with the CCM and the equally popular CUF clashing in closely run elections – particularly in 2001 and 2005 when there were outbreaks of violence between their supporters after tense and closely contested elections. As a result, since 2010 Zanzibar has been administered under a government of national unity following the approval of a power-sharing agreement between the CCM and CUF. At elections Zanzibaris vote not only for a national Tanzanian president, but also for a Zanzibari president and assembly.

Pemba

Pemba has never been the centre of any ruling empire and has almost always been under proxy control by Unguja. There is nothing on Pemba that holds as much historical or cultural significance as Stone Town, but it is the site of many historical ruins that bear testament to its role in the spice trade and early commerce with the other Indian Ocean dynasties. Most date back to the Arab domination when Pemba was seized by the Sultan of Muscat (Oman) in the 17th century. European traders and explorers rarely landed on Pemba, except for water and a few days' rest from a storm. This was in direct contrast to Zanzibar where the Europeans exerted influence and in some cases administrative control. What has survived in more prevelance on Pemba than on Zanzibar are the ocean-going dhows, which still today transport local goods and ply the run to and from Wete to Shimoni in Kenya, and when the winds are favourable, through to northern Mozambique. Unlike Zanzibar, Pemba's landscape is more rolling, with green hills and fertile valleys, and it has a very jagged coastline. As such most of the island has always been and is today dominated by small scale farming including cloves (see Clove production page 132). Fishing too is a major income-provider, thanks to the offshore Pemba Channel, which is one of the most profitable fishing grounds on the Swahili Coast.

Practicalities

Getting there

Air

Tanzania has three international airports: Dar es Salaam's **Julius Nyerere International Airport (JNIA)**, which is 13 km southwest of the city centre along Julius K Nyerere Road; Zanzibar's **Abeid Amani Karume International Airport (ZNZ)**, 7 km southeast of Stone Town; and **Kilimanjaro International Airport (KIA)**, halfway between Arusha and Moshi, about 40 km from each. Most travellers to Zanzibar and Pemba either arrive at Dar es Salaam first and then continue to the islands on a short flight or by ferry, or on flights from Nairobi in Kenya, as well as charter flights from Europe, direct to Zanzibar's Abeid Amani Karume International Airport.

> **Tip...**
> Airport information can be found on the websites of the Tanzania Airports Authority (www.taa.go.tz.), and the Zanzibar Airports Authority (www.zaa.go.tz).

From Europe

There are no direct scheduled flights to either Dar es Salaam or Zanzibar from the UK. Flying time to either is a very minimum of 11¼ hours and there will be at least one change of plane. The options to Dar are **Kenya Airways** via Nairobi; **Turkish Airlines** via Istanbul; **Egypt Air** via Cairo; **Swissair** via Zurich and Nairobi; **KLM** via Amsterdam; **Emirates** via Dubai; **Ethiopian Airlines** via Addis Ababa; **Etihad Airways** via Abu Dhabi; and Qatar Airways via Doha. To Zanzibar, **Ethiopian Airlines** has flights via Nairobi, **Qatar Airways** via Nairobi, and **Fly 540**, **Kenya Airways** and **Precision Air** via Nairobi which can be included in flights from Europe with **Kenya Airways**, **KLM** or **British Airways**. Italy, Spain and Switzerland have charter flights directly to Zanzibar. Otherwise the option is to get to Dar and then continue on to Zanzibar or Pemba on one of the domestic airlines (below).

> **Tip...**
> Jet lag is not an issue if flying from Europe to Tanzania as there is only a minimal time difference.

From North America

There are no direct flights from the US or Canada to Tanzania and routes go via Europe or the Middle East (above), which means there may be at least two changes of planes. To use the same airline for all or much of the journey, consider **KLM** from New York, or **Ethiopian Airlines** from Toronto. Another alternative from going via Europe or the Middle East is with **Delta Airlines** who have a code-share agreement with **South African Airways** and flights go from Atlanta and New York to Johannesburg, from where **South African Airways** fly to Dar, **Fastjet** to Zanzibar with a touchdown in Dar, and **Mango** directly to Zanzibar.

From Australia, New Zealand and Asia

There are no direct flights from Australia and New Zealand to Tanzania, but a number of indirect routes go via Asia and South Africa. **Qantas** and **South African Airways** fly between Australia and Johannesburg; **Singapore Airlines** fly between Australia and New Zealand and Johannesburg via Singapore; and **Malaysia Airlines** fly between Australia and New Zealand and Johannesburg via Kuala Lumpur. From Johannesburg there are connections to Dar es Salaam with **South African Airways**, **Fastjet** to Zanzibar with a touchdown in Dar, and **Mango** directly to Zanzibar. Alternatively you can go via Kenya or the Middle East (above).

Airlines

British Airways, www.britishairways.com.
Delta, www.delta.com.
Egypt Air, www.egyptair.com.
Emirates, www.emirates.com.
Etihad Airways, www.etihad.com.
Ethiopian Airlines, www.ethiopianairlines.com.
Fastjet, www.fastjet.com .
Kenya Airways, www.kenya-airways.com.
Fly 540, www.fly540.com.
KLM,www.klm.com.
Lufthansa, www.lufthansa.com.

Malaysia Airlines, www.malaysiaairlines.com.
Mango, www.flymango.com.
Precision Air, www.precisionairtz.com.
Qantas, www.qantas.com.au.
Qatar Airways, www.qatarairways.com.
Singapore Airlines, www.singaporeair.com.
South African Airways, www.flysaa.com.
Swissair, www.swissair.com.
Turkish Airlines, www.turkishairlines.com.

Rail

There are two railway lines operating passenger services in Tanzania: the Central Line between Kigoma and Mwanza and Dar es Salaam, and the TAZARA (Tanzania and Zambia Railway Authority) line between Kapiri Mposhi in Zambia and Dar es Salaam. For details of both services, see page 47.

Road

There are a number of road border crossings between Tanzania and its neighbouring countries. The most popular route for those heading to or from the Zanzibar Archipelago is from Nairobi in Kenya, perhaps visiting the national parks and game reserves in the Northern Circuit around Arusha or climbing Mount Kilimanjaro near Moshi on the way. The main road crossing with Kenya is at Namanga, about halfway along the A104 road between Nairobi and Arusha. As this border receives thousands of tourists on safari each week en route between the Kenyan and Tanzanian parks, it is reasonably quick and efficient.

Bus

There are regular shuttle buses connecting Nairobi with Arusha (seven hours) and Moshi (7½ hours), and long-distance buses ply the route from Arusha via Moshi to Dar es Salaam (see Transport page 43 for details of these services).

Car

If you are driving, border crossings between Tanzania and its neighbours is straightforward as long as your vehicle's paperwork is in order. For all cars you must have a vehicle registration document (if it's not in the name of the driver, a letter of authorization is also required), and a driving licence printed in English with a photograph. You will be required to get a Temporary Import Permit or TIP from the customs desk at the border, and (if you don't already have it) take out third-party insurance for Tanzania from one of the insurance companies who have kiosks at the border. For a foreign-registered vehicle, you will also need a Carnet de Passage en Douanes, which is an international customs document that allows you to temporarily import a vehicle duty-free and is issued by a body in your own country (such as the RAC in the UK). Most car hire companies will not allow you to take a rented vehicle out of Tanzania, but some may consider it if you only want to go to Kenya (the same goes for hiring a car in Kenya and only going to Tanzania).

Tip...
If you are travelling around East Africa in your own car and want to go to Zanzibar, there are a few campsites/lodges in Dar es Salaam that for a fee will allow you to safely park a vehicle for a few days while you are on the islands.

Getting around

Air

Flights to the islands from the mainland are enjoyable and scenic; the views of the turquoise ocean plied by dhows, sandy atolls and tiny forested islands are quite incredible from the small low-flying planes. There are numerous daily flights between Dar es Salaam's Julius Nyerere International Airport and Zanzibar's Abeid Amani Karume International Airport, which take 20 minutes and cost from around US$80 one-way. The airlines that offer these include **Air Excel**, **Air Tanzania**, **Auric Air**, **Coastal Aviation**, **Fast Jet**, **Precision Air**, **Regional Air** and **ZanAir**. There are also a few daily flights from Zanzibar to Pemba's Karume Airport, which take 30 minutes and cost from US$95 one-way, with **Auric Air**, **Coastal Aviation** and **ZanAir**. For airline details, see Dar page 43 and Zanzibar page 82. All tickets can be booked online, through a tour operator or can be bought directly from the airline town offices or desks at the airports. For those going on a broader exploration of Tanzania by air, these flights can be linked to several flights taking in the safari destinations too – again, either organized yourself directly with the airlines or through a tour operator.

> **Tip...**
> The smaller airlines will only fly with the required minimum of passengers (sometimes this is only two people). The schedules to Pemba can change regularly, and flights will be cancelled if there are not enough takers, so it's essential to continually check with the airlines even on the day of departure.

Air charter

Several companies offer small planes for charter, especially on the routes between the parks and islands. The advantage is by booking the whole plane, you can decide on departure times and it may work out economical for groups of four to six people. The following can organize charter flights: **Air Excel**, Arusha, T027-254 8429, www.air excelonline.com.

Auric Air, Arusha, T0688-723 274, www.auricair.com.
Flightlink, Dar, T022-211 3820, www.flightlinkaircharters.com.
Regional Air, Arusha, T0784-285 753, www.regionaltanzania.com,
Zantas Air, Arusha, T0688-434 343, www.zantasair.com.

Road

Boda-boda

The use of *boda-boda* bicycle taxis started in the 1970s and they are now a ubiquitous form of East African transport. These days bicycle *boda-bodas* have largely been replaced by mopeds or more powerful motorbikes depending on

ON THE ROAD

Overland tours

Overland truck multi-week tours are a popular and hassle free way of exploring East Africa and most itineraries visit many of Tanzania's places of interest by road. It's a great adventure, and lots of fun for the camaraderie and company, but be aware its group and participatory travel and you'll have to help with making camp and preparing meals, etc. The standard route most tours take is from Nairobi on a two-week loop via some of the Kenya's national parks into Uganda, to go chimpanzee and mountain gorilla tracking, before returning to Nairobi to head south to Tanzania's Northern Circuit parks. The route then continues to Dar es Salaam, for an excursion to Zanzibar, and then on through Malawi and Zambia to Victoria Falls. Another three weeks takes you from there to Cape Town in South Africa via Botswana and Namibia. The itinerary also runs in reverse from Cape Town to Nairobi. There are several overland companies with departures almost weekly from Nairobi, Livingstone/Victoria Falls and Cape Town. If you're flying into Kilimanjaro or Dar es Salaam airports, there is also the option of joining one of these circuits from there.

Overland operators:
Acacia Africa, www.acacia-africa.com.
Africa Travel Co, www.africatravelco.com.
African Trails, www.africantrails.co.uk.
Dragoman, www.dragoman.com.
Exodus, www.exodus.co.uk.

G Adventures, www.gadventures.com.
Gecko's Grassroots Adventures, www.geckosadventures.com.
Intrepid, www.intrepidtravel.com.
Oasis Overland, www.oasisoverland.co.uk.
Tucan Travel, www.tucantravel.com.

the terrain. In Tanzania these are also called *piki-pikis*. They can be flagged down in the street and are useful for short journeys, but bear in mind they have a very poor safety record and accidents are common – always ensure the driver gives you a spare crash helmut. Agree the price before getting on.

Bus and dala-dala

There is an efficient network of privately run buses across the country. Larger non-stop buses cover the longer distances, and minibuses (*dala-dalas*) cover the shorter routes between the small towns and villages and stop along the way to pick up and drop people off. If you have problems finding the right vehicle, just ask around and someone will direct you. Most buses and *dala-dalas* will only leave when full; you can join an almost full vehicle and leave promptly, or wait in a half empty one for an hour or two on a less busy route. On the main long-distance bus routes it is sometimes also possible to book ahead at a kiosk at the bus station – known as bus 'stage' or 'stand in Tanzania. *Dala-dalas* are also the most popular form of urban transport. They follow routes along the main roads in the towns and cities (most have a sign indicating their route and destination on the front)

ON THE ROAD

Dala-dalas

These public transport vehicles are privately owned minibus shared taxis, which were introduced in Dar es Salaam in the 1970s as a response to the shortage of public transport for the growing population. Before minibuses came along, pick-up trucks with benches in the open back were used and some of these can still be seen on Zanzibar and Pemba. Now widespread all over East Africa (and called *matatus* in Kenya and Uganda), *dala-dalas* generally run on fixed routes picking up passengers at central locations, and will also stop anywhere along their route to drop someone off or allow a prospective passenger to board. In fact a 60-km journey could take up to three hours since stops are so frequent, back-tracking sometimes even occurs, and the driver will wait around for as long as he deems it advantageous to swell his numbers. The basic crew of each *dala-dala* is made up of two people: the driver (clearly picked for the ability to drive fast rather than well) and the conductor, or in Dar slang *Mgiga debe* – literally 'he who beats on a tin can', and so named because he slaps the vehicle to indicate to the driver that they are ready to depart. It is his job to collect money and issue tickets, harangue passengers who fail to make room for one more, as well as to entertain the remainder of the bus with hair-raising acrobatic stunts such as hanging out of the open door. Supplementing this basic crew at either end of the journey is a tout, who bawls out the intended destination and route, attempting to attract or, if necessary, intimidate people (at times this stretches to actual manhandling of passengers) into entering his *dala-dala*. It is a system that appears to work to everyone's advantage other than that of the passenger, who suffers the consequent overcrowding and the suicidal driving as *dala-dala* competes with *dala-dala* to arrive first and leave fullest. Nevertheless they are by far the most prevalent mode of urban and rural transport in Tanzania and are cheap: US$0.30 for a short journey, rising to US$1.50 for a longer one – from one side of Zanzibar to the other for example. If you are in no hurry, a ride on a *dala-dala* can be fun – you could be accompanied by a chicken on your lap or a bucket of fresh fish on the set next to you – and it's a great way to meet and chat to the local people.

and can be flagged down on the street for short journeys in the direction you are going (see box). By law, all public service vehicles have to be speed governed at 80 kph, standing is not permitted and everyone gets their own seat with a seat belt. However, these rules are often flaunted and overcrowding and reckless and fast driving can occur – do not continue in a vehicle if you are not comfortable. Petty theft can be a problem on vehicles and at stands/stages – keep an eye on your belongings and keep any valuables out of sight.

Car

Driving is on the left side of the road. The key main tarmac roads between the towns and cities are in good condition, but away from these, most of the minor roads are unmade gravel with potholes. Fuel is available along the main highways and towns, but only the larger pertol stations in Dar es Salaam will except credit cards so you will need cash. If you break down, it is common practice in East Africa to place a bundle of leaves 50 m or so before and behind the vehicle to warn oncoming motorists. Also slow down if you see this – a broken down vehicle may be blocking the road ahead.

Car hire Most people visiting Tanzania's coast or islands will not have much need to hire a car. Although if you do want to head out from Dar es Salaam, there are car rental agencies in Dar (see page 44). The option on Zanzibar and Pemba is to hire a small 4WD jeep (usually a Toyota or Suzuki) for a couple of days of exploration – this is fairly easy on Zanzibar but very difficult on Pemba, simply because there are not many vehicles available. If you are confident about driving in Tanzania, you can hire a car on a self-drive basis, or alternatively most companies can also organize drivers for additional expense (effectively this is comparable to hiring a taxi but on a daily rate). To hire a car you generally need a credit card, to be over 23 and have a full driving licence; it does not have to be an international licence, your home country one will do as long as it's got a photograph with an English translation if necessary. On the islands it is also necessary to get your licence endorsed by the local police – a simple procedure that the rental company will sort out. Costs vary between the different car hire companies but are from around US\$40-60 per day for a normal saloon car in Dar es Salaam, and USS\$30-50 per day for a small car on Zanzibar. Deals can be made for more than seven days' car hire. It is important to shop around and ask the companies what is and what is not included in the rates. Things to consider include whether you take out a limited mileage package or unlimited mileage depending on how you many kilometres you think you will drive, and what the provisions are in the event of a breakdown. It's also a good idea to take out the collision damage waiver premium as even the smallest accident can be very expensive. Finally, 20% VAT is added to all costs.

It's possible to rent 125cc scooters on Zanzibar, which are a good way to explore Stone Town and around; costs are US\$25-30 per day with insurance and helmets – ensure it's in good mechanical order before you set off.

> **Tip...**
> If self-driving on Zanzibar, there are few roads but they are often poorly signposted – just as useful as a map or GPS-enabled phone is some limited Kiswahili in order to ask for directions.

Cycling

If you can handle the heat and humidity, then cycling in Zanzibar can be an excellent way to explore; in fact, it will soon become apparent that most Zanzibaris own bikes. Many beach resorts will rent out bikes for around US\$5-10 per day and some offer free bikes to guests. You can also approach local people, who may lend you their own bike for a few hours in exchange for payment. Watch out for motorists though, as they generally have little respect for cyclists and expect them to get out of the way or leave the road when they want to pass.

Ferry
The ferry services between Dar es Salaam and Zanzibar are quick, efficient, enjoyable and well priced. Less so for the ferry services between Zanzibar and Pemba, which only run twice a week; for details of all these see Dar page 44. If you are already in Dar es Salaam, or coming off a bus from Arusha and Moshi in northern Tanzania or elsewhere in the country, the Zanzibar ferry is a good option. However, if flying into Dar, bear in mind that while the distance between Julius Nyerere International Airport and the ferry terminal on Sokoine Drive in the city centre is only 12 km, thanks to the horrendous Dar traffic, this can take up to 1½ hours in a taxi (sometimes longer in rush hour). You might want to consider not only the timings, but the cost too; a taxi/ferry combination may not be more economical than a cheap flight to Zanzibar.

Hitchhiking
In the Western sense (standing beside the road and requesting a free ride) hitchhiking is not an option. In any case the most likely vehicles to stop if you are standing on the side of the road are *dala-dalas* or *boda-bodas* and then of course you will have to pay. However, in very remote areas (only likely on Pemba Island) if you are stuck where there is no public transport, private motorists/truck drivers may offer you a ride but it is only polite to offer payment as a thank you.

Minibus
By far the most convenient way to reach the tourist resorts around Zanzibar – Paje, Jambiani, Bwejuu, Nungwi, Kendwa etc – is to book a seat on one of the daily tourist minibuses from Stone Town. These will usually take you right to a hotel door for about US$15, and can be booked the day before at any Stone Town hotel or tour operator. The minibuses usually leave Stone Town at around 0800 and return from their various destinations in the mid-afternoon. Although not always the most modern-looking vehicles, they are fairly reliable and comfortable and there's space for luggage.

Taxi
Airports, hotels and town centre locations are well served by taxis, some good and some very run-down but serviceable. Hotel staff, even at the smallest locations, will rustle up a taxi even when there is not one waiting outside. If you visit an out-of-town centre location, it is wise to ask the taxi to wait or get their mobile phone number. Taxis don't have meters, so you should establish the fare (*bei gani?* – how much?) before you set off. Prices are generally fair, as drivers simply won't take you if you offer a fare that's too low. A common practice is for a driver to set off and *then* go and get petrol using part of your fare to pay for it, so often the first

Sensitivity to Zanzibar culture

Zanzibar has a relaxed and sympathetic attitude to visitors. However, the islands are predominantly Muslim and, as such, Zanzibaris feel uncomfortable with some Western dress styles. In the towns and villages, it is courteous for women to dress modestly, covering the upper arms and body, with dress or skirt hemlines below the knee. Wearing bikinis, cropped tops, vests that reveal bra straps, or shorts causes offence. For men there is no restriction beyond what is considered decent in the West, but walking around the towns bare-chested or revealing shoulders or with no shoes is considered offensive. However, at hotel swimming pools and on the beach, it is acceptable to wear swimwear, but, if a fisherman or harvester wanders by, it is polite to cover up. Zanzibaris are either very vocal in expressing their offence or, by contrast, are too polite to say anything. It is because of the latter behaviour that many tourists continue not to heed this advice. It is worth remembering that while you may see other tourists wandering around in inappropriate dress, this doesn't mean that you should do the same. Behave like a responsible tourist and cover up. Other sensitivities to consider are during the holy month of Ramadan when most Muslims fast during daylight hours. It is considered the height of bad manners to eat, drink or smoke in the street or public places at this time. Although alcohol is freely available, drunken behaviour is not regarded with tolerance and is considered offensive by most non-drinking Muslims. Finally, public displays of affection are also considered to be inappropriate.

part of a journey is spent sitting in a petrol station. Also be aware that taxi drivers never seem to have change, so try and accumulate some small notes for taxi rides.

Maps

The best map and travel guide store in the UK is **Stanfords** ① *12-14 Long Acre, Covent Garden, London WC2E 9LP, T0207-836 1321, and 29 Corn Street, Bristol, BS1 1HT, T0117-929 9966, www.stanfords.co.uk*. The **Michelin Map of Africa: Central and South** ① *www.michelintravel.com*, covers Tanzania in detail. In South Africa, **Map Studio** ① *T+27 (0)21-460 5400, www.mapstudio.co.za*, produces a wide range of maps covering much of Africa, which are available to buy online. Once in Tanzania you can pick up locally produced maps of Zanzibar in the bookshops and at some hotels in Stone Town, where you may also be able to get ones of the most popular parks, such as the Serengeti, if you are going further afield in Tanzania.

Essentials A-Z

Accident and emergency

Police, fire and ambulance T112.

Bargaining

While most prices in shops are set, the exception are curio shops where a little good-natured bargaining is possible, especially if it's quiet or you are buying a number of things. Bargaining is very much expected in the street markets, whether you are buying an apple or a blanket. Generally traders will attempt to overcharge tourists who are unaware of local prices. Start lower than you would expect to pay, be polite and good humoured and if the final price doesn't suit – walk away. You may be called back for more negotiation if your final price was too high, or the trader may let you go, in which case your price was too low. While in Dar es Salaam on the mainland, hotel prices are fairly consistent all year round, those on the islands are seasonal; if it's out of season or things look quiet, it's quite reasonable to bargain with the hotel manager over the cost of a room – especially if you are staying more than a couple of nights or there are a few of you.

Children

Zanzibar has great appeal for families: lots of fun can be had at the beach, the sea is warm and safe, and most accommodation has swimming pools and offers activities such as snorkelling or boat trips. There are significant discounts on room rates, and reductions on entry fees and excursion rates for children under 16, and under 5s usually go free.

Most beach resorts are completely child-friendly, although there is a handful aimed at honeymooners where children are not permitted at all. In the family-orientated ones, there are either specific family rooms or adjoining rooms, and often extra amenities such as children's dining, baby-sitting, children's swimming pools or kids' clubs. At the smaller independent places, you may be able to organize rooms next to each other sharing a patio, and putting extra beds in rooms is common practice on Zanzibar. Eating is not too tricky from a kid's point of view. Zanzibari food is not overly fancy or hot, and common options include fish, rice, chips and pasta, with lots of tropical fruit and treats such as pancakes. Many children enjoy hotel buffets and love the street food stalls at Stone Town's Forodhani Market (page 59).

Supplies of disposable nappies, formula milk powders and puréed foods are reasonable in Dar es Salaam and Stone Town, but they are expensive and not available elsewhere, so you may want consider bringing enough of these with you. It is important to remember that children have an increased risk of gastro-enteritis, malaria and sunburn and are more likely to develop complications, so care must be taken to minimize risks. See Health, page 156, for more details.

Tip...
If you wander on foot around the alleyways of Stone Town, make sure that children watch out for scooters and bicycles.

BACKGROUND
Zanzibar during Ramadan

Almost the entire population of the Zanzibar Archipelago is Muslim, and therefore the celebration of Ramadan is an important and closely adhered to event. Ramadan is the ninth month in the Islamic calendar, and marks the revelation of the Quran by Allah to Prophet Mohammed. Muslims fast from sunrise to sunset for the full 30 days, and also refrain from drinking, smoking, arguing, sex and swearing among other 'sinful' things, and it is a time for spiritual reflection, prayer and charity. Visitors must remember that during Ramadan on the islands, it is considered very offensive to eat, drink and smoke in public during the day when most people are fasting. Some Muslim-owned restaurants are completely closed, while others respect the day fasting time and close their terraces and patios for service outside, but visitors are allowed to eat and drink inside. While on the beach during Ramadan, it will be business as usual in terms of alcoholic drinks and meals, but remember to follow Ramadan etiquette if you leave the hotel or resort property.

Customs and duty free

The official customs allowance for visitors over 18 years includes 200 cigarettes, 50 cigars, 250 g of tobacco, 2 litres of wine, 1 litre of spirits, 50 ml of perfume and 250 ml of eau de toilette. There is no duty on any equipment for your own use (such as a laptops or cameras). Once in Tanzania, be careful about buying or accepting any wildlife-derived object (as well as coral and sea shells). Any souvenir made from an endangered species is prohibited. If you were to buy such items, you should always consider the environmental and social impact of your purchase, and it cannot be taken out of Tanzania. Attempts to smuggle controlled products can result in confiscation, fines and imprisonment under the Convention on Trade in Endangered Species (CITES), (www.cites.org).

Disabled travellers

There are few specific facilities for disabled people in Tanzania and wheelchairs are not accommodated on public road transport, or with ease on the ferries to Zanzibar (there are steep gangplanks and stairs on board). However, a beach holiday is very manageable and the option is to fly directly to Zanzibar and arrange a vehicle transfer to a hotel or resort. Note though on the smaller planes, like those from Dar es Salaam to Zanzibar, some lifting assistance may be needed to get on. Stone Town is tricky to navigate in a wheelchair because of the narrow alleyways and uneven pavements; but not impossible. While there is little specific disabled-equipped accommodation, most rooms on the beach are at ground level (cottages and the like), although make sure there's a pool – swimming in the sea often isn't possible around low tide when the water recedes over the reefs (especially on the east coast). Some excursions on Zanzibar are do-able; wheelchairs can be lifted on to boats and the Spice Tour is in a vehicle in any case. Tanzanians themselves will do their very best to help, and with a little bit of pre-organizing, being disabled should not deter you from visiting.

Electricity

230 volts AC at 50 Hz. Square 3-pin British-type sockets. Travellers with round-pin plugs will require adaptors. Hotels usually have 2-pin round sockets for razors, phones etc. There are still occasional power cuts in Zanzibar, but it's becoming less frequent, and most hotels and businesses have back-up generators. However, visitors are advised not to leave expensive electrical appliances plugged in when not in use, due to occasional power surges.

Embassies and consulates

For a list of Tanzanian embassies and consulates abroad, see http://embassy. goabroad.com.

Gay and lesbian travellers

Homosexuality is illegal in Tanzania and is considered a criminal offence, so discretion is advised. However, there is a general toleration by ordinary people of discreet behaviour, especially by those in the tourism industry. There are no specific gay clubs or bars.

Health

See your GP or travel clinic at least 6 weeks before your departure for general advice on travel risks, malaria and vaccinations. Make sure you have travel insurance, get a dental check, know your own blood group and, if you suffer from a long-term condition such as diabetes or epilepsy, make sure someone knows or that you have a Medic Alert bracelet/necklace (www. medicalert.org.uk). If you wear glasses, take a copy of your prescription.

Vaccinations
Confirm that your primary courses and boosters are up to date (diphtheria, typhoid, polio and tetanus). Note: Travellers to only Tanzania do not require a yellow fever vaccination certificate. However, travellers from non-endemic countries that travel through Tanzania will be asked to show the certificate after departing Tanzania and arriving at other destinations, which include all land borders in Tanzania and very possibly your home country.

Health risks
Bites and stings
There are a few insects and small creatures in Tanzania that, if you are unlucky, may bite or sting you. These rarely cause any more problems than mild irritation and can be relieved by cool baths, antihistamine tablets, or mild corticosteroid creams. However, if bites and stings fester they can become infected in the humid climate, when you may have to progress to antiseptic or antibiotic cream or, even better, powder, which are all available locally. If the redness around the infection spreads or you develop a fever, a course of antibiotics may be required.

Diarrhoea
Diarrhoea can refer either to loose stools or an increased frequency of bowel movement, both of which can be a nuisance, but symptoms should be relatively short lived. Adults can use an antidiarrhoeal medication to control the

symptoms but only for up to 24 hrs. In addition, keep well hydrated by drinking plenty of fluids and eat bland foods. Oral rehydration sachets taken after each loose stool are a useful way to keep well hydrated. These should always be used when treating children and the elderly. Bacterial traveller's diarrhoea is the most common form; if there are no signs of improvement, the diarrhoea is likely to be viral and not bacterial and antibiotics may be required. Also seek medical help if there is blood in the stools and/or fever.

The standard advice to prevent problems is to be careful with water and ice for drinking. If you have any doubts then boil the water or filter and treat it. Food can also transmit disease. Be wary of salads (what were they washed in, who handled them), re-heated foods or food that has been left out in the sun having been cooked earlier in the day. There is a simple adage that says wash it, peel it, boil it or forget it. Also be wary of unpasteurized dairy products as these can transmit a range of diseases.

Hepatitis
Hepatitis means inflammation of the liver. Viral causes of the disease can be acquired anywhere in the world. The most obvious symptom is a yellowing of your skin or the whites of your eyes. However, prior to this all that you may notice is itching and tiredness. Pre-travel hepatitis A vaccine is the best bet. Hepatitis B (for which there is a vaccine) is spread through blood and unprotected sexual intercourse: both of these can be avoided.

HIV
Africa has the highest infection rates of HIV in the world. Efforts to stem the rate of infection have had limited success, as many of the factors that need addressing such as social change, poverty and gender inequalities are long-term processes. Visitors should be aware of the dangers of infection from unprotected sex and always use a condom. If you have to have medical treatment, ensure any equipment used is taken from a sealed pack or is freshly sterilized. If you have to have a blood transfusion, ask for screened blood.

Malaria
Malaria is present in almost all of Tanzania and prophylactics are advised. However, the prevalence of malaria on the Zanzibar Archipelago is these days regarded as low-risk (schemes to eradicate the disease have paid dividends). But for short-term travellers and holidaymakers (especially children), taking some sort of medicine to prevent malaria still makes sense as a precaution. Take expert advice before you leave home, and ensure you finish the recommended course of anti-malarials even if means taking them after you have arrived home. It can start as something just resembling an attack of flu. You may feel tired, lethargic, headachy, feverish, or, more seriously, develop fits, followed by coma and then death. Have a low index of suspicion because it is very easy to write off vague symptoms, which may actually be malaria. If you have a temperature, go to a doctor as soon as you can and ask for a

> **Tip...**
> When snorkelling and diving, it is prohibited to touch or stand on coral reefs, but accidental contact may occur; cuts from coral can be painful and may quickly develop into an infected wound if not treated quickly.

malaria test. On your return home, if you suffer any of these symptoms, get tested as soon as possible.

To prevent mosquito bites wear clothes that cover arms and legs and use effective insect repellents. Repellents containing 30-50% DEET (Di-ethyltoluamide) are recommended; lemon eucalyptus (Mosiguard) is a reasonable alternative. Rooms with a/c or fans also help ward off mosquitoes at night, and almost every bed on Zanzibar has a mosquito net so there is no need to bring one.

Rabies

Avoid dogs and monkeys that are behaving strangely. If you are bitten by a domestic or wild animal, do not leave things to chance: scrub the wound with soap and water and/or disinfectant, try to at least determine the animal's ownership, and seek medical assistance at once. The course of treatment depends on whether you have already been satisfactorily vaccinated against rabies.

Sun

The jua kali ('hot sun' in Kiswahili) beats down fiercely on Tanzania's coast and islands – amplified by the pale white bleached sands of the beaches. Be sensible and always protect yourself adequately against the sun. Apply a high-factor sunscreen and also make sure it screens against UVB. Keep children in the shade at the sun's peak – from 1100 to 1500 – and ensure kids wear hats and ideally full swimsuits covering at least shoulders and torsos. Prevent heat exhaustion and heatstroke by drinking enough fluids throughout the day (your urine will be pale if you are drinking enough). Symptoms of heat exhaustion and heatstroke include dizziness, tiredness and headache. Use rehydration salts mixed with water to replenish fluids and salts and find somewhere cool and shady to recover. If you suspect heatstroke rather than heat exhaustion, you need to cool the body down quickly (cold showers are particularly effective).

If you get sick

There are private hospitals in Dar es Salaam and Stone Town, which have 24-hour emergency departments and pharmacies, and have a high standard of healthcare. In other areas of Tanzania, facilities range from government hospitals to rural clinics, but these can be poorly equipped and under staffed. For extreme emergencies or surgery, visitors with adequate health insurance will be transferred to a private hospital in Nairobi, Kenya, which has the best medical facilities in East Africa.

Dar es Salaam

Aga Khan Hospital, Barak Obama Dr at the junction with Ufukoni Rd, T022-211 5151-4, www.agakhanhospitals.org. **AMI Trauma Centre Hospital**, 589 Yacht Club Rd, Msasani Peninsula, T022-260 2500/501, www.amiplc.com.

Stone Town

The main public hospital is **Mnazi Mmoja Hospital**, Kuanda Rd near the State House, T024-223 1071. A better bet are the private hospitals: **Dr Mehta's Hospital, opposite the High Court**, off Vuga Rd, T024-223 1566; www.drmehtashospital.com; **Zanzibar Medical Group**, off Kenyatta Rd, T024-223 3134.

Pemba Island

The main public hospital is **Abdalla Mzee Hospital**, in Mkoani, but this is poorly equipped and in the event of an emergency you are strongly advised to get to Dar or at the very least Zanzibar. For diving medical emergencies, the nearest hyperbaric re-compression chamber is in Likoni in Kenya, which is reached by air; all divers are required to have adequate hyperbaric-medical insurance.

> **Tip...**
> It is essential to have travel insurance as hospital bills need to be paid at the time of admittance, so keep all paperwork to make a claim.

Websites
www.btha.org British Travel Health Association.
www.cdc.gov US government site that gives excellent advice on travel health and details of disease outbreaks.
www.fco.gov.uk British Foreign and Commonwealth Office travel site has useful information on each country, people, climate and a list of UK embassies/consulates.
www.fitfortravel.nhs.uk A-Z of vaccine/health advice for each country.
www.travelhealth.co.uk Independent travel health site with advice on health risks, vaccination and travel insurance.
www.who.int World Health Organization, updates of disease outbreaks.

Insurance

Before departure, it is vital to take out comprehensive travel insurance. There are a wide variety of policies to choose from, so shop around. At the very least, the policy should cover medical expenses, including repatriation to your home country in the event of a medical emergency. If you are going to be active in Tanzania, ensure the policy covers whatever activity you will be doing (for example, trekking or diving). There is no substitute for suitable precautions against petty crime, but if you do have something stolen while in Tanzania, report the incident to the nearest police station and ensure you get a police report and case number. You will need these to make any claim from your insurance company.

Internet

Despite the decreasing need for them, there are still a few internet cafés around Dar es Salaam and Stone Town, but these days most online access is via Wi-Fi at hotels, resorts and cafés. Costs vary from free, at coffee shops and at more expensive accommodation where they offer it as part of the rates, to expensive, when you have to buy a voucher with a password, when it may cost up to US$5 for an hour's access. If you are using a 3G mobile phone or device, remember that data charges will be expensive if it's on roaming with your home service provider – be sure to disable data roaming on your phone and use local Wi-Fi instead. There's also the option of using a local Tanzanian SIM card (also see page 163), and a USB/dongle connection on your laptop, and use local pay-as-you-go data bundles. All this can be organized at any of the mobile phone shops (there are plenty in Dar es Salaam and a few outlets in Stone Town – look for the signs hanging over small shops).

> **Tip...**
> As well as the hotels and some of the restaurants/cafés, Wi-Fi hotspots in Stone Town are at the airport, ferry terminal and Forodhani Gardens.

There are several mobile networks – the four major operators are Vodacom, Airtel, Tigo and Zantel.

Language

Tanzania is a welcoming country and the first word that you will hear and come to know is the Kiswahili greeting '*Jambo*' – 'hello', often followed by '*Hakuna matata*' – 'no problem'! Lengthy greetings are important in Tanzania, and respect is accorded to elderly people, usually by the greeting '*Shikamoo, mzee*' to a man and '*Shikamoo, mama*' to a woman.

There are a number of local languages, but most people in Tanzania, as in all East Africa, speak Kiswahili and some English. Kiswahili is the official language of Tanzania and is taught in primary schools. English is generally used in business and is taught in secondary schools. A little Kiswahili goes a long way, and most Tanzanians will be thrilled to hear visitors attempt to use it. Since the language was originally written down by the British colonists, words are pronounced just as they are spelt.

Media

Newspapers and magazines

Tanzania has several English-language newspapers. The best are the *Daily News* (www.dailynews.co.tz) and the *Guardian* (www.ippmedia.com), which both cover eastern and southern African news and syndicated international news and are available online. There are also a number of newspapers published in Kiswahili. An excellent regional paper, *The East African* (www.theeastafrican.co.ke), published in Nairobi, comes out weekly and provides good Tanzanian coverage and provides the most objective reporting on East African issues.

Radio

Radio Tanzania broadcasts in Kiswahili, and news bulletins tend to contain a lot of local coverage. There are several popular FM stations that can be picked up in the cities, such as Radio Free Africa, Clouds FM and Radio One FM, which mostly broadcast imported pop, rap and hip-hop music. *BBC World Service* is broadcast to Tanzania; check the website for frequencies (www.bbc.co.uk/worldservice).

Television

Television Tanzania began to transmit in 1994, and it's widely believed that Tanzania was the last country in the world to get TV. Prior to that, Julius Nyerere believed (in accordance with his socialist principles) that TV would increase the divide between rich and poor. There are now numerous national and local stations (Dar es Salaam broadcasts no fewer than 15), which have a mixture of English and Kiswahili home-grown programmes and foreign imports. Most hotels have DSTV (Digital Satellite Television), South African satellite TV, with scores of channels including news and movies. The most popular with Tanzanians are the sports channels for coverage of European football.

Money

US$1=TSh 2190, £1=TSh 3150, €1=TSh 2465 (Mar 2016)

Currency

The Tanzanian currency is the Tanzanian Shilling (shilingi), not to be confused with the Kenyan and Uganda Shilling which are different currencies. The written abbreviation is either TSh or using /= after the amount, ie 500/=).

Notes currently in circulation are TSh500, 1000, 2000, 5000 and 10,000. Coins are TSh 50, 100 and 200. A TSh500 coin was issued in 2014, which will eventually replace the TSh500 note. As it is not a hard currency, it cannot be brought into or taken out of the country; however, there are no restrictions on the amount of foreign currency that can be brought into Tanzania. Many hotels require payment in US$, in particular for accommodation, but also for food and drink and for some tours.

Changing money

There are banks with ATMs and bureaux de change (known as forex bureaux) in the major centres and international airports (see below). All banks have a foreign exchange service, and bank hours are Mon-Fri 0830-1500, Sat 0830-1330. Forex bureaux are open longer hours and some open on Sun. The easiest currencies to exchange are US dollars, UK pounds and Euros. If you are bringing US dollars in cash, try and bring newer notes – because of the prevalence of forgery, many banks and bureaux de change do not accept US dollar bills more than 5 years old. Sometimes lower denomination bills attract a lower exchange rate than higher denominations. On Zanzibar, many hotels and tour operators publish their rates in US$ (and in some cases Euros), but they can also be paid in TSh – just ensure that you are getting a reasonable exchange rate. Visitors should not change money on the black market as it is illegal.

ATMs, credit and debit cards

Visa is the most widely accepted card, followed by MasterCard; AMEX and Diners far less so. Remember your bank at home will charge a small fee for withdrawing from an ATM abroad with a debit and credit card. Cards are accepted by the large hotels, airlines, main car hire firms, tour operators and travel agents. An additional levy of 5% may be charged, so check first if paying a sizeable bill. In Dar es Salaam, as well as banks, many shopping malls and petrol stations also have ATMs. However, on the islands, a little bit of planning ahead is required. On Zanzibar, the only banks and ATMs are in Stone Town (and there are ATMs at the airport), so ensure you get enough cash before heading to the north or east coasts unless you intend to use only a credit card at the resorts. On Pemba, while there are branches of the **People's Bank of Zanzibar** in the 3 towns: Mkoani, Chake Chake and Wete, none of them presently have ATMs and must not be relied upon to change foreign currency – it is essential to bring cash from Zanzibar or the mainland.

Tip...
ATMs generally only dispatch notes in increments of 10,000 TSh, which are often too large for people to have change – break bigger notes when you can and save small change for taxis, snacks and drinks, souvenirs and the like.

Currency cards

Pre-paid currency cards allow you to preload money from your bank account, fixed at the day's exchange rate, and are accepted anywhere that you can use a debit or credit card. They are issued by specialist money changing companies, such as Travelex, Caxton FX and the post office. You can top up and check your balance by phone, online and sometimes by text.

Opening hours

Banks Mon-Fri, 0830-1530, Sat 0830-1330. Forex bureaux are open longer hours 7 days a week. **Post offices** Mon-Fri 0800-1630, Sat 0900-1200.
Shops Generally Mon-Sat 0800-1700 or 1800. In Dar es Salaam the shopping malls and larger branches of the supermarkets stay open until late in the evening and are open on Sun morning. On Zanzibar it is the Muslim tradition to open every day but to close for a couple of hours in the afternoon and stay open later; until around 1900-2000.

Post

The **Tanzania Post Office** (www.posta.co.tz) has branches across the country, even in the smallest of towns. The postal system is fairly reliable, and letters to Europe take about 5-7 days and to the US about 10 days. If sending parcels, they must be no longer than 105 cm and have to be wrapped in brown paper and string. There is no point doing this before getting to the post office as you will be asked to undo it so that the parcel can be checked for export duty. Items have been known to go missing, so post anything of personal value through the fast post service known as **EMS**, a registered postal service available at all post offices, or with a courier company such as **DHL** (www.dhl.co.tz), which has offices in the major towns.

Public holidays

All along the coast and on the islands the **Islamic calendar** is followed and festivals are celebrated. These include **Id-ul-Fitr** (end of Ramadan, variable); **Id-ul-Haji** (Festival of Sacrifice, variable);

Islamic New Year (Jun) and **Prophet's birthday** (Aug).

1 Jan	**New Year's Day**
12 Jan	**Zanzibar Revolution Day** (Zanzibar)
Mar/Apr	**Good Friday; Easter Monday**
26 Apr	**Union Day**
1 May	**Labour Day**
8 Aug	**Farmers' Day**
14 Oct	**Nyerere Day**
9 Dec	**Independence & Republic Day**
25 Dec	**Christmas Day**
26 Dec	**Boxing Day**

Safety

The majority of the people you will meet are honest and ready to help you, so there is no need to get paranoid about your safety. However, theft from tourists in Tanzania does occur. The most common crimes are pickpocketing, purse-snatching and thefts from vehicles, and many robberies happen in crowded places such as markets and bus stations. General common sense rules apply: don't exhibit anything valuable and keep wallets and purses out of sight; always keep car doors locked and windows wound up; lock room doors at night as noisy fans and a/c can provide cover for sneak thieves; do not accept any food or drink from strangers as it may be drugged and used to facilitate a robbery; avoid deserted areas (including beaches) and always take taxis at night. Note that during elections on Zanzibar and Pemba every five years (the last general election was in 2015) there are sometimes sporadic outbreaks of political violence. The tourist areas are rarely affected – for example, in Stone Town most political activism takes place in the surrounding neighbourhoods and not in the historic centre itself – but nonetheless, heed local advice and avoid mass gatherings. If travelling during election times, the best place to be is on the beach.

Telephone *IDD 000. Country code 255.*

Tanzania's landline telephone system is run by Tanzania Telecommunications Company Ltd (TTCL; www.ttcl.co.tz). But the need for public coin or card phones has become virtually non-existent.. Additionally the landline service on the islands hardly works at all anymore. Almost everybody carries a mobile phone, and as such most businesses nearly always use a mobile number – you will see from listings for hotels and restaurants in this book that mobile numbers are offered instead of landline numbers: they start T07. You can use your own mobile phone in Tanzania if it's on international roaming, or you can buy a local pay-as-you-go SIM and top-up cards. There are several mobile networks – the four major operators are Vodacom, Airtel, Tigo and Zantel – and you can go to their phone shops, and also buy from roadside vendors anywhere, even in the smallest of settlements.

Time

GMT +3.

Tipping

It is customary to tip around 10% for good service, which is not obligatory or expected but greatly appreciated by hotel and restaurant staff, most of whom receive very low pay. You can make individual tips, or most large hotels and beach resorts have tip boxes in reception for you to make a contribution at the end of your stay, which is shared among all staff. Taxi drivers don't need tipping since the price of a fare is usually negotiated first.

Tour operators

If you book an organized tour with a travel agent in your own country, they may also be able to book flights and other transfers and accommodation arrangements too. If you are after an all-inclusive package holiday to Zanzibar, this is usually the cheapest way to go. However, within Tanzania there are many good tour operators offering trips in Tanzania and East Africa, and all the local airlines and most of the

Tip...
If you find a taxi driver or tour guide you like, get their mobile number as this is the best way to reach them.

accommodation has their own websites, so there is no reason why you cannot deal with them directly too.

UK and Ireland

Abercrombie & Kent, www.abercrombiekent.co.uk.

Acacia Africa, www.acacia-africa.com.

Africa Travel Centre, www.africatravel.co.uk.

Africa Travel Resource, www.africatravelresource.com.

Expert Africa, www.expertafrica.com.

Global Village, www.globalvillage-travel.com.

Hayes & Jarvis, www.hayesandjarvis.co.uk.

Kuoni, www.kuoni.co.uk.

Okavango Tours and Safaris, www.okavango.com.

Pure Zanzibar, www.zanzibar.co.uk.

Real Africa www.realafrica.co.uk.

Rainbow Tours, www.rainbowtours.co.uk.

Somak, www.somak.co.uk.

Steppes Africa, www.steppestravel.co.uk.

Tanzania Odyssey, T020-8704 1216, www.tanzaniaodyssey.com.

Thomson Tailormade, www.thomsonworldwide.com.

Tribes Travel, www.tribes.co.uk.

Tropical Sky, www.tropicalsky.ie.

Africa

African Budget Safaris, www.africanbudgetsafaris.com.

Go2Africa, www.go2africa.com.

Predators Safari Club, www.predators-safaris.com.

Pulse Africa, www.pulseafrica.com.

Simba Safaris, www.simbasafaris.com.

Sunny Safaris, www.sunnysafaris.com

Thompsons Holidays, www.thompsons.co.za.

Zanzibar Travel, www.zanzibartravel.co.za.

Australia

Classic Safari Company, www.classicsafaricompany.com.au.

Peregrine Travel, www.peregrine.net.au.

The Africa Safari Co, www.africasafarico.com.au.

North America

Adventure Centre, www.adventure-centre.com.

Africa Adventure Company, www.africa-adventure.com.

African Horizons, www.africanhorizons.com.

Bushtracks, www.bushtracks.com.

Ker & Downey, www.kerdowney.com

Visas and immigration

Your passport must have at least 2 blank pages and be valid for at least 6 months after your planned arrival date in Tanzania. Almost all visitors require a visa, with the exception of some African countries, including South African passport-holders who are allowed a visa-free stay of up to 30 days. Visa requirements are the same on Zanzibar and Pemba as they are for mainland Tanzania. However, if you've already arrived in Tanzania and then go to the islands, as they are administered semi-autonomously, you may be asked to show your passport again to an immigration official on entry and exit.

A transit visa valid for 14 days costs US$30 per person; a single-entry visa valid for 3 months costs US$50 (the exception are US citizens for whom a single entry is US$100); a multi-entry visa valid for 12 months costs US$100. Single-entry and transit visas can be obtained on arrival at the airports or border crossings, but multiple-entry visas can only be obtained in advance through Tanzania's embassies. Visas are paid for in US$ cash, but the airports and borders frequented by tourists, such as Zanzibar's Abeid Amani Karume International Airport, will also accept Euros or UK pounds.

Visas can be extended (but before they expire) to a maximum of 6 months at the Immigration Headquarters, Loliondo St, Kurasini, Dar es Salaam, T022-285 0575, Mon-Fri, 0730-1530 or on Zanzibar, go to the port in Stone Town. You will be asked to show proof of funds (a credit card should be sufficient) and your return or onward airline ticket or tour voucher. Occasionally, independent travellers not on a tour may be asked for these at point of entry; those travelling through Tanzania on the way to somewhere else on a 14-day transit visa will most certainly be asked for these. For more information visit www.immigration.go.tz.

> **Tip...**
> Tanzania, Kenya and Uganda have an agreement that allows holders of single-entry visas to move freely between all 3 countries without the need for re-entry permits as long as your visas remain valid; this also covers travel to Zanzibar.

Weights and measures

Metric.

Tanzania Odyssey

Tailor-made Safaris and Honeymoons to Tanzania and Zanzibar. We have been specialists to Tanzania for 20 years and charge no mark-up on any itinerary. Please call or email us for expert advice.

Our internet site contains a wealth of information about the lodges and parks, and includes an extensive **on-line video library**.

www.tanzaniaodyssey.com

UK: 5 The Mews, 6 Putney Common, London, SW15 1HL
Tel: (UK) 44 020 8704 1216

USA: 1209 Meadowbrook Drive, Portland, Texas 78374 USA
Tel: (US)1 866 356 4691

info@:tanzaniaodyssey.com

Index

Entries in **bold** *refer to maps*

FOOTPRINT
Features

Advertisers' index

Credits

Footprint credits
Editor: Stephanie Rebello
Production and layout: Emma Bryer
and Patrick Dawson
Maps: Kevin Feeney
Colour section: Patrick Dawson

Publisher: Felicity Laughton
         Patrick Dawson
Marketing: Kirsty Holmes
Sales: Diane McEntee
Advertising and content partnerships:
Debbie Wylde

Photography credits
Front cover: meunierd/Shutterstock.com.
Back cover: Top: Mint Images/SuperStock.
com. Bottom: Luisa Puccini/Shutterstock.com.

Colour section
Inside front cover: Martchan/Shutterstock.
com; africa924/Shutterstock.com; nelik/
shutterstock.com; Alessandro Travagli/
SuperStock.com. **Page 1**: Magdalena
Paluchowska/Shutterstock.com. **Page 2**:
Rikard Stadler/Shutterstock.com. **Page 4**:
DOZIER Marc/SuperStock.com; Andrew
McConnell/SuperStock.com. **Page 5**: Ian
Cumming/SuperStock.com; Ivan Pavlov/
Shutterstock.com; trevor kittelty@
Shutterstock.com; LOOK-foto/SuperStock.
com. **Page 7**: Kristina Vackova/Shutterstock.
com; lkpro/Shutterstock com; Roger de
la Harpe/SuperStock.com; Aleksandar
Todorovic/Shutterstock.com. **Page 8**: Peter
Wollinga/Shutterstock com.

Duotones Page 26 and 46: Magdalena
Paluchowska/Shutterstock.com. **Page 124**:
Jacojvr/Dreamstime.com.

Printed in Spain by GraphyCems

Publishing information
Footprint Zanzibar & Pemba
2nd edition
© Footprint Handbooks Ltd
May 2016

ISBN: 978 1 910120 83 5
CIP DATA: A catalogue record for this
book is available from the British Library

® Footprint Handbooks and the
Footprint mark are a registered
trademark of Footprint Handbooks Ltd

Published by Footprint
6 Riverside Court
Lower Bristol Road
Bath BA2 3DZ, UK
T +44 (0)1225 469141
F +44 (0)1225 469461
footprinttravelguides.com

Distributed in the USA by
National Book Network, Inc.

Every effort has been made to ensure
that the facts in this guidebook are
accurate. However, travellers should still
obtain advice from consulates, airlines,
etc about travel and visa requirements
before travelling. The authors and
publishers cannot accept responsibility
for any loss, injury or inconvenience
caused.